171190

THE ENVIRONMENT
COMMITTEES

This book is printed on 100 percent recycled paper

The Ralph Nader Congress Project

A Study of the House and Senate Interior, Agriculture, and Science Committees

The Ralph Nader Congress Project

Grossman Publishers

A DIVISION OF THE VIKING PRESS
NEW YORK 1975

THE ENVIRONMENT COMMITTEES

Library of Congress Cataloging in Publication Data

Ralph Nader Congress Project.
    The environment committees.

    Includes bibliographical references and index.
    1. Environmental policy—United States. 2. United
States. Congress—Committees. I. Title.
HC110.E5R28 1975   301.31′0973   75-14170
ISBN 0-670-29719-4

Contributors

Part I. *The Interior Committees*
Arthur J. Magida
A.B. Marlboro College (1967); M.A., Georgetown University
(1972); Environmental Reporter, *National Journal*

Part II. *The Agriculture Committees*
Joanne Engeke
Ruth Glushien
Richard Guttman
Bruce G. Rosenthal

Part III. *The Science Committees*
Mark Nadel, Project Director
Douglas Harbit
Judith Lichten
Thomas Lichten
Bruce G. Rosenthal

Contents

Introduction

This volume studies how Congress develops policies for land, food, space, and science. These areas can be subsumed under the environmental rubric, but it is only in recent years that the members of such committees as Interior or Agriculture have been exposed to any appreciable environmental appeals. There is some response by some committee members to matters of health and safety, and to the longer-range need to preserve resources and temper the quantity of agricultural production with concern for the soil and the consumer. But the giveaway heritage of Interior and Agriculture, under the ever present watch of special interest lobbyists, remains a dominant force.

Because they can dispense rights, subsidies, and government business, the environment committees attract powerful claimants. The committees on Interior and Agriculture are heavily weighted with members from the states where these claimants are entrenched economically and politically. The flow of campaign funds, the impact of voting blocs, and, not infrequently, the economic interests of the legislators themselves feed a business-congressional fraternity that attains the unity of a common ideological fervor. In the past two sessions a more diversified membership has emerged in some of these committees, and two powerful chairmen, Wayne Aspinall of House Interior and Insular Affairs and Robert Poage of House Agriculture, have been toppled—the former by a primary opponent in Colorado and the latter by the House Democratic Caucus in January 1975.

The question of distributional justice continually challenges these committees. Rarely has the challenge been met. Millions of Americans went hungry or were exposed to harmful pesticides while the Agriculture committees for years denied the problem; then, after they could no longer do so, ignored it; then, after they could no longer do that, acted but still avoided their legislative oversight duties to make sure programs were implemented and not abused. In similar prejudice, these committees for decades produced policies that made the rich farmer richer, agribusiness more dominant, and the small farmers and sharecroppers impoverished if not driven from the land altogether.

Parallel leanings have characterized the Interior committees. The lucrative grazing permits, mineral leases, and timber-cutting rights on the vast federally owned lands have been largely granted at the expense of taxpayers, consumers, and future generations for whom the government is supposed to hold and manage these national assets. The Bureau of Land Management, one of the least known and studied agencies in Washington as far as the general public is concerned, has the immense discretion to manage the public lands with minimum accountability. In these times, when the BLM is deciding on private corporate leasing of oil-bearing and geothermal-bearing land, the need to make these bureaucratic anonymities visible and responsive to the public interest is increasingly obvious.

The science committees, developing out of the space programs, should be moving from legislative boosterism to more serious inquiries and decisions surrounding federal science policy. These involve the allocation of research and development dollars in crucial areas such as energy, and shaping a humane science effort by the federal government guided by the well-being of the people instead of the insulated supremacy of the knowledge-production industries and professions.

Changes are coming, albeit unevenly, to the Interior and Agriculture committees. Consumer interests are meeting with increasing strength a number of bills reported to the House and Senate floors by the Agriculture committees on behalf of producer interests, ending some automatic rubber-stamping of committee legislation.

The rights of native Americans are receiving greater Interior committee respect, compared to the horrid years when legislators and staff on these committees were pushing to terminate the reservation land base that is the hope of Indian economic development and the binding force for Indian cultural survival. The arrival of champions such as South Dakota Senator James Abourezk, who grew up on an Indian reservation, has further humanized the congressional environment for these citizens.

Changes in a direction opposite to blatant corporate-commercial domination are modest, as the unsuccessful attempts to pass a modest land use bill reveal. This is especially apparent against the background of the strip-mining drive, soaring food prices, the Russian grain deal, the milk fund scandal, and the rising voice of migrant workers and small farmers vis-à-vis the concentrating tide of agribusiness and its subsidies, their waste and inefficiencies in the care of the land. In 1968 a Select Committee on Nutrition and Human Needs, chaired by Senator George McGovern, was established when a majority of senators lost any hope in trying to persuade the Agriculture Committee to pay attention to the needs of the poor and to the food processing industry's abuse of the nutrition and other rights of consumers.

The pace of public interest change on these committees has been slowed by the Nixon-Ford occupancy of the White House during the awakening of the citizen-consumer movement in the country. Minority rule by veto, plus the absence of constructive program proposals by the White House, can brake all but the most informed momentum on Capitol Hill. This volume does not merely illustrate how the very few make critical decisions for the very many, but also makes less remote and more accessible to citizens those legislative committees who have so much of our world in their hands. For the people to retrieve more control requires the initiation of informed civic attention toward the lawmakers who have fostered and now sustain the injustices of their power.

Ralph Nader

I

THE HOUSE AND SENATE INTERIOR AND INSULAR AFFAIRS COMMITTEES

Arthur J. Magida

1

Land, Law, and Loopholes: Uncle Sam and Grandmother Earth

In retrospect, 1973 was a usual year, a very usual year, for the Interior and Insular Affairs Committees of the Senate and the House of Representatives. Though they gave the Indians, Eskimos, and Aleuts of Alaska title to 40,000,000 acres of Alaskan land and $925,000,000 under the Alaska Native Land Claims Act, and made significant headway toward the development of a national land use policy, they spent most of their time deliberating such crucial issues as:

· A bill to give the Fort Belknap (Montana) Indian Community five acres valued at $200 (H.R. 10702);
· Twenty-four contracts for private-business concessions in national parks; and

3

· Whether to permit sessions of the Virgin Islands' legislature at places other than the islands' capital, Charlotte Amalie, on St. Thomas.

Some congressional committees, such as Appropriations and Foreign Affairs, have fairly well-defined jurisdictions, narrow and specific in contrast to the vagueness and the broad jurisdiction of the Interior committees. For instance, included in the jurisdiction of the Agriculture committees are farming, agricultural colleges and extension services, rural development, and animal welfare. The title of the Appropriations committees succinctly defines their jurisdiction: appropriating funds for the support and implementation of government programs. But the Interior committees are insatiable sponges, absorbing a colorful miscellany of responsibilities. Their domains are nominally the public land of the United States, but with a little imagination this can include almost anything—and usually does. In the Ninety-third Congress the committees' fourteen subcommittees* dealt with a variety of subjects.

They were concerned with the environment, Indian lands and the Indian nations, minerals and energy fuels, mining, wilderness areas, and governing the territories owned by the United States. If Astronaut Neil Armstrong had had the audacity to declare that the moon was American territory rather than to announce that he had just made a "giant step for mankind," then the Territorial and Insular Affairs subcommittees would undoubtedly now be considering junkets to the moon for oversight purposes.

One of the chief reasons why Congress has become the target for so much vitriol in recent years is that its pace of work is so glacial. For years, critics have been complaining that Congress is

---

* Each committee has seven subcommittees. The Senate committee's subcommittees are Indian Affairs; Minerals, Materials and Fuels; Parks and Recreation; Public Lands; Territories and Insular Affairs; Water and Power Resources; and a Special Subcommittee on Legislative Oversight. In the House, the subcommittees are Indian Affairs; Mines and Mining; National Parks and Recreation; Public Lands; Territorial and Insular Affairs; Irrigation and Reclamation; and the Environment.

so lethargic that it is certainly comatose and perhaps verging on the moribund. They have debated whether Congress should consult an efficiency expert or a funeral director. Members of Congress are besieged with tremendous and numbing tasks. Though they are cued and aided by an army of experts, aides and clerks, they can get by only so far with their help. For it is the members who are ultimately responsible for legislation, not their aides. It is they who must put their votes where their consciences are or where their best political interests lie. It is they who must answer quorum and roll calls, who must debate legal, economic, political, and social intricacies. It is they who must decide which hearings they will attend among those of the two or three subcommittees they are assigned to on each of the two or three full committees of which they are members. It is they who must have the expertise, and the patience, to serve adequately on these committees.

Considering the Interior committees' primary jurisdiction, the public lands—one-third of the nation's area (755 million of the country's 2 billion, 271 million acres)—it is not surprising that many members of Congress are eager to have their name read at quorum calls of the Interior committees.[1] Especially in the West, the economies of the states are inextricably linked to the use of public lands. Over 95 percent of Alaska is federal land, 86.4 percent of Nevada, 66.5 percent of Utah, and 63.9 percent of Idaho. In California, the nation's most populous state, 44.3 percent of the land is owned by the federal government.[2] Over 64 million acres of federal land throughout the country are leased to oil and gas companies for current and future production. Though no figures have been compiled for the mineral production of public land, the western states produce 90 percent of the domestic copper supply, 95 percent of the mercury and silver, 100 percent of nickel, molybdenum and potash, and about 50 percent of the lead. Most of the domestic reserves of nonferrous minerals are located in the western states. Timber sales by the Bureau of Land Management in the West and Minnesota combined amount to more than $80 million annually. Revenues from permits to graze cattle on public land raise almost $7.7 million annually. The total value of resources extracted from public land each year has been estimated at over $2 billion, and all these vast riches fall under the aegis of the Interior committees.

In fact, it could even be contended that the West was not won on the battlegrounds of the Indian wars, but in the meeting rooms of the Interior committees. The present Interior committees were created by the Legislative Reorganization Act of 1946, but their precursor, the House Public Lands Committee, was created in 1805 after the United States made its first great acquisition of public land, the Louisiana Purchase.

From their very inception the committees were oriented toward the West, and so have been most of the bills that have passed through the committees on their way to the law books. From the mid-1800s, with the surge of western development, Congress has churned out laws that encouraged western mining, exploration, railroad construction, and, later, grazing, drilling, and logging. Though these were intended to make the West enticing and practical for the pioneer, they eventually made it more enticing for the wealthy. For instance, land exploiters used an 1850 bill for the disposal of "swamp and overflow" lands to acquire millions of acres at $1.25 an acre. Though no more than 500,000 acres of California was ever swampland, two million acres of the Golden State were sold under this law. According to editor Horace Greeley, most of this land was "so dry that there was not enough muck to supply a single small frog." One of the state's largest landowners, Henry Miller, had a team of horses drag a small boat around a dusty tract so he could claim that it was swampland.

The Federal Homestead Act of 1862 was also abused so that wealthy men could acquire huge estates of hundreds of thousands of acres. Some paid a token fee to hundreds of "dummy" claimants to acquire their holdings. Others acquired water rights and cut off all water flowing onto neighboring properties until these could be purchased at ridiculously cheap prices. Henry Miller used this ploy to garner a million acres along the Kern and San Joaquin rivers.

The Desert Land Act, passed in the mid-1870s, was also most profitable for the wealthy and the stealthy. This law authorized the disposal of desert land to encourage settlement and eventual irrigation. Though each settler was limited to 640 acres, William Carr, Lloyd Tevis, and James Haggin used "dummy" claimants to acquire 70,000 acres. After this dusty trio was apprehended, they contended that a 640-acre tract was unprofitable to irrigate. The government apparently thought so too: in the early 1900s the Interior committees authorized millions of dollars to encourage private developers by irrigating the same lands they had earlier sold at bargain prices.

One of the biggest land giveaways in this country occurred in the last half of the nineteenth century. To stimulate the construction of railroad tracks to link the East and the West, Congress gave massive land grants to the railroad companies. Some of it was for permanent right of way; *all* of it was free. Though the railroads have either sold the land at inflated prices or still use it for logging, mining, drilling, and, now, subdividing for recreational purposes, this was explicitly prohibited by a proviso in the original land grants: "all such lands . . . which shall not be disposed of or sold by said company within three years after the entire road shall have been completed, shall be subject to settlement and preemption like other lands, at a price not exceeding $1.25 per acre, to be paid to said company."

In a related manner the Interior committees have apparently thought that what is good for the surface of America is also good for what is underneath it. It was not sufficient simply to grant or sell over one billion acres of surface land between 1795 and 1970.[3] What was underneath the land was a responsibility of the Interior committees, and it also had to be mined, drilled, and scraped. The first major law related to mining was the Mineral Location Law of 1872, which gave miners carte blanche to explore and claim all public lands for such "locatable minerals" as gold, copper, and silver. This law, which is still in effect after more than a hundred years, gave mining rights to the first person to stake a claim on a site. The rights are in perpetuity if a minimum of $100 worth of work a year is done on a claim.

The Mineral Location Law was written in the days when the "Bear-Went-Over-the-Mountain" syndrome was at its height, when Americans had an insatiable appetite for land that could be temporarily appeased by clambering over the next ridge into the next valley and staking another claim. There was no thought of conserving land or natural resources. Nature was graciously bountiful and man her presumptive beneficiary. To make a claim on public lands under the Mineral Location Law, it is necessary only to dig a ten-foot "discovery hole." There is no mention of filling in the hole or repairing any damage done to the land. The miner is entitled to unlimited free access to his claims and has wide discretion in what he can do on adjacent public lands as long as it is related to his mining.

Though the scope and means of mining have changed considerably since the 1872 law was written, until the House (but not the Senate) passed a bill in the Ninety-second Congress (1971–72), the Interior committees had steadily refrained from reviewing the impact of the law or proposing new acts that would be more applicable to contemporary coal mining. In the 1970s over 450 million acres are vulnerable to either strip or deep mining for coal. Approximately two million acres of this land have already been ripped apart by strip mining, and about two-thirds of that have been abandoned without any attempt at reclamation after the coal was extracted from it. Stripping tears into about 4,650 acres each week, according to the federal government's Council on Environmental Quality.[4]

The total number of claims subject to the law's absolute rights of access and use has been estimated at over one million, with 250,000 in Southern California alone. A possible effect of this enormous number of claims is that, even disregarding the environmental impact of working the claims, the construction of many miles of access roads causes severe environmental damages.

Non-locatable (or leased) minerals include oil, gas, phosphates, coal, lignite, peat, oil shale, sodium, potash, and sulphur, and these resources have been handled differently from all other minerals, which are known as locatable minerals. To regulate the government's leasing of its oil, gas, and sulphur preserves, Congress passed the Mineral Leasing Act of 1920 and later the Mineral Leasing Act of 1947. These laws gave considerable latitude to the Bureau of Land Management of the Department of the Interior in administering leases and setting terms. However, the present lease forms granted by the BLM are a reversal of *caveat emptor*. They should read, "Let the Buyer Take What He Will." For instance, one of the form's provisions prohibits the lessee from undertaking operations that *"unnecessarily* cause soil erosion, water pollution, or vegetation damage [italics added]." In effect, then, mining interests may not burn down a forest capriciously but it is permissible if it is related to mining, and such relationships are broadly construed.

The BLM is responsible for the Minerals Disposals Act of 1947, which regulates mining of sand, gravel, and pumice. Rather than leasing mines or mineral sites, this act simply sells the mineral to the purchaser through an ordinary sales contract, and the purchaser digs it out of the ground. Again the BLM contract gives the purchaser extraordinary discretion. Its vague language asks him to have "due regard" for stream bank erosion and to avoid "unnecessary" disturbances to underground water supplies "where possible." BLM contracts generally disregard possible water pollution, erosion, the effects of construction of access roads, or threats to wildlife habitats.

Despite the power that the BLM enjoys in administering over 470,300,000 acres, there has been virtually no oversight by the Interior committees of its administration or the effects of its policies.[5] The rare oversight hearings are held only when outrages and disasters are sensational enough to make headlines, such as oil spills from off-shore drilling or mining disasters. And once the hearings are held, and the public and BLM critics have been placated, the Interior committees again return to their somnolence and the BLM to its omnipotence.

The BLM's jurisdiction includes livestock grazing. It received this authority under the Taylor Grazing Act of 1934, which was ostensibly meant to prevent overgrazing, "to provide for . . . orderly use [and] improvement" of grazing land, and to "stabilize" the livestock industry, which depends on the open range. Whether the BLM actually meets these mandates is debatable. It currently allows massive grazing of federal lands with only token fees charged. Since the Taylor Act was written in the 1930s, when the nation was more concerned about helping the economy than protecting the environment, it did not deal with ecological perils of excessive and irresponsible livestock grazing.

For example, there are an estimated one million cattle and sheep grazing on public land in California. One-third of these are in national forests. Since the BLM allows these animals to graze on federal land, it is also indirectly responsible for their welfare. To protect them from coyotes, the Interior Department's National Wildlife Service began a program of massive poisoning in the late 1960s. These poisons have decimated not only coyotes, but also owls and other predators essential to the ecological cycles of the federal lands. So many of these ancillary predators have been killed that there is now a proliferation of rats, rabbits, and other animals usually eaten by them. So the Wildlife Service's solution has been to poison these other animals as well. The Interior committees have not been eager to investigate the BLM's animal warfare—although they did hold extensive hearings on the fate of the American bald eagle, the symbol of what's right with America.

The BLM also has the authority to reclassify public lands so they can be used for game refuges, parks, scenic river projects, and other public purposes, and to retract these classifications and sell the lands to private citizens. The BLM had no explicit guidelines for disposal or reclassification until 1961, when Interior Secretary Stewart Udall instructed the Bureau that public lands could not be sold and opened to settlement unless the applicant could prove that the use to which he would put the land would be at least equal in value and purpose to the use the government had made of it.

Almost 50,000,000 acres have been classified as parks, recreation areas, or wildlife preserves by either Congress or the BLM. These are maintained by the Fish and Wildlife Service or the National Park Service.* Included in this acreage are the National Forest System, which was created to preserve timber resources, and the National Park System and the National Wildlife System, both set up to preserve lands withdrawn from the private domain.

The vagueness of the laws specifying the powers of the BLM, the Fish and Wildlife Service, and the National Park Service was explained succinctly by a former chairman of the House Interior Committee, Wayne Aspinall (D., Col.): "The people in the [Nixon] administration—and it would be the same thing in Democratic administrations—would rather write their own rules than to have the Congress of the United States tell them there are certain policies they have to conform to." But Udall, Interior Secretary in both the Kennedy and the Johnson administrations, admitted that "there is an appeal about Congress having the power [to establish national land policy], but there wouldn't be any national parks and forests today if Congress had that power." And the present Interior Secretary, Rogers C. B. Morton, agrees with Udall's assessment of Congress' ability to establish an impartial and nonpartisan land use policy: "You're dealing with a different ball game when you're getting into the public land policy.

* The Interior committees have jurisdiction over the National Park Service. In the House, the Fish and Wildlife Service falls under the Merchant Marine and Fisheries Committee; in the Senate, under the Commerce Committee.

You've got this economic interest . . . it's partisan, regional versus national, development versus nondevelopment . . . user versus non-user. . . ."

While the BLM and the other divisions of the Interior Department establish policy, while livestock graze on public lands for token fees, while waters are polluted and discolored from strip mining, the Interior committees sit in oak-paneled rooms on Capitol Hill listening with equal calm to palliatives from industry representatives and thorny criticism from conservationists. They keep the traditions of their committees alive, the traditions of being favorably disposed toward industry and land developers and forgetting the public interest. Through a consistent practice of inaction, procrastination, and inadequate action they further permit the deterioration of the nation's land.

2

The Land Lords:
Rich Man, Poor Man,
Beggar Man, Thief,
Banker, Realtor, Indian Chief

A committee is attractive to a member of Congress for one of two reasons. Its jurisdiction may inherently appeal to the member's philosophy or interests, or he may prefer a committee whose function has a direct relationship to his district or state, so that he can exploit his membership with his constituents. In the first category would be such committees as those for Government Operations, Un-American Activities, and the District of Columbia, which might even be a political liability at home, since no direct benefits accrue to a congressman's constituents from their representative's membership on them.

13

During three recent congresses these committees were the least attractive to freshmen members. In the House of Representatives, only 7 percent of the freshmen requested appointments to the Government Operations Committee, 3 percent to the District of Columbia Committee, and 2 percent to the Un-American Activities Committee.[1] By contrast, 32 percent of the entering representatives asked for appointments to the Banking and Currency Committee or the Interstate and Foreign Commerce Committee and 27 percent to the Public Works Committees, committees which have extraordinary potential for providing visible aid to constituents.

The more popular committees, then, seem to be those that offer a member of Congress an opportunity to serve his constituents first, and then the nation. It is not surprising that the House Interior Committee, which authorized $2,034,220,000 worth of projects in 1971 alone, was the fifth most popular committee among freshmen during recent sessions of Congress.[2]

A conscientious member of an Interior committee can parlay the committee's authorizations into comparative wealth for his district or state. In 1971 the Interior Department spent $10 per capita throughout the entire United States, but the districts of the Interior committees' members averaged $64 per capita, more than six times the national average. Some of the senior members of the committee had the Interior Department pour even more cash into their districts. According to their *Congress Project Profiles*, Representative Harold T. Johnson (D., Calif.) obtained $71 per capita for his California district; Republican Representative Sam Steiger's Arizona district corralled $115, and the Washington district of Democrat Tom Foley $182.[3]

Since the Interior committees offer their members enormous opportunities to pork-barrel funds into their home states and districts, and since an inordinate proportion of the projects funded by the committees are in the West, the committees are extremely attractive to westerners.* As one member of the House Interior Committee candidly admits:

> I was attracted to it, very frankly, because it's a bread and butter committee for my state. I guess about the only thing about it that is not of great interest to my state is insular affairs. I was able to get two or three bills of great importance to my state last year. I had vested interests I wanted to protect, to be frank.[4]

Such candor may be exceptional, but the congressman's reasoning is typical. Every congressman from Alaska has sat on the Interior committees because over 95 percent of the state is public land. Every delegate from the Virgin Islands and Guam has been on the House Interior Committee's Territories and Insular Affairs Subcommittee because this body ultimately governs these territories.† In the Ninety-third Congress exactly half the Senate committee came from the West, and 46 percent of the House committee had their districts either along the Pacific or in the Rocky Mountains. (See Tables 1 and 2.) Only 7 percent of the members of either committee represented eastern states. The committees' geographical representation, then, is almost directly proportional to the size of each area's public lands.

The Interior committees are rarely considered *national* committees geared toward national problems, but rather regional committees obsessed with local issues. With rare exceptions, such as a bill that set codes for every national forest or the exceptional measure the Ninety-third Congress passed (but President Ford vetoed), demanding reclamation on every strip-mining site in the

---

* For the purpose of this study, "western states" include Alaska and Hawaii, as well as those traditionally classified as western—Washington, Oregon, California, Montana, Wyoming, Colorado, New Mexico, Arizona, Utah, Nevada, and Idaho.
† The Virgin Islands and Guam have had nonvoting delegates in the House of Representatives only since the 92nd Congress. They have no representation in the Senate.

country, virtually every bill the committees produce is tailored to remedy some local situation—adding acreage to a national park or buying a pond for the Fish and Wildlife Service. Except for the Land Use Planning Bill, which was killed by the House Rules Committee in February 1974, neither the House nor the Senate committee has ever taken a comprehensive view of the land and resource needs of the country.

THE HOUSE COMMITTEE
AND ITS LEADERSHIP

Though the House and the Senate committees have virtually identical geographical representation, some important structural changes have recently occurred in the House committee. Changes in membership and leadership, a revolt by Young Turks in 1970 that caused basic changes in the committee's rules, more power wielded by the subcommittee chairmen, and a less conservative membership have all produced a committee about which environmentalists are increasingly enthusiastic and industrialists are increasingly worried.

The Tyranny of Chairman Wayne Aspinall

The single most important reason for the changes in the House Committee was the defeat of the committee's chairman, seventy-six-year old Wayne Aspinall, in the 1972 Democratic primary in Colorado's fourth congressional district. Aspinall came from a mining and agricultural district where handouts from the Interior Committee could be of major significance. During his twenty-four years in the House, Aspinall sent over one billion dollars worth of pork-barreling back to his district. This was much appreciated, especially by gasoline and mining interests. His campaign coffers were filled with contributions from executives of such industrial giants as Kennecott Copper, Shell Oil, American Metal Climax, Humble Oil, and the Oil Shale Corporation. The chairman made no pretense of his allegiance to business and his hostility toward

TABLE 1.

Geographic Distribution—Senate Interior Committee (93rd Congress)

Region	Democrats			Republicans			Total	
	From the Region	No.	Percent of Committee	From the Region	No.	Percent of Committee	No.	Percent of Committee
West	Jackson—Wash. Bible—Nev. Church—Idaho Metcalf—Mont. Haskell—Colo.	5	36	Fannin—Ariz. Hansen—Wyo. Hatfield—Ore. McClure—Idaho	4	29	9	64
East	— —	—	—	Buckley—N.Y.	1	7	1	7
Midwest	Abourezk—S. Dak. Nelson—Wis.	2	14	Bartlett—Okla.	1	15	3	22
South	Johnston—La.	1	7	— —	—	—	1	7
Total	— —	8	57	— —	6	43	14	100

TABLE 2.

Geographic Distribution—House Interior Committee (93rd Congress)

Region	Democrats			Republicans			Total	
	From the Region	No.	Percent of Committee	From the Region	No.	Percent of Committee	No.	Percent of Committee
West	Johnson—Calif. Udall—Ariz. Burton—Calif. Foley—Wash. Meeds—Wash. Melcher—Mont. Roncalio—Wyo. Runnels—N.M. Burke—Calif. Owens—Utah Mink—Hawaii	11	27	Hosmer—Calif. Steiger—Ariz. Ketchum—Calif. Clausen—Calif. Lujan—N.M. Dellenback—Ore. Towell—Nev. Young—Ill. Symms—Idaho	9	22	20	48
East	Vigorito—Pa. Bingham—N.Y.	2	3	Cronin—Mass.	1	3	3	7
Midwest	Kastenmeier—Wis. Seiberling—Ohio Jones—Okla.	3	7	Skubitz—Kans. Sebelius—Kans. Regula—Ohio Camp—Okla.	4	8	7	17

TABLE 2. (continued)

Region	Democrats			Republicans			Total	
	From the Region	No.	Percent of Committee	From the Region	No.	Percent of Committee	No.	Percent of Committee
South	Haley—Fla. Taylor—N.C. Kazen—Tex. Stephens—Ga.	4	10	Steelman—Tex. Martin—N.C. Bauman—Md.	3	7	7	17
North Central	O'Hara—Mich.	1	3	Ruppe—Mich.	1	3	2	5
Guam	Won Pat	1	3	— —	—	—	1	3
Virgin Islands	de Lugo	1	3	— —	—	—	1	3
Total	— —	23	56	— —	18	44	41	100

conservationists. He once remarked that "Mother Nature is actually one of the worst environmentalists,"[5] and he showed his contempt for conservationists when he snorted at them as people "who treat those lands as a place to play and have a good time."[6] Aspinall wanted to turn natural resources into cash, not into glens and parks for posterity. As one environmentalist put it, Aspinall "did more damage to the American earth than any other human being in this century."

Aspinall was first elected to the House in 1948 after seventeen years in the Colorado Senate and House of Representatives. In 1958 he succeeded Representative Clair Engle (D., Calif.) as chairman of the Interior Committee. Aspinall was the heir apparent, successor both by dint of his seniority and by the personal preference of Engle. Engle had given him a subcommittee to head so he would know how to pound the gavel correctly and dampen opposition. It became apparent soon after Aspinall assumed the chairmanship that his conception of a chairman's task did not mean that a chairman *led* a committee—to Aspinall, the chairman *was* the committee.

Aspinall presided dictatorially over the full committee from the head of a horseshoe-shaped table. Hanging behind him was a portrait of himself mounted in a gilt frame. He selected each member of the committee's staff himself, to be sure that they reflected his views. One subcommittee chairman was so frustrated by the committee's staffing that he used an ingenious ploy to hire a staff member who would be compatible with his own political and conservationist beliefs. As chairman of another committee's subcommittee, the dissident hired a staff member for that other subcommittee but used him for the Interior subcommittee. Aspinall may have fumed, but for once he was completely stymied.

Aspinall set the agenda and time for every meeting of each subcommittee, and he attended virtually every meeting. Though he did not necessarily preside at subcommittee hearings, his truculence and technical expertise enabled him to dominate the proceedings. One committee member, Representative Lloyd Meeds (D., Wash.), recalled in an interview that there was an unwritten rule that "no new legislation was considered at a subcommittee unless Aspinall was there."

The chairman himself decided which bills would pass, which would languish in limbo, and which would be squashed immediately. As one Senate Interior Committee staff member lamented, "If Aspinall said go, it went. If he said don't go, it stopped." Furthermore, if Aspinall liked a bill, it did not merely go through the committee, but through the entire House. His power and influence were such that his stamp of approval guaranteed a bill's passage. He was like the Grand Inquisitor whose casual nod determined life or death. From 1958 through 1971 the Interior Committee reported over 1,000 bills to the House floor. Not one of those bills was defeated. Aspinall took great pride in this feat: "I've had over 1,000 bills before Congress," he liked to remind visitors, "and never lost a one."

However, by the end of the 1960s chinks began to appear in the walls that Aspinall had placed around his fiefdom. In 1967, Representative Phillip Burton (D., Calif.), one of the more liberal and voluble members of the committee, persuaded several senior liberal Democrats to take advantage of seven Democratic vacancies on the committee to weaken Aspinall's power. If they could not maneuver a palace coup, at least they could force Aspinall to recognize the provinces, to distribute power throughout the committee and to distribute it equally. Six of the seven openings went to fairly liberal Democrats: Robert W. Kastenmeier (Wis.), James G. O'Hara (Mich.), William F. Ryan (N.Y.), Patsy T. Mink (Hawaii), Lloyd Meeds (Wash.), and Abraham Kazen (Tex.). The seventh spot on the committee went to James Kee (W. Va.), who was slightly more conservative than the other six. The new liberal incursion gave Aspinall's opposition a lever to use against him.

By the Ninety-third Congress, two of the six liberals who had joined the committee in 1967 headed two of its seven subcommittees. These were Patsy Mink, chairman of the Mines and Mining Subcommittee, and Lloyd Meeds, chairman of the Indian Affairs Subcommittee.

The final *coup de grâce* to Aspinall's autocracy was a combination of the Reorganization Act of 1970 and the uprising of "Young Turks" in the Ninety-second Congress. Together they undermined the foundations of Aspinall's power, his control over the committee's staff and subcommittees. The clause of the Reorganization Act most applicable to the Aspinall regime was its requirement that one-third of each full committee's staff be selected by its minority members. At the beginning of the next Congress, an improbable coalition emerged in the committee. The Democrats wanted to share Aspinall's power and break his stranglehold on the committee; the Republicans wanted to gain a more autonomous staff. Headed by Burton, the coalition included such GOP stalwarts as Craig Hosmer and Sam Steiger, both of whom are unpopular with conservationists. The amendments in the committee's rules forced by the coup introduced three major changes: 1) the Democratic Caucus could veto the selection of subcommittee chairmen; 2) subcommittees gained autonomy to set their own agendas and meeting times; and 3) under certain circumstances the Democrats could select their own delegates to House-Senate conferences which iron out differences on completed legislation. The vote on the rule changes was approved by a close 13 to 12 vote.

Although it was so narrow a defeat, Aspinall was personally hurt. According to a member of the Interior Committee staff, Aspinall said after the coup that if any of his subcommittee chairmen had told him they were not given enough responsibility, he "wouldn't have hesitated to give them more."

To reinforce his waning power, Aspinall created a Subcommittee on the Environment whose jurisdiction was broad enough to include almost any bill referred to the committee. Aspinall made himself chairman and appointed the ranking minority member of the full committee, John P. Saylor (R., Pa.), the ranking minority member of the new subcommittee. While Aspinall strained to coopt the new committee rules, those who had championed them were reluctant actually to use them. The only subcommittee chairman who exercised his new freedom to select the staff for his subcommittee was Phil Burton, who appointed only two staff members, including a secretary.[7] As Saylor noted in an interview, "The subcommittee chairmen were never ready to assume the authority given to them." And the Committee's minority counsel, Charles J. Leppert, later recalled that "Aspinall still had complete power here. He could still withhold legislation from a subcommittee, even under the new rules. In other words, you could get subcommittee staff, but no legislation to work on. Burton was the only one to take Aspinall on, and he got away with it."[8]

To retaliate against Burton for appointing two staff members, Aspinall opposed the only major piece of legislation to come out of Burton's Territorial Subcommittee during that Congress, a bill to provide nonvoting delegates to Congress for Guam and the Virgin Islands. Despite Aspinall's opposition, the bill was approved by the committee and enacted by Congress.

As Aspinall's power in Washington eroded during the Ninety-second Congress, so did his power back in Colorado. Early in 1972 Alan Merson, a law professor in his forties teaching at Denver University, announced that he would challenge Aspinall for the Democratic nomination. Aspinall, seventy-six in April, was initially reluctant to enter the race. He was concerned about his health and had already seen a sizable proportion of his most highly valued legislation passed into law. Perhaps land use was the only area in which he still wished to have some legislation passed. Aside from his health and age, the other key factor that militated against Aspinall was redistricting. When Aspinall ran for his seat in 1970, the fourth district had contained thirty-five counties, most of them rural and most of them friendly to him. But in the spring of 1972 the state legislature cut the fourth district to nineteen counties. One of these included 100,000 residents of suburban Denver, which was hardly typical of the rural areas from which Aspinall had traditionally drawn his support.

After months of deliberation, Aspinall declared his candidacy in June, just a month before his party's nominating convention. He had waited too long. Merson won the nomination and the top slot on the primary ballot. He was aided financially and morally by environmental groups. The League of Conservation Voters contributed $16,300 to his campaign. Aspinall was nominated to the Environmental Action Group's "Dirty Dozen," the twelve members of Congress who made the most, and the worst, legislative contributions "to the ecological problems that confront us today."[9] *Field and Stream* magazine bolstered the anti-Aspinall forces when it rated members of Congress and cast Aspinall "In a Class by Himself: The Man Who Absolutely Must Go."[10]

As his campaign against Merson mounted, Aspinall expected the "main issues in this campaign" to be "age and the attacks on me by extreme environmentalists." But after 52.7 percent of the 31,544 voters decided not to return him to Congress, he attributed his defeat solely to redistricting.[11]

The voters' decision was in marked, almost startling, contrast to Aspinall's victory in the Democratic primary just two years before, when he had smashed Richard L. Perchlik's effort to unseat him by getting 72 percent of the vote.[12]

Industrialists mourned when they heard that Aspinall would not be ruling the Interior roost for the Ninety-third Congress. Thomas Cavanagh, a lobbyist for 42,000 sheep- and cattle-grazing permittees, praised Aspinall as a man who "surely understood our problems. His leaving is a real blow." The general counsel for the American Petroleum Institute, Stark Ritchie, conceded that "Obviously, we thought Chairman Aspinall did a great job. He realized the importance of multiple use [of federally controlled lands] because you can't just lock out certain areas of the country for energy production."[13] But conservationists were elated. "Aspinall was a terribly tyrannical chairman, a robber baron presiding over a committee that treated the public lands voraciously," said the chairman of the League of Conservation Voters, Marion B. Edey.[14]

John Saylor, Ranking Minority Member

One member of the committee who shared the joy of the conservationists was the ranking minority member, John Saylor. As the Ninety-third Congress began, Saylor whispered to a conservationist, "Y'know, for the first time I think this committee will be fun." But Saylor did not rejoice for partisan reasons. He was almost as much a conservationist as any member of the Audubon Society or the Sierra Club. One environmentalist said as he looked at the picture of Saylor above his desk, "We revere Saylor around here. We call him St. John." A staff member of a national conservation group commented that Saylor "practiced conservation for thirty years, when nobody ever heard of the word."

Saylor was a maverick, the head of his party on the committee who was alienated from his party. According to Joe Skubitz (R., Kans.), the third-ranking Republican on the committee in the Ninety-second Congress, "Even as ranking member, he doesn't really have rapport with our side of the aisle." Saylor was not reluctant to dissent from the views of his party. While 62 percent of the GOP congressmen voted for all bills consonant with President Nixon's policies during the Ninety-first Congress, Saylor voted for less than half of them. During the first session of the Ninety-second Congress he voted with the majority of the Republican Party only 55 percent of the time.[15]

Saylor was not one to hide his conscience or his votes. He frequently sent messages to the Nixon administration in the same tone as his November 20, 1969, wire to John Volpe, Secretary of the Department of Transportation:

> DOT decision to allow operation of "training strip" at Everglades National Park to begin Monday, Nov. 24, the worst step department has taken since January 20, 1969 [the be-

ginning of the Nixon administration]. Decision indicates Administration has turned its back on conservation, has broken its pledge to the American people to protect the Nation's environment, and has caved-in to profit political pressure. . . . Decision is back alley politics at its worst and is unworthy of the Department's responsibility to the public. Predict the Nation's conservationists will rise as a body to trample on DOT as your decision tramples on the public.[16]

The conservationists never did "trample on" the Transportation Department, and Saylor's disgust with the Nixon administration remained undiminished, yet his faith in the American people never wavered. On November 25, 1969, he sent an equally angry telegram to Interior Secretary Walter J. Hickel after the Interior Department had proposed that it suspend an increase of the fees for grazing livestock on public lands:

The previous Administration [the Johnson administration] made a decision which was long overdue to correct an abuse by vested interest groups of our public land. That decision provided for an annual increase of our grazing fees over a ten year period with the first increase having gone into effect and the remaining nine to be automatic. Your suspending that decision indicates that this Administration has once again broken its pledge to the American people and surrendered to profit and political pressures . . . these public lands are not the private domain of the grazers but belong to all the American people. Your decision is unworthy of the Department of the Interior's responsibility to the American people.[17]

Saylor's devotion to the environment earned him awards from the National Parks Association, the National Wildlife Federation, the Pennsylvania Outdoor Writers Association, The Belle Baruch Foundation, the Pennsylvania Roadside Council, the Sierra Club and the Izaak Walton League.[18]

The differences between Saylor and Aspinall were glaring. In 1971 the Pennsylvania congressman voted for 90 percent of the legislation favored by the League of Conservation Voters. That same year, Aspinall voted for only 30 percent of LCV-favored bills. The next year, 1972, Aspinall did not vote for a single bill that the League favored, whereas Saylor voted for 60 percent of these bills. Of the 435 members of the House in 1971, Saylor was ranked 122nd by the LCV; Aspinall was ranked 405th.

Saylor had a solid political base in his twelfth district in Pennsylvania. In 1970 he garnered 58 percent of the vote. Two years later his opponent in the GOP primary was neatly dispatched with a 72 to 28 percent tally, and the incumbent did almost as well in the following general election by attracting 68 percent of the vote.

So secure was Saylor's seat in the House that it seemed he could remain until he decided to retire. However, before he had a chance to retire voluntarily, the sixty-five-year-old representative had a fatal heart attack in October of 1973.

Chairman James A. Haley and a Relaxed New Era

Saylor's death in the middle of the Ninety-third Congress completely changed the complexion of the leadership of the House Interior Committee. Aspinall had been succeeded at the beginning of the Ninety-third by seventy-four-year-old James A. Haley (D., Fla.), who seemed to prefer lighting his cigar to lighting a fire under the committee, and Saylor was succeeded by fifty-eight-year-old Craig Hosmer, a Californian who apparently thought it was his obligation to preserve the truculence and antienvironmentalism of Aspinall.

As one committee member's staff assistant said, "Haley was like soap. He didn't take over—he floated to the top." Haley has never distinguished himself in Congress; in fact he seems to have entered politics through its back door, to fill a vacuum in his vocational life after having gone through one of the more scarring experiences that society can impose—jail. In 1944, when Haley was vice-president of Ringling Brothers–Barnum & Bailey Circus, a fire in the big top in Hartford, Connecticut, killed 185 people and injured another 500.[19] Haley and four other Ringling employees were convicted of involuntary manslaughter. Although he was given a prison sentence of not less than a year and a day and not more than five years, Haley was released for good behavior after serving eight months and seventeen days. In 1947, three years after his release, Haley was elected to the Florida House of Representatives, and by 1952 he was in the House of Representatives.

Haley's major concerns seem to be preserving the free enterprise system with a minimum of governmental control and combating any international threat —or what he conceives as a threat —with a maximum of military might. He has a 92 percent rating from the conservative Americans for Constitutional Action and a 100 percent rating from the pro-military American Security Council.[20]

Haley's antipathy to a livable, breathable environment was cleverly masked in a February, 1971, news release when he stated that:

> As a member of the House Committee on Interior and Insular Affairs, I have devoted in recent years a great deal of thought to the pollution problem, in as much as that committee, of which I am the ranking member, has jurisdiction over a considerable body of anti-pollution legislation.[21]

Since he maintains that he has given pollution "a great deal of thought," he cannot assert that his votes on the matter have been rashly spontaneous. He voted against a bill to empower the Environmental Protection Agency to set and enforce standards protecting rivers and streams from pollution. He opposed a bill to require the use of the "best available" water pollution control by 1981. Nor did he favor allowing environmental advocates the same rights as those charged with pollution to appeal EPA rulings in court. He also fought a one-year moratorium on stream channelization. (Although channelization improves navigability and flood control, environmentalists contend that the process degrades water quality, promotes soil erosion, and destroys wildlife and fish.)

But since January 1973, when Haley became chairman of the committee, it has become difficult to determine exactly where he stands on issues, or whether he has any opinion at all. He votes at subcommittee or full committee meetings only when there is a tie. He speaks in the committee only when there is a parliamentary rule to be enforced or a witness to be introduced. Aspinall was a tyrant, but at least every member of the committee knew exactly what he stood for, and there was a direction to the committee. The other members may not have liked it, but at least the dimensions of their lives in their work on the committee were defined. Haley is the antithesis. Under him the committee has lost its structure and its direction. Times of flux are provocative and intellectually stimulating, because the necessity to cope with new questions summons creative forces to seek new answers. The Haley chairmanship has tapped just these forces on the committee. The members have become more self-reliant and independent, less willing to compromise because there is less need to do so. The brick wall Aspinall had constructed vanished the day Haley became chairman, because Haley has none of Aspinall's obstinacy, hostility, or obstructionism. He is more of a caretaker than an activist chairman in the Aspinall tradition.

The nexus of the full committee used to be its chairman; now power is equally distributed among each of the seven subcommittees.* Though the Aspinall staff has been retained, the growth of the subcommittees' staffs, and the increase in their influence, has

* The fate of the full committee and especially of its subcommittees since Aspinall's departure has confirmed Representative Morris Udall's comments in October 1972: "[Aspinall] was a tireless worker. By sheer force of personality he dominated the committee, and the subcommittees weren't really autonomous. In fact, they had hardly any power at all. Under Haley, I think you're going to see an entirely different kind of committee in which the subcommittee chairmen will play a much larger role." See Paul L. Leventhal, "Turnover in Key Committees' Chairmanships Foreshadows Policy Changes in 93rd Congress," *National Journal*, October 11, 1972, p. 1755.

forced the full committee's staff to deal with administrative matters rather than legislative issues. This has rejuvenated the subcommittees and virtually killed the full committee. Aspinall went into each Congress with a clear idea of the legislation he expected to be passed that year and a definite schedule of priorities and hearings. The full committee no longer views legislation as a complete package as it did in the Aspinall days. It has become an improvisational committee with no broad plans or strategies, considering each bill as an entity in itself with little relation to whatever preceded or should follow it.

These changes have made the committee more accessible to lobbyists, especially to those from conservation or public interest groups. The lack of an autocratic chairman allows each committee member to be more decisive; it leaves him personally responsible for the way he casts his vote. One lobbyist for a national conservation group cheerfully reported that he does not feel the hostility from the committee that he did when Aspinall was chairman. A representative of another environmental group said that almost everyone on the committee is now willing to listen to him, even some of those who used to be members of Aspinall's inner circle.

Craig Hosmer, Archconservative, New Ranking Minority Member

If this new openness is compensation for Aspinall's reign, there is also an ironic compensation for the years when John Saylor was the ranking minority member. Since Saylor's death in October 1973, the ranking minority member has been the late Republican's antithesis, Craig Hosmer, from Southern California. The director of a Washington-based environmental group has tagged Hosmer "one of the most unreasonable men in the Congress . . . he is almost contemptuous of the views of citizens." In 1970 Hosmer voted for none of the bills supported by the League of Conservation Voters; the next year he favored a slim 16 percent of the LCV-preferred bills. That year the LCV ranked him 329th of the 435 members of the House.

Hosmer's priorities when he is confronted with a choice between economic and environmental matters were apparent in his interrogation of Representative John F. Seiberling (D., Ohio) during the fall 1971 hearings on a strip mining bill:

> MR. HOSMER: . . . you have strongly recommended, either one of two courses: either . . . shutting down the mines, or the alternative course of a 5-year moratorium . . . you come to this committee with these recommendations . . . without recognizing the costs, or equating the costs of these alternatives against the cost of other alternatives. Is that what you mean to tell us?
>
> MR. SEIBERLING: I know that the cost of continuing to operate strip mines is unacceptable.
>
> MR. HOSMER: You don't know what it is.
>
> MR. SEIBERLING: In terms of the environment . . . I can say that the cost of continuing the present course is unacceptable, and to me . . . MR. HOSMER, I presume that this committee is dedicated to the same proposition that I am: namely, that whatever it costs to keep a livable world for ourselves and our children is a cost we have to pay.
>
> MR. HOSMER: We are not talking about a livable world; we are talking about a world which is decent and clean *and acceptable*. We are not talking about life and death, and you know we are not talking about life and death. We are talking about strip mining.
>
> MR. SEIBERLING: In terms of what is happening to the State of Ohio we are talking about life and death.
>
> MR. HOSMER: All right, when you shut down my kilowatts in the Nation's largest metropolitan area, southern California, because you won't let the coal come up from the mine, you are going to kill a lot of my people simply because our industrial society must support those people with food; it must support them with shelter; it must support them with pharmaceuticals; . . . It costs people in

terms of human lives when you turn that energy off. I,
sir, no more than you, wish to see the land desecrated, and
I think we can arrive at decisions which will prevent the
land from being desecrated, but I think we can also make
up our mind that we are going to have to accept a certain
amount in order to perpetuate a society in which just not
the strongest physically, can continue to survive.

MR. SEIBERLING: Well—

MR. HOSMER: These are the things that people forget when
they take extremist positions in environmental matters or
in any other phase of our national life.[22]

Luckily for the many who disagree with Hosmer, they won't
have him to kick them around any more. The fifty-nine-year-old
congressman will be retiring at the end of the Ninety-third Congress. In his retirement announcement he reiterated the truism
that "long seniority helps a Congressman serve his constituency
well." Then, after twenty-four years in the House, he conceded
that "from time to time it is also healthy for fresh talent to move
up to governmental responsibility."[23]

Those who may some day succeed Hosmer and Haley are a
diverse crew. Some would preserve an environment that would
make Lewis and Clark feel at home. Others, in the Aspinall mold,
would not protest if smokestacks replaced trees on every horizon.
Although the Democratic members of the committee have consistently been more concerned with preserving the environment than
their Republican counterparts have been, alignments on the
committee do not necessarily follow party labels. In 1973 Democrats Jonathan Bingham (N.Y.) and Robert Kastenmeier (Wis.)
had 95 and 100 percent ratings from the League of Conservation
Voters, while Democrat Harold Runnels (N.M.) had a 7 percent
LCV rating.* Republicans Alan Steelman (Tex.) and John Del-

---

* The May 17, 1974, issue of *New Times* magazine named Runnels one
of the "ten dumbest" members of Congress. Runnels' nickname, "Mud,"
was acquired, the magazine reported, from the way he made his money—
selling mud for drilling oil wells. As one reporter said of Runnels, "Harold

lenback (Ore.) had 65 and 58 percent LCV ratings, while John Happy Camp (Okla.) had a zero percent rating.*

Since each member of a committee must necessarily be responsive to different constituencies, it is elucidating to view some of the committee members individually, since that may explain not only why they vote the way they do, but whether they might vote otherwise if they came from other districts. Here, then, are short profiles of the subcommittee chairmen, as well as of a few members who have distinguished themselves either by notable aid to environmentalists or by excessive help to private interests.

House Interior Subcommittee Chairmen

Next in line to succeed Chairman Haley is sixty-two-year-old Roy A. Taylor (D., N.C.), who heads the National Parks and Recreation Subcommittee. A lobbyist for a conservation group who has worked for many years with Taylor assesses him as "hard-working and conscientious," a congressman who "knows his subject thoroughly." Taylor is dedicated to preserving and extending the national parks system. He considers it necessary for ameliorating urban malaise and providing a counterpoint to the congestion and pollution of our cities. When Taylor intones such paeans as "Na-

---

has the native shrewdness of a boy who grew up barefoot in Arkansas and made $1 million selling mud. . . . He's always playing the angles."

According to *New Times*, "the dumbest thing that Runnels ever did" was to purchase confidential material from Pentagon sources so that he could ask better questions at Armed Services Committee hearings. The Arkansas representative later admitted, "I've done many dumb things in my life, like engaging these young men to give me information. But if you don't learn from your mistakes you're really dumb." The magazine concluded that "Runnels may be redeemable." ("The Ten Dumbest Congressmen," by Nina Totenberg, *New Times*, May 17, 1974, vol. 2, no. 10, p. 24).

* Bingham has consistently had one of the highest LCV ratings of any member of Congress. During the past four years his LCV ratings have averaged 96 percent: 95 percent in 1973, 96 percent in 1972, 93 percent in 1971, and 100 percent in 1970. Happy Camp, on the other hand, has consistently had one of the lowest LCV ratings on Capitol Hill. He has averaged 8 percent for the past four years: 0 percent in 1973, 15 percent in 1972, 17 percent in 1971, and 0 percent again, in 1970.

ture's a great healer—nature provides inspiration," he sounds like a latter-day Frederick Law Olmsted, the late-nineteenth-century landscape architect who perceived the dangers of increasing American urbanization. Taylor repeatedly insists that "We've become a nation of urban centers, and a lot of our problems are caused by too much crowding. We need to do more to create open spaces and disperse them near urban centers so people can get to them."[24] Taylor once admonished a witness who appeared before his subcommittee:

> Did you ever stop to think that the national parks—the proper use of our natural resources—is an aid in solving these human problems [of our cities]? Our problem in the big cities is crowding too many people on top of people. Parks give them a place we can get out and get back to nature . . .[25]

Taylor may realize and appreciate the economic benefits of national parks on the immediate environment, but his paramount reason for their establishment is to secure a spot of rest and respite for the public. He has recalled that

> I live close to the Smoky Mountain National Park and the whole economy of that area revolves around the park. In every county [in his district adjacent to the park], you find numerous motels and filling stations or businesses of every kind that are there because the park is there. I think the economic growth [of a proposed park in Minnesota] will quickly offset the immediate tax loss.[26]

When some Minnesota residents resisted the proposal for a park in their state, Taylor reminded them, "The economic benefits of this park reach far beyond the two counties affected. They reach over most of the state. They will bring visitors into your big cities who will go up there to the park."[27] Then Taylor returned to his theme, the *raison d'être* for all national parks: "[that they] are created for the recreational enjoyment of people and for the preservation of natural resources . . . If we had to depend on dollars as a reason for the creation of national parks, I fear that we could not justify creating many."[28]

The third-ranking Democrat on the committee is the chairman of its Water and Power Resources Subcommittee, California's Harold T. Johnson, who has been described by a Republican on the committee, Don Clauson, as a man "who has forgotten more about water than most of us [on the Interior Committee] will ever know." Not only does Johnson rule Interior's Water Subcommittee, he also exerts powerful influence as a ranking member of the Public Works Committee's Water Resources Subcommittee.

Johnson has not especially courted the favors of environmentalists, and they do not especially like him either. In 1973 he voted for only 31 percent of the legislation preferred by the League of Conservation Voters. He supported both the $35,000,-000 Disney ski complex at Mineral King and the Mammoth Pass-Mineret Summit Trans-Sierra Highway—both in California, and both vigorously opposed by environmentalists. The Disney project, near Sequoia National Park, would have covered over 300 acres and affected another 13,000 acres, and would have required the construction of a $25,000,000 high-speed highway and a 66,000-volt power line across the national park—all this despite the fact that Mineral King had become a game refuge under a 1926 law.

The Mammoth Pass-Mineret Summit Trans-Sierra Highway, according to the Nader Task Force on Land Use in California, will combine astronomical construction costs, difficult maintenance, and minimal traffic. More than a hundred miles of the highway will be above the 5,000-foot level where snowfall is heaviest. Despite two federal studies discouraging its construction, the road will be built as part of the federal highway system, mostly to please truckers and San Joaquin farmers who want their own highway across the Sierra.

Johnson's policies have been appreciated by industrialists. His 1972 campaign was supported by the Del Monte Corporation, one of the largest landowners in California; the Southern Pacific

Company, the largest private landholder in Johnson's district; the Union Oil Company of California; and Southwest Forest Industries.[29]

Morris K. Udall, chairman of the Environmental Subcommittee, is the only Democrat among Arizona's six-man delegation to Washington. Though some conservation groups are wary of "Mo" because of his eagerness to make compromises to assure a bill's passage, most people in Washington associate Udall with pro-environmental causes. Brock Evans of the Sierra Club affectionately tagged Udall "our champion on land use and the Alaska pipeline" fights. He sponsored an amendment to the Alaska Native Claims Act, which cleared the way for the pipeline, to help preserve lands in public ownership. He sponsored a land use bill which cleared the Interior Committee in January 1974 by a 26–11 vote but was defeated by a 9–4 vote in the Rules Committee. "Having witnessed the abuse of some of Arizona's most beautiful and scenic land," Udall commented, "land use reform has become a kind of personal cause with me."[30]

Referring to the chairman of the Territorial Subcommittee, the Washington director of a national conservation group lamented that "if there should be a puppet that we can pull 100 percent of the time, it should be [Phillip] Burton." But the California Democrat is irascible and unpredictable, a man who likes to assert his own independence and his own sense of priorities. And Burton's sympathies lie inherently with labor, sometimes at the expense of the environment. One indication of his labor orientation is his attendance on the Education and Labor Committee compared to that on the Interior Committee. In 1970–71, the Education and Labor Committee met ninety-three times. Burton either attended or gave his proxy to someone to cast at seventy-six of these sessions, 83 percent of the meetings. But during 1970 Burton attended only four of the Interior Committee's meetings, 27 percent.[31]

One reason why Burton's support is valuable is that he really has three votes. As chairman of the Territorial Subcommittee, he has great influence over the votes of the representatives of Guam and the Virgin Islands who sit on his subcommittee. One committee member's administrative aide reported that Burton frequently blackmails Guam's Antonio Borja Won Pat and the Virgin Islands' Ron de Lugo, both Democrats, with the threat that either they vote with him or their islands "won't get a damn thing this year."

The chairman of the Public Lands Subcommittee, Montana's John Melcher, is a former veterinarian who represents a state in which almost 30 percent of the land is under federal jurisdiction. Though Melcher has averaged a 73 percent rating from the League of Conservation Voters from 1970 to 1973, he is a pragmatist who seems to base his votes on each bill's individual merits rather than on how it meshes with a general scheme for the use of federal lands. For instance, Melcher has strongly supported every bill to regulate strip mining. "If land can't be restored," he insists, "it shouldn't be mined."[32] But he also led the successful fight for the San Carlos Mineral Strip Bill, which critics charged would cost the government at least $362.5 million, to get ranchers off publicly owned lands.[33] The bill authorized $2.5 million to be paid to Arizona ranchers to compensate them for terminating permission to graze their cattle on formerly public land, the San Carlos mineral strip, which had been returned to the San Carlos Apache Indians of Arizona. George Alderson, then the legislative director of the Friends of the Earth, predicted that the bill "would set an unacceptable precedent and enthrone livestock grazing as the dominant use of public lands being used under permits," adding that: "the long-standing national policy is that such permits are privileges, revocable by the government whenever there is good reason to do so."[34] Alderson's fight against the bill was aided by the Interior Department, which confirmed: "The principle has been well established that grazing permits confer no vested rights but merely a privilege which may be withdrawn without compensation."[35]

The Department agreed with Alderson that compensating the

Arizona ranchers would establish a "dangerous precedent," since leases held by ranchers for public lands are worth altogether "at least" $362.5 million.[36]

But Melcher refuted the opinions of experienced conservationists and the Interior Department. Introducing the bill on the House floor on September 18, 1973, he said:

> The valid rights of the ranchers have to be considered. Under the circumstances and conditions of the settling of the San Carlos mineral strip, these ranchers find what they have for generations been assured was their legal right is not their right, and they are suddenly going to be dislodged from the ranches.
>
> They are going to have to leave their ranching operations on the strip.
>
> The Interior Committee believes that equity requires that these ranchers be reimbursed for their land, their improvements and the loss of their grazing rights.[37]

Melcher was opposed almost single-handedly by John Saylor, dean of the House conservationists. Saylor ominously warned:

> . . . if we pass this piece of legislation, and it becomes law, we will have undermined the entire management structure of our public grazing lands. We have a long and well established policy that grazing permits on public lands confer no vested rights, but merely confer a privilege which can be taken away or withdrawn at any time.[38]

The bill's "dangerous precedent," Saylor forecast,

> could expose the United States to substantial liability whenever it declared public land to use with which grazing is inconsistent such as a national monument or wildlife refuge. The precedent could also inhibit the future granting of grazing permits in many areas where the projected use is uncertain, as there would be a desire to avoid exposure to liability based on subsequent determinations.[39]

But neither the House nor the Senate agreed with Saylor, Alderson, or the Interior Department. Apparently more willing to placate a group of ranchers on the Arizona desert than to consider the ramifications of the San Carlos bill on the future of grants for use of public land, Congress passed the bill in December 1973. The San Carlos Indians now have their land, the Arizona ranchers now have their $2.5 million, and the United States government now has a potential $362.5 million liability, thanks to the pugnacious determination of John Melcher.

Patsy Mink (D., Hawaii) was a relatively inconspicuous member of the Interior Committee from her arrival on the committee at the beginning of the Ninetieth Congress until her accession to the chairmanship of the Mines and Mining Subcommittee at the beginning of the Ninety-third. It was not that she was unconcerned about the committee, but she seemed to be more concerned with her assignment to the Education and Labor Committee and her brief campaign for the Democratic presidential nomination in 1972.

Mink's interest in the Interior Committee has increased since she has headed the Mines and Mining Subcommittee. Environmentalists have especially admired her fight for the Surface Mining Bill (H.R. 11500), especially because she first advocated the complete prohibition of surface mining throughout the country. In fact, conservationists have trusted her more on the strip-mining bill than they have Udall, the chairman of the environmental subcommittee which held joint hearings with Mink's subcommittee on H.R. 11500. Mink, they say, fights first for her principles and compromises only as a last resort.

The chairman of the Indian Affairs Subcommittee, Lloyd Meeds (D., Wash.), is considered a friend by the Indians but is viewed ambivalently by conservationists. Meeds came to Congress in 1964 as an environmentalist. He was one of the major advocates of the North Cascades National Park, which preserved over 500,000 acres of woodland when it was created in 1968. He was also a major sponsor of the Youth Conservation Corps, similar to the Civilian Conservation Corps of the 1930s.

But Meeds's uncertainty on other environmental issues, especially when they affect his home district, was indicated in his March 1972 newsletter to his constituents. On the newsletter's fourth page Meeds reiterated his support for the trans-Alaska pipeline. Although the Alaskan route threatened a considerable risk of ecological destruction from oil spills along a shipping route that passed Alaska, western Canada and parts of Washington, Meeds predicted:

> Building the proposed Trans-Alaska Pipeline system can create at least 6,000 jobs in the Puget Sound region by 1980, not counting jobs in the existing and future oil refineries.
> . . . Like the people who would scrap pollution regulations to save jobs, the extreme environmentalists are also negative. They are unrealistic. They would like to kill the pipeline and "keep oil tankers out of Puget Sound."
> Some of these extremists would ignore the economy and turn the United States into a museum . . .[40]

On the other hand, in the newsletter's first three pages Meeds refuted the January 14, 1972, claims of Weyerhaeuser, the giant timber company, that it was closing its sulphite mill in Everett, Washington, because of stringent environmental standards. The *Seattle Times* called this part of the newsletter "a bombshell."[41] Weyerhaeuser had asserted that it was closing the plant because it would cost $52 million to construct a new mill or $10 million to outfit an old one with a recovery process that would meet environmental standards. The federal Environmental Protection Agency had estimated that the chemical level of Everett's Point Gardner Bay wastes equaled the wastes of five to six million human beings.[42] Meeds charged, however, that environmental standards were entirely irrelevant to the plant's closing. The Everett mill had been dependent upon one East Coast customer for 65 percent of its business. In 1969 Weyerhaeuser had opened a plant in New Bern, North Carolina, a plant that was closer to the eastern markets and located in a state with lax labor laws. As one employee in the New Bern plant told Meeds's staff, "Weyerhaeuser started hiring men in 1969. They told a lot of guys that the old Everett mill was to be phased out and replaced with a plant here."[43]

Meeds rebuffed not only Weyerhaeuser's claims, but those of many of his constituents who had demanded that environmental laws be changed to permit the continued operation of the Everett plant: "One pulp mill nearing death is not going to be revived by changing pollution laws. Abandoning these regulations would injure our water quality and be unfair to the vast majority of Pacific Northwest pulp mills that are cleaning up . . ."[44]

As for whether the plant's closing would ruin the area's economy:

> Economic recovery depends on the spirit of the people. Other communities have been shellshocked but have come back. We've been bitter before too, but being negative never brought in a new payroll. That's why we have to count our blessings, not our miseries. Let's stop staring hopelessly at the ground and start looking ahead . . . We need a new, positive view of the future . . .[45]

Just as Meeds criticized many in his district, he himself was also severely castigated. Shortly after the newsletter was mailed, he met in Everett with an angry delegation from the Association of Western Pulp and Paper Workers. Despite Meeds's long prolabor record, he said that this meeting was "the most acrimonious . . . I've ever had. . . . I'll be very disappointed if this hasn't done some good—if it hasn't caused people to think. But so far it has been a political minus for me. People don't want to hear what they don't like to hear." He thought a moment, then added, "I hope I haven't pushed enough people over the line to vote against me and throw me out of office."[46]

If there is any member of the House Interior Committee whose name causes conservationists to become apoplectic, it is Sam Steiger (R., Ariz.), the ranking Republican on the Public Lands Subcommittee. Steiger received a 5 percent rating from the League of Conservation Voters in 1973. His average LCV rating for the preceding four years was 13 percent. One environmental lobbyist tagged the Arizona representative a "criminal of the first rank; a rude, nasty person."

Steiger seems to derive a certain pleasure from being exuberantly tactless. He has admitted that "I make as many people mad as possible."[47] One of the many people whom he has incensed is Congressman Udall, who blamed Steiger personally, as a member of the Rules Committee, for "sandbagging" the land use bill that Udall and others had carefully nurtured through the Interior Committee. Steiger's truculent attitude toward environmental groups was apparent during his questioning of the Sierra Club's Brock Evans in the 1973 hearings on the trans-Alaska pipeline:

> MR. STEIGER: . . . Mr. Evans, I am constantly impressed at the certainty with which your group and yourself are able to predict disaster in the light of your track record. Were you a member, active member, of the Sierra Club when the Sierra Club was predicting the Amchitka disaster?
>
> MR. EVANS: I was a member of the Sierra Club; right.
>
> MR. STEIGER: Do you recall that incident?
>
> MR. EVANS: Sure.
>
> MR. STEIGER: Do you consider the Amchitka underground exploration as a disaster today?
>
> MR. EVANS: It depends. If you consider the destruction of 1,000 sea otter a disaster; yes. But we have to be concerned about that.
>
> MR. STEIGER: . . . I think this group would be irresponsible if they did not recognize that, at the very best, your enthusiasm to predict disasters does not represent a balanced equation with your expertise in this area. Therefore, at the same time that you would cry out for an objective, scientific appraisal, you are apparently far more interested in rhetoric than in fact. This is the reason, frankly, I am

going to support very strongly the language that seems as a legislative fact of life, the fact that in this instance, NEPA [the National Environmental Protection Act] has been complied with and therefore we should not tolerate any further tampering with the judicial process by well-meaning but apparently misguided groups.

It is a direct reaction and rather an unsavory one, I might add, but a direct reaction to the excesses to the movement you obviously are very much involved with. . . .

MR. MELCHER [Chairman of the Public Lands Subcommittee conducting the Alaska pipeline hearings]: Thank you very much, Brock, for your testimony, and for your candid replies to our questions. You are always welcome here.[48]

Steiger's uninhibited bias against environmentalists is thoroughly appreciated by private interests. His 1972 reelection campaign was financed with the generous help of the Union Oil Company of California; the Atchison, Topeka and Santa Fe Railroad; Southwest Forest Industries Inc.; and personal contributions from two members of the Pew family of Philadelphia, which owns the controlling interest in the Sun Oil Company.[49]

Steiger's campaign financing was in direct contrast to that of the other Arizona representative who sits on the committee. Contributing to Udall's 1972 campaign were eleven unions, including the national AFL-CIO and eight of its affiliates, the United Auto Workers, and the Teamsters. Not one cent came from a major industrial group.[50]

THE SENATE INTERIOR COMMITTEE

The organization of the Senate Interior Committee resembles neither of the models presented to describe the House committee. The Senate committee is a hybrid of the Aspinall autocracy and the Haley anarchy. Compared to the Aspinall committee, the Senate committee is loose and unstructured; its chairman is concerned, though not obsessed, with environmental problems; and each member of the committee is treated with respect and allowed a certain amount of independence. But the Senate committee does not give its subcommittees as much freedom as does the Haley committee in the House. The full committee's staff is also the staff for the six subcommittees, and the committee chairman appoints members of the staff to become *ad hoc* authorities on issues as they arise.

Chairman Henry Jackson

The committee has been operating as it does now since 1963, when Henry Jackson, (D., Wash.), then fifty-one, succeeded Clinton Anderson as its chairman. Jackson is a man who generates very mixed opinions. He has been sardonically described by the *New York Times* as "a persistent if not profound thinker . . . an earnest plodder rather than a zealous crusader"; he has been praised adoringly by the committee's chief counsel, William Van Ness, as a man "too intellectually honest to take cheap shots"; and his embittered opponent for the 1970 Democratic senatorial nomination, Carl Maxey, said in 1972 that he had "just begun to realize the full scope of his [Jackson's] vindictiveness."[51]

Jackson is a man who inspires either great loyalty and confidence or considerable suspicion and hostility. Robert Kennedy tried to persuade his brother to select Jackson as his running mate in 1960, but the older Kennedy preferred Sam Rayburn's advice that he put Lyndon Johnson on the ticket. It is common knowledge in Washington that President-elect Nixon asked Jackson to be his Secretary of Defense. When Jackson refused, he was asked to join the Nixon administration as Secretary of State, and he refused that too.[52]

But Jackson also has an unenviable knack for making enemies. He vehemently opposed two of the Democratic Party's most recent liberal contenders for the presidency, Eugene McCarthy and George McGovern. In 1972 McCarthy threatened to bolt from the party if Jackson were tapped for the presidential nomination.

Liberals like Senator Fred Harris and Representatives Shirley Chisholm and Allard Lowenstein warned that a fourth party was inevitable if Jackson was nominated in 1972.*

Jackson evokes such disparate reactions from members of both parties because he is that rarity, a moderate Democrat, who has strong ties to labor, advocates a mighty cold war military posture for the United States, and advocates strong social programs. He has voted for Medicare, for such assistance to the poor as Project Headstart, and for unemployment benefits to migrant workers, but he has also opposed cutting the level of U. S. troops in Europe, opposed reducing the Defense Department's budget, and opposed banning the use of chemical defoliants. He was one of the Senate's most faithful adherents to the "domino theory," which rationalized the United States presence in Vietnam. Jackson usually buttressed his arguments for the continuation of the war by asking rhetorically whether there was any doubt that an American withdrawal from Vietnam or a humiliating compromise would open the doors to a vast extension of Chinese and/or Soviet influence in Asia.[53]

Jackson's balance between moderately liberal domestic policies and a traditionally conservative foreign relations and military posture is reflected in the ratings he receives from interest groups. He has voted against only one of the 120 issues that the AFL-CIO's political wing, COPE (Committee on Political Education), has favored since he arrived in Washington. During 1973 he voted for none of the nine bills favored by the National Chamber of Commerce, and in 1971–72 for only one of the nine issues favored by the National Associated Businessmen. He has a 55 percent 1973

---

* Jackson did manage to record a considerable protest vote at his party's 1972 convention. Once McGovern's nomination was a certainty, Jackson's aides rounded up enough delegates to demonstrate that there was a substantial alternative. The Washington senator finished second, with 534 votes, while McGovern won the nomination with 1,715 votes. See "Energy Crisis, Economy Bolster Jackson for 1976." Jules Witcover, *Washington Post*, Feb. 11, 1974, p. A4.

rating from the Americans for Democratic Action and an 80 percent 1971–72 rating from the pro-military American Security Council.

Jackson, then, is a man divided between his views of the domestic needs of the nation and its international security. The senator's split priorities are reflected in his environmental policies. In 1971, for example, he received a 53 percent rating from the League of Conservation Voters. As one environmentalist said, Jackson has the "power to do good or evil," and the decision he makes from an environmental viewpoint is mostly contingent on how the environmental standard would affect the nation's military strength. For instance, though both the trans-Alaska pipeline and the supersonic transport plane (SST) were bitterly opposed by environmentalists, Jackson supported them on the grounds that they were necessary for economic and military security. During the March 24, 1971, debate on restoring the funds for the development of the SST, Jackson denounced the environmentalists' anti-SST tactics, charging that the SST debate had been churned and provoked by "predictions of environmental disaster by people not qualified to speak on the issues they raise."[54] He lamented the environmentalists' opposition and wondered aloud why the "real environmental problems, real problems in technology assessment do not receive the attention from Congress, from environmentalists and from the media which has been given to the SST."[55]

But rather than chastise his colleagues, Jackson mostly wanted to remind them that the facts, as he saw them, were that if the SST was terminated

> 13,000 American scientists, engineers and technicians and working men will be out of jobs tomorrow; 4,900 of these people work for the Boeing Co. in my State. They will enter a labor market already staggering under an unemployment rate of 18 percent. They will join 71,500 people in the Seattle area who are unemployed, 66,000 who are receiving welfare, 72,000 who are receiving food stamps.[56]

Jackson, who has been called "the senator from Boeing," predicted that if the SST funds were rejected his fellow senators would be deluged with complaints from their constituents. They would hear, he said somewhat histrionically,

> of the misery, the tragedy, and the insecurity of being unemployed at a time when unemployment stands at a 9-year high and unemployment nationally stands at 6 percent.
>
> I would urge my colleagues in the Senate to think about what they say to these American men and women before they vote this afternoon. They will find little comfort in the discussions of "priorities" I have had to date.[57]

But apparently the Senate preferred to suffer the complaints of those who lost their jobs through the cancellation of the SST program rather than the pangs of their own consciences from voting for a measure they opposed. Fifty-one senators voted against providing funds for the SST, while forty-six favored the funding. Jackson was among the minority.

In a different vein, Jackson was the Interior Committee's major proponent for some recent legislation that has advanced the environmental cause: the Eastern Wilderness Areas Act, the Surface Mining Regulation Act (S. 425), and especially the National Environmental Policy Act. NEPA is one of the most important pieces of legislation to originate in the Interior Committee. It established the President's Council on Environmental Quality and articulated the first real national policies and goals on environment. It also established stringent environmental standards for all federal agencies by requiring them to file environmental impact statements with the Council on Environmental Quality before beginning any new program.

During the 1969 NEPA hearings Jackson said that he had introduced the bill because

> our present knowledge, our established policies, and our existing institutions are not adequate to deal with the growing environmental problems and crises the nation faces.

The inadequacy of present knowledge, policies and institutions is reflected in our nation's history, in our national attitudes, and in our contemporary life. We see this inadequacy all around us: haphazard urban growth, the loss of open spaces, strip-mining, air and water pollution, soil erosion, deforestation, faltering transportation systems, a proliferation of pesticides and chemicals, and a landscape cluttered with billboards, powerlines and junkyards.

Today it is clear that we cannot continue to perpetuate the mistakes of the past. We no longer have the margins for error and mistakes that we once enjoyed.[58]

Although Jackson was one of the sixty-seven senators who voted for the Emergency Energy Act (S. 2589) on February 19, 1974, he did so most reluctantly. During the debate on the bill, Jackson, whom one observer called "the Toscanini of energy legislation,"[59] assailed the Nixon administration because it was still

committed to the 19th century notion that the way to deal with the energy shortage is to limit demand by raising consumer prices.

The White House either does not know or does not care that this foolish and intellectually indefensible policy has cruel and disastrous consequences for the poor and the middle class. It is a stupid policy because it is counterproductive to the national interest. It is an unfair policy because it enables the affluent to buy their way out and, at the same time, it gives the oil companies billions of dollars in unearned profits.[60]

It is comments like these which raise the hackles of the oil industry and, as one of Jackson's aides said, makes "the energy industry think that Scoop is out to nationalize it."

Lee Metcalf, Chairman of the Minerals, Materials and Fuels Subcommittee

From the environmentalists' viewpoint, the best man on the committee is Lee Metcalf; industry sees him as the worst. One conservationist described the Montana Democrat as "one of the most reliable committee members"; a committee staff member tagged Metcalf a "tried-and-true liberal, dedicated to the environment and suspicious of big business," including businesses in his home state, which is heavily dependent on mining.

Since his arrival in Washington, Metcalf has been particularly concerned with preserving the environment. As a freshman representative in the Eighty-third Congress (1953–54) he worked hard to defeat the D'Ewart Grazing Bill (H.R. 4023), which would have made grazing permits for public lands tantamount to ownership. Metcalf warned that this would have made the "monopolization of public lands certain."[61] During the second session of the same Congress he was the floor leader of the forces that halted the Ellsworth Timber Exchange Bill. If passed, the bill would have required the federal government to make partial payment for its timberland purchases with timberland from other federal lands, including national forests and parks and wildlife refuges. Metcalf described this as "trading trees for stumps," since federal purchases of timberland would include land comdemned for inundation behind new dams.[62]

In 1962, the second year Metcalf was in the Senate, he introduced the Save Our Streams (SOS) Bill, which was designed to curtail the destruction of recreation facilities and fish and wildlife caused by the construction of the Interstate Highway System. The bill would have required that highway planning satisfy environmental standards. Though the bill failed, Metcalf introduced it again in 1963, and this time he obtained a compromise when the Kennedy administration ordered coordination between highway construction and conservation. The intent of the SOS Bill has been included in the National Environmental Policy Act, which requires every activity of the federal government to satisfy minimal environmental standards.

Metcalf has publicized the discouraging fact that fifty-five members of the National Industrial Pollution Control Council, established by President Nixon in 1970, are leaders in the indus-

tries that contribute the most to environmental pollution. Metcalf
stated frankly:

> The purpose of industry advisory committees to Government
> is to enhance corporate image, to create an illusion of action
> and to impede Government officials who are attempting to
> enforce law and order and gather the data upon which en-
> forcement is based.
>
> The President and the large corporation heads who serve
> on his new Council have voices so powerful that they can
> drown out the cries of a hundred Senators. But business
> advisory councils and public relations ploys will not preserve
> the environment. They will hasten its destruction, because
> they impede enforcement.[63]

There is perhaps no better subcommittee for Metcalf to head
than the Interior Committee's Minerals, Materials and Fuels Subcommittee. For many years he has been interested in regulation of
the minerals and utilities industries. The thesis of the 1967 book,
Overcharge, which he wrote with his executive secretary, Vic
Reinemer, was that state regulation of these industries has failed
because most of the nation's top legal, accounting, and technical
talent has been monopolized by the utilities and has not been
available to the regulatory commissions and the public. Among
the strong regulatory measures that Metcalf has recently supported are the 1973 surface mining bill (S. 425) and a bill to
regulate the development of the nation's mineral resources on
public lands (S. 3086). When Metcalf introduced the latter bill
on February 28, 1974, he noted that:

> Mining often involves the destruction of other resources to
> some extent. In many cases, timber must be removed, wild-
> life habitat must be disturbed, natural waterways must be
> changed, overburden must be set aside, wastes must be dis-
> posed of, roads must be pushed through undisturbed areas,
> water must be diverted, and may become contaminated, and
> holes must be drilled . . .[64]

Metcalf admitted that "these and other activities are essential to obtain minerals needed by the economy," but he urged that the nation "balance mineral development with other resource values and other potential land uses." For years, he lamented, "the scales have been tipped in favor of the mineral developer," and he went on to say:

> I believe that the general public will accept the balance principle, with one exception. This is: When in doubt, err on the side of the environment. Deferred development almost always can take place in the future, but environmental damage may be difficult if not impossible to repair.[65]

Frank Church, Chairman of the Water and Power Resources Subcommittee

One of the most crassly pragmatic members of the committee is the chairman of its Water and Power Resources Subcommittee. Frank Church is from Idaho, a state rich in mining and timber, whose farmland is watered by over 5,000 small diversion dams and 15,000 miles of irrigation canals.[66] One environmental lobbyist praised the Idaho Democrat as "first class on environmental issues. If there were more men in the Congress like him, we'd have a better country." Another gave Church slightly more tepid praise: "Church is not going far enough, but if you consider his constituency, he's doing pretty well. I'd give him fairly consistent good marks on environment issues."[67]

But as election time approaches, environmental concerns recede and Church remembers those influential and affluent interests back home, timber men and mining operators. Ten months before election day 1974, one conservationist complained that he could not even get Church to endorse a national historical site.

For the first years after Church's election to the Senate in 1956, he usually supported as much environmentally oriented legislation as any other member of the committee. In 1962 he was the floor manager for the Wilderness Act, which established the National Wilderness Preservation System. In 1972 Church recalled that the bill was known in Idaho as the "Church Wilderness bill." It was opposed by all the major private interests in his state: miners, foresters, cattlemen, sheepmen, the Chamber of Commerce, and all but one of the state's newspapers.

> My father-in-law, who was once governor, was pacing the floor on the evening before the vote on my reelection. He finally came over to me and said, "I would like to know how you expect to be elected." All the groups were against me. They were saying I was going to make a playground for Eastern millionaires, and that our source of livelihood would be ruined. I told my father-in-law, "Well, maybe the people will not be against me." And they weren't—I won.[68]

To Church, his vindication at the polls "illustrated for the first time that Idaho people cared a great deal about the outdoors. . . . From that point on, men in public life in Idaho began to recognize that times were changing, that the [men] long dominant in Idaho could no longer . . . preserve their rights to the public domain as against the public interest."[69]

As chairman of the Water and Power Resources Subcommittee, Church has been interested in developing new sources of energy, particularly since the country is entering "an energy crisis of major proportions," accompanied by "electrical brownouts and spiraling costs of all energy forms."[70] The energy dilemma, as Church predicted, is turning out to be "one of the most critical national problems of the next few decades."[71] During the summer and fall of 1973, Church chaired three days of subcommittee hearings on present and future technology in the field of geothermal energy. He said that this power source has a potential for great applicability, which gives it a "high priority" for development and use.[72]

Alan Bible, Parks and Recreation Subcommittee Chairman

One of the committee's most powerful men will be retiring at the end of the Ninety-third Congress. Nevada's Alan Bible has been chairman of two key subcommittees, the Interior Committee's Parks and Recreation Subcommittee and the Appropriations Committee's Interior Subcommittee. Bible is responsible not only for shaping the subcommittee's legislation on parks and recreation, but also for determining which of the committee's bills will receive funds for their implementation. At Interior Appropriation Subcommittee's hearings Bible is a tough, brusque questioner. He frequently interrupts witnesses—even if they are fellow senators —to ask about the validity of statistics they are presenting, about the necessity of certain programs that could be shaved from the appropriations budget, about the relationship between state and federal programs to avoid duplication and save money.

Bible seems more closely aligned to his state's ranching and mining interests than to the ecological interests of conservationists. For instance, he has constantly opposed any increase in grazing fees on public lands. During 1969 hearings on grazing increases, Bible commented:

> . . . it appears that we are about to embark on the umpteenth chapter of a serial that could well be entitled "The Perils of the User of the Public Domain" or "How long can the livestock rancher continue to operate under the ill-advised and fantastic increase in grazing fees charged for the use of public lands. . . ."
>
> As I advised the former Secretary of the Interior in my letter of December 5, urging a moratorium on the proposed grazing fee increase, I was being forced to the conclusion that the proposal, if implemented, would be a first step in the eventual elimination of domestic livestock grazing from the public domain lands.[73]

Floyd K. Haskell, Public Lands Subcommittee Chairman

The chairman of the Public Lands Subcommittee, Floyd K. Haskell, has had one of the most independent political histories of any of the members of the Senate Interior Committee. In 1964 Haskell was elected as a Republican to the Colorado State Legislature and was appointed by the state GOP House Caucus as the assistant majority leader. One of the new representative's chief concerns was American military involvement in Indochina. In 1967 he sponsored and successfully fought through the Colorado House a resolution criticizing American conduct in Vietnam. In 1970, the day after President Nixon ordered United States troops into Cambodia, Haskell switched parties and became a Democrat.

In 1972 Haskell unseated powerful five-term Republican Senator Gordon Allott. Since his arrival in Washington he has been alternately praised and criticized by environmentalists. On the favorable side, one conservationist calls him "great"; another said he was a "very, very good senator, one of the best new senators in town." Almost everyone praised his strong opposition to the trans-Alaska pipeline. During the 1973 floor debate on the pipeline bill, Haskell proposed an amendment that would delay any transportation of oil from Alaska's North Slope until the U.S. Comptroller General, with the cooperation of the director of the National Science Foundation, had studied the relative merits of the two suggested routes for the pipeline. The alternatives were either the trans-Alaska route, which was ecologically less damaging and which would supply the western states, or one across Canada, which would deliver the oil directly to the more needy midwestern and eastern states. Haskell advised his colleagues:

> Those who favor the trans-Alaska route should favor my amendment. If they are confident their route is in the best interest of the Nation as a whole and can withstand careful scrutiny, they should join in the amendment. Similarly those who favor the trans-Canada route would have an opportunity to prove their case.
>
> Right now we do not have the information on which to make a decision. This is admitted in the Department of the Interior's environmental impact statement on the trans-Alaska route which states:
>
> Data does not exist to definitely state the relative efficien-

cies of TAPS [Trans-Alaska Pipeline System] and Mac-
Kenzie Valley Pipeline System.

We have an obligation to secure the information and to
make a decision.[74]

However, Haskell has also been criticized by environmental
groups. Though he has often opposed ecologically destructive legislation, environmentalists are disappointed by his diffidence. His
inexperience on the committee is too readily apparent; his lack of
expertise is too much of a handicap. In committee debates Haskell is amenable, quick to compromise, sometimes to yield completely to the opposition. He seems to lack the doggedness that
comes with intimate knowledge of the Senate and of a committee's affairs. Though he may espouse certain bills or amendments,
he occasionally does so with a sense of dread and pessimism. His
March 1974 form-letter response to letters from constituents
urging him to support a wilderness review clause for a Bureau of
Land Management bill typifies this attitude. "I favor such a
clause," he wrote, "but am not at all confident that a majority of
my colleagues on the committee feel the same. Even if such a
provision were to survive committee scrutiny, I am certain that
there would be a battle over it once it hits the Senate floor."[75]

James Abourezk, Indian Affairs Subcommittee Chairman

As far as Indians are concerned, there could hardly be a better
chairman of the Indian Affairs Subcommittee than James
Abourezk (D., S. Dak.). They usually consider him their best
friend in Congress and admire him for his sensitive awareness of
the Indian cause. They are relieved to have a friendly and concerned chairman of the subcommittee that is responsible for their
health, education, and lands.

Though Abourezk is usually tagged a liberal, he seems to be
more comfortable in the populist mold than in the liberal. He is
an outspoken critic both of congressional procedures and of his

own party. He once confessed that "when I listen to people on the floor, it is a lot of bullshit."[76]

Abourezk loathes compromise and tenaciously protects his principles. For instance, the defeated Energy Emergency Act was intended to roll back the price of domestic crude oil to $5.25 per barrel, and to give the president the option to raise it 35 percent to $7.09. Abourezk introduced an amendment that would have sent the Act back to the conference committee and instructed the conferees to roll the price back even further. The senator was severely criticized by his colleagues for refusing to compromise on a roll-back price, but he maintained his stance, and his amendment was soundly defeated, 37 to 62,* on February 19, 1974. Abourezk stated that the surge in oil prices "and the so-called energy crisis are part of a hoax, a scheme to blackmail the American people by making them believe there is a shortage when there is none." He said:

> According to the Federal Trade Commission's July 1973 investigation of the petroleum industry, the top 20 major oil companies in 1970 controlled over 93 per cent of domestic proven oil reserves. Also in 1970, 20 companies—16 of which are the same—controlled over 87 percent of gasoline refining capacity. Many of these same companies, according to the November 1973 report of the Senate Permanent Investigations Subcommittee, were the ones primarily responsible for restricting outputs in 1972 and 1973 directly causing both fuel and oil and gasoline shortages. That the current fuel shortages have been caused by a shortage of crude oil in the world and the Arab embargo, as the oil companies and the Nixon administration would have this Congress and the public believe, is not so. The fuel shortages have been caused by the deliberate and joint actions of the major oil companies and the Nixon administration. By voting in favor of the conference report [on the Energy Emergency Act] the

---

* Interior Committee members who supported Abourezk's amendment were Bartlett, Buckley, Fannin, Hansen, and Johnston. Opposing were Bible, Church, Haskell, Jackson, Metcalf, Metzenbaum, and Nelson.

Senate would capitulate to the power of the oil oligopoly and force the American people to give in to the biggest holdup in history.

. . . As far as I am concerned, and as far as many of my constituents are concerned, the fuel shortages have been skillfully contrived and the so-called energy crisis is nothing but a hoax. It is a hoax designed to fleece the American people—to increase oil company profits; to achieve their legislative objectives; to eliminate competition at every level; to raise prices; to forestall environmental safeguards and to grant to the executive branch of Government unlimited dictatorial power.[77]

Though Abourezk's instinctive balking at compromise limits his effectiveness as a senator, he does respond to the promptings of his conscience which is much more than can be said for many members of Congress.

J. Bennett Johnston, Jr., Territories and Insular Affairs Subcommittee Chairman

The chairman of the Territories and Insular Affairs Subcommittee is a first-termer from Louisiana. According to the 1974 *Almanac of American Politics*, since J. Bennett Johnston, Jr., arrived in the Senate in 1972, with the support of 55 percent of his constituents, he "has come out as one of the more conservative Southern Democrats."[78] Johnson is from one of the most richly oil-endowed states in the nation, and he is closely allied with the oil interests. He supported the trans-Alaska pipeline, is not especially sympathetic toward government regulation of oil prices, and has proposed a small tax on imported oil whose first $100,000,000 would establish a fund to be used to clean the pollution caused by oil spills. The remainder would be used for conservation purposes.

Paul J. Fannin and Clifford P. Hansen

The Committee's two senior Republicans, Paul J. Fannin (Ariz.) and Clifford P. Hansen (Wyo.), have been called "the two most rapacious men in Congress" by an environmentalist. Whenever a mining, grazing, or oil interest wants anything, it is reputed, the first man to see is Paul Fannin. He fulminates against government regulation of oil prices, proposed increases in grazing fees on public lands, and strict controls of mining. Predictably, he opposed the price rollback in the Energy Emergency Act, but for reasons exactly opposite to Abourezk's. He contended that

> during the past half century the free market created a very complex but very effective system of supplying the gasoline needs of our people. We are only now beginning to realize just how great this system was. It provided abundant supply at low prices. Attempting to manipulate this system through government controls has proved to be an overwhelming task.
>
> I believe the cure to our energy crisis lies in moving back toward the free market, not away from it. It would take a new Government bureaucracy of gigantic proportions to administer a rationing program with any effectiveness and equity.
>
> . . . I believe that if we could let the free market work, it would provide us with the very controls that no government can impose. It would provide the most efficient usage of our various energy resources at the most reasonable prices for consumers. Equally important, it would leave the people with freedom of choice.[79]

Joining Fannin as a handmaiden of the oil and mining interests is Clifford Hansen, ranking minority member of the Parks and Recreation Subcommittee. Hansen stuffs the *Congressional Record* with reprints on topics like: "Oil Hunters Aid Sealife—IOCC Told," and "Cheap Foreign Oil-Gas Myth Laid to Rest," from such magazines as *Oil Daily*. His recurrent theme is that "One of the greatest things [the government] could do would be to do less in the way of regulation and control, particularly in the area of gas pricing and also in recognizing the real need for incentives— price and tax incentives."[80]

Because of his steadfast opposition to government regulation of oil prices, Hansen opposed the oil price rollback that was part of the Energy Emergency Act. "It is possible," Hansen warned,

> that rigid price controls over a 3-year period will result in an intensified energy crunch with devastating effects on the economy.
>
> In the longer run it will lead to higher prices, because not even the U.S. Congress can repeal the law of supply and demand.
>
> Our national goals of energy self-sufficiency and elimination of waste are frustrated by the price rollback provision. Governmental interference with the free market price mechanism during this time of rapid changes in the industry and the world situation threatens the development of a sound energy base.[81]

Exploiters of the nation's natural resources greet Hansen's remarks and votes with enthusiasm and money. His 1972 campaign, for example, was assisted by contributions from the chairman of the board of Olin Mathiesen, a chemical manufacturer ($3,000); a member of the Pew family, which has the controlling interest in Sun Oil Company ($2,000); and an executive of the Atlantic Richfield Petroleum Company ($1,000).[82]

For another example of Hansen's political philosophy, the Grand Teton National Park has always featured prominently in his career. Hansen, who was county commissioner of Teton County and a leading cattleman in the area when the park was first established in 1943, strongly opposed its establishment.* Since then he has worked just as diligently to have the park's acres used and misused by private individuals, including himself. Since 1950 he has been one of three ranchers whose cattle are

---

* Hansen attacked the establishment of the park with hysterical manifestos as: ". . . an enemy has invaded our peaceful valley and threatened to take away from us our properties, our livelihoods, and the heritage of our sons and daughters. . . ." ("Senator Hansen's Cattle in the Park," by Bernard D. Shanks, *Progressive*, Sept. 1972, p. 39).

allowed to graze within the park. In 1971 a graduate student at Michigan State University's Department of Resource Development, Bernard D. Shanks, wrote:

> The National Park Service permits the continuation of several questionable grazing permits, and maintains cattle for Wyoming's U.S. Senator Hansen and two of his cattlemen associates. To prevent Hansen's cattle from wandering onto the park highways where the heavy traffic would take its toll, the cattle are protected by park fences. Senator Hansen, who has frequently spoken out against increases in the grazing fees, has no apparent hesitation about the Park Service spending over $264,000 in a 10-year period to care for his cattle. On public land the Park Service has built miles of fence and maintains ditches and gates for irrigated pasture land. It pays for irrigators every summer and rather than permitting the area to return to its original ecological state the Park Service "improves" the grass cover.[83]

Though the superintendent of the Grand Teton Park, Howard H. Chapman, denied Shanks's allegations that "Hansen and his two friends secured their permits by a brazen political power play," he failed to answer, or even acknowledge Shanks's accusations that the Park Service had spent over $264,000 to maintain the senator's cattle.[84]

In 1968, a Grand Teton issue again reared its snow-topped head. That year, Hansen began to urge that an airport runway lying within the park be extended from 6,300 to 10,000 feet to accommodate jets. George Hartzog, Jr., the director of the National Park Service, sternly vetoed the project because it would be "a violation of the obligation with which we have been charged by the people of this country through Congress."[85] However, few things are as powerful as an idea that is backed by a member of the U.S. Senate. Though Hartzog had vetoed the Jackson Hole Airport extension, Congress did not. Funds for the extension—$2,215,000—were finally included in the 1972 supplemental appropriations act. Representative Julia Butler Hansen (D.,

Wash.), who chairs the House Appropriations subcommittee that handles funding for national parks, attributed the appropriation to the indefatigable efforts of the Wyoming delegation, the two senators, Hansen and Gale McGee, and Representative Teno Roncalio, a member of the House Interior Committee.[86]

Conservationists and scientists alike were aghast at the probable effects of the increased jet noise and emissions on Grand Teton's tranquility. Park wildlife will severely suffer, according to Dr. William Robertson, Jr., National Park Service ornithologist. Nesting birds, he said, react to the shadows and noises of low-flying jets by repeated "panic flights" which disrupt critical incubation rhythms and lead to desertion of the nest. "Nest abandonment by the larger birds is a distinct possibility," Robertson cautioned.[87]

Another specialist, Dr. Robert F. Sawyer, professor of mechanical and aeronautical engineering, added, "This type of development should be avoided at all costs. The noise and visual impact would seem completely and fundamentally contrary to the essence and function of a national park."[88]

But Senator Hansen seemed oblivious to the destruction of the once pastoral park. He was more concerned with the alleged benefits of the jetport. Though the citizens opposing the jetport contended that only 1 percent of the tourists coming to Jackson arrive by air, Hansen insisted that "the area had a 'great number of visitors' who arrived by air."[89]

Casting about for other reasons to support the jetport, the senator displayed a certain chauvinistic pride. In 1972, the centennial year for the National Park System, "the attention of the world will be focused" on the system and its components, including Grand Teton, Hansen said. Possibly assuming that the park would be deluged with visitors from around the globe, he urged that "adequate facilities providing access to the park by air should be available."[90]

Hansen finally got his funds and Jackson Hole Airport finally got its additional 3,700 feet, taxiways, feeder lanes, parking aprons, $13,000 worth of sewer piping, jet noise, and air pollution; but the Grand Teton area never got the surge of visitors that Hansen predicted would be attracted by the jetport. A typical reaction to Hansen's coup was that of Congresswoman Hansen. When she finally discovered that her subcommittee's appropriation for "improvements" really meant jetport construction, she said indignantly, "It's the craziest thing I ever heard."[91]

3

The Land Rapers:
They Got the Bread,
We Got the Crust

In the summer and fall of 1973, radios across the United States were pulsating with the words of a song by John Prine about the depredations of strip mining in western Kentucky. The town of Paradise, in Prine's lament, was sacked, gouged, and shoveled until there was nothing left but black piles of slag, deep ravines along coal seams, and the angry glare of sunlight on long-deserted homes. Paradise is a long way from Washington, but what happens in the town mourned in John Prine's ballad and what happens in the town where the nation's laws are made is inextricably linked. For years, coal companies throughout the country were able to convince Congress that strip mining should be regulated by the state governments. They persuaded the state legislators—except those in West

Virginia and Pennsylvania, the states with the toughest strip-mining laws in the nation—to pass laws with big enough loopholes to make them completely ineffectual.

Strip mining is a scourge that has swept through Appalachia, the coal fields of central Illinois, Indiana, western Kentucky, and Kansas, and the fields of the Far West. The U.S. Bureau of Mines estimates that there are over three trillion tons of unmined coal in the United States, half of which can be recovered by modern technology. It has been estimated that 356 billion tons can be mined by underground mining methods and 45 billion tons by strip mining. Thus the ratio of coal that can be mined by underground methods to coal that can be surface mined is about eight to one.[1]

Although there is more coal to be mined through underground methods, stripping is more attractive to the mining companies for one elementary economic reason: stripping is cheaper, from 75 cents to $2.50 per ton cheaper, than deep-mining coal. No tunnels need be dug, practically no safety measures observed. One man working a stripping machine can produce as much coal per day as fifteen to twenty men can produce in an underground mine. The underground mine operator must make huge capital investments before he can dig his first ton of coal, but the stripper's major outlays are only in earth-moving equipment and explosives. Months and often years are necessary to bring a new underground mine into full production; the stripper can bring coal to market within a few days.

Stripping is also more efficient. The giant claws of a stripping machine can gouge out 80 to 90 percent of a coal seam; deep mining recovers only 50 percent.[2]

Although stripping is more profitable for the mining companies, it is certainly not profitable for the areas where it occurs. The taxable value of the land has decreased as strip mining continues, and since strip mining employs fewer men than deep mining, the displaced population no longer contributes to the tax rolls. The tax base in the heavily strip-mined areas of Appalachia has sagged by 33 percent.[3] Stripping claims 4,650 acres in the United States each week. The U.S. Geological Survey has reported that a total of approximately 3,000 square miles has already been exploited. If stripping is used to extract the remainder of what is thought to be available, an additional 71,000 square miles, equivalent to the combined area of Pennsylvania and West Virginia, will be ripped apart. Most of the area that could be destroyed is in the western states, where 77 percent of America's total strippable coal is located.[4]

Coal companies, showing a rare concern for miners, argue that deep mining is an inherently dangerous profession. This argument is demolished by the example of mining in Europe. The United Kingdom, which has three times as many miners as the United States, has one-quarter the number of fatalities and has made considerably more progress in combating black-lung disease.[5] In a good year for safety in American mines, there were .84 fatalities per 100,000 man shifts. In a poor year for safety in Germany, there were .77.[6] One strip-mining critic has claimed that the safety record of mines worked by slave labor in Nazi Germany was better than that of American mines.

Though it cannot be denied that tragedies occur in both types of mining, those that are written into the script of the strip mine seem grimmer because they include people who are not even involved in mining. The residents of Buffalo Creek Hollow in Amherstdale, West Virginia, worried for years about the mud and rock slides that came down from the strip mines high on the mountain above them. Their fears were not misplaced. On February 26, 1972, a coal company dam made from slag burst, releasing a thirty-foot wall of water that killed 125 people in the valley. This situation was similar to that faced by the folks in Fayette County, West Virginia, where, according to Mr. and Mrs. Harvey Kincaid, "When the rains come, and there isn't anything to stop the drainage, the mountains slide, and the spoil banks falls down to the next highest highwall, and so on until the mountain slides."[7] The bulldozers and shovels of the strip miners tear ruthlessly at the earth's surface. The grave of the infant child of Mrs. Bige Richie of Knott County, Kentucky, was uncovered, thrown over a hill and covered with boulders and dirt by miners.[8] In 1971 Ohio's Representative Wayne Hays recalled a revealing conversation with a shovel operator:

> "You know, there are some old family burial plots in the county and a lot of them are unmarked. Did you ever run into them?" He said, "Oh yes, I turned up six of them." I said, "What did you do with them?" He said, "I put them in the bottom of the pit and I covered them up real fast."[9]

The companies' contempt for the people is matched by their neglect of the land once they have extracted the black wealth of coal from it. The American record of reclamation contrasts abominally with that in Germany and Great Britain, where strip-mined coal comprises less than 10 percent of the total production, as compared to over 50 percent in the United States. Reclamation costs in Germany range from $3,000 to $4,500 per acre; while in Great Britain they run as high as $7,179 per acre and average about $4,000. According to Representative Ken Hechler (D., W. Va.), reclamation in the U.S.

> is sharply different in outlook than in Great Britain and Germany where true reclamation means reforestation and a thorough and intelligent restoration of the land. All too often aesthetics are the ruling yardstick of reclamation success in this country.[10]

The government has estimated that American industry spends between $200 and $600 per acre to restore the land after stripping.[11]

As Hechler has further lamented about strip mining:

> Under our cowboy capitalist approach to mining, we have placed heavy emphasis on how you extract the minerals from the ground in the quickest and cheapest fashion. Coming from a state which specializes in extractive industry I

regret we also have a few extractive politicians who take out more than they put in, with very little reclamation.[12]

For years the lack of congressional concern for the environment and the successful lobbying by utilities and coal companies inhibited individual members of Congress from voicing support for the regulation of strip mining. Slowly the ice began to break. In 1968 Senator Jackson, chairman of the Senate Interior Committee, held brief hearings on strip mining. Nothing further was heard from the Senate on the subject for another three years. In 1972, during the closing days of the Ninety-second Congress, the Subcommittee on Minerals, Materials and Fuels, headed by Senator Frank Moss (D., Utah), released a weak strip-mining bill (S. 630).

Since the bill was introduced September 18, 1972, and the last session of the Ninety-second Congress was held October 18, the Senate did not have much time to review and debate the bill. Furthermore, since it was not considered to be an emergency bill that could not wait for consideration until the next Congress, the harried senators did not give it top priority. On October 6, two and a half weeks after the bill was first introduced, Senator Jackson offered a substitute bill in the form of an amendment to the original bill, but the Senate never debated or voted on either the original bill or Jackson's amendment. Time flies, and so do members of Congress at the end of a session. As the senators returned to their homes and districts or went off on junkets at the end of the Ninety-second Congress, they left untouched a surface mining bill that could have prevented the ravaging of 4,000 acres each week.

It may seem surprising that its opponents were distraught and its supporters exuberant at the death of the bill. The president of the National Coal Association, Carl Bagge, a member of the Federal Power Commission from 1965 to 1971, explained that his group "had hoped to get the whole issue behind us, we earnestly sought and fought for a bill." He was saddened, he said, because it was "tragic that we'll have another year of rhetoric" whose increased clamor might produce a "myopic" bill rather than a "realistic" bill with a "balanced approach."[13]

The environmentalists were elated because they realized that the death of the bill was actually a reprieve. It gave them time to lobby for a stronger bill, and it gave members of Congress time to travel to Appalachia or other strip-mining areas and see for themselves the ravages of strip surface mining.

In contrast to the bill produced by the Senate Interior Committee and strangled in the end-of-Congress rush, the bill from the House Interior Committee, the Coal Mine Surface Area Protection Act of 1972 (H.R. 6482), was debated at leisure by the House. Unlike the Senate bill, this one did not attempt to regulate the surface mining of every mineral, but limited itself to coal. Thus, its provisions were more specific and detailed, easier to enforce and less complex. Reported to the full House on September 28, 1972, three weeks before the end of the Ninety-second Congress, H.R. 6482 would have prohibited stripping on slopes steeper than 20 degrees unless a mining company demonstrated that the land could be reclaimed and that sedimentation, land slides, and water pollution could be prevented. It empowered the Interior Secretary to establish regulations that would prevent formation of "spoil banks," earth dumped down a slope after mining, on slopes steeper than 14 degrees. But as one member of the House Interior Committee staff said, the bill, "contrary to a lot of people's opinion, did not prohibit strip mining above a certain slope angle. It merely set stricter reclamation requirements for steeper slopes."[14] After debate on October 11, the bill was passed by 265 to 75. This was an overwhelming margin, the more impressive because there had been a barrage of lobbying against the bill by the coal industry and because this was the first strip-mining regulation ever to reach the floor of the House.

The huge margin in the House and the considerable support the bill had received from the Senate Interior Committee made it seem inevitable that some bill regulating strip mining would come out of the Ninety-third Congress. As the new Congress convened, one of the first priorities of both Interior committees was an effective and enforceable strip-mining bill. During four days in March 1973 the Senate Interior Committee held hearings on two bills: S. 923, the Nixon administration's strip-mining bill,* and S. 425, which was virtually identical to Jackson's substitute for the bill the Senate committee had released during the last days of the Ninety-second Congress. For four days in April and two days in May, the House Interior Committee held hearings on fifteen different strip-mining bills. Five of these bills were sponsored by eleven members of the committee.†

Since both committees were moving toward regulatory legislation, the two antagonists most interested in the results—the environmentalists on the one hand, the coal industry and the utilities on the other—rallied their troops for the imminent Armageddon on Capitol Hill. The coal industry said that it was "mature" and that it was ready to accept strip-mining regulations, but that it should not be unduly penalized for its mistakes of the past. "All the bills being considered need to be substantially modified in order to be realistic," cautioned William E. Hynan, National Coal Association vice-president for law, in June, 1973. Edwin R. Phelps, president of the Phelps Coal Company, the nation's largest coal producer, told the Environmental and Mines and Mining subcommittees of the House Interior Committee‡ on May 14,

---

* It is rare that a bill draws such opposition as the administration's strip-mining bill evoked from Representative Melcher. In March 1974 Melcher denounced S. 923 as "gutless" legislation that "smells so bad it must be dead and should be buried as quickly as possible." The Democrat accused President Nixon of submitting a "business as usual" bill because he was "trying to walk the line between the coal operators and the ecologists." ("Nixon's Strip-Mining Bill Defended and Assailed," *New York Times*, Anthony Ripley, March 14, 1973.)

† The eleven members were Mink, Seiberling, Saylor, Hosmer, Sebelius, Martin, Udall, Foley, Melcher, Camp, and Steiger. The different bills they sponsored were H.R. 1000, H.R. 4863, H.R. 6603 and H.R. 3.

‡ Since logically both subcommittees could have jurisdiction over surface mining, their chairmen, Morris Udall and Patsy Mink, held joint hearings and issued a joint report to the full committee.

1973, that some of the proposed legislation "very likely will hurt mine reclamation in this country." He maintained that the mining companies have the technology and the will to reclaim land after it has been stripped. Furthermore, they may have the technology in the near future to reclaim on fairly steep slopes. "To prohibit mining in a certain area, for example, above a certain degree of slope, would be a grave mistake," Phelps warned, because mining and reclamation which is impractical in some areas now may be quite feasible next year because of new developments in technology."[15] Phelps insisted that the coal industry could now meet most of the proposed federal standards for reclamation, but he preferred to distinguish between the aesthetics and the technology of reclamation:

> Some legislative proposals contain undefined references to the "environment" and "natural beauty." I recognize the good intentions behind these terms, but they can be mischievous in effect. Beauty is indeed in the eye of the beholder and impossible to define . . . Requiring that lands be returned to beneficial use can be enforced; requiring that they be restored to a natural beauty makes enforcement a matter of taste.[16]

Phelps may have been correct to assume that the creation of beauty is not a bureaucratic task, but he failed to acknowledge that restoring land to "beneficial use" could simply mean preparing it for another exploitive industry that would ravage the land once more.

While the industry proclaimed its willingness to accept and to work with strip mining laws, the environmentalists marshaled to prevent the industry's walking away with a bill so weak that mining companies could strip a lane forty feet deep across the entire country and justify their failure to reclaim it by calling it a new natural wonder. Although most environmental groups favored a complete ban on strip mining, they were willing to lobby for a bill that would simply regulate it. Louise C. Dunlap, who spearheaded the environmentalists' campaign as a coordinator of the Coalition Against Strip Mining, contended that the conservationist's position was not "inconsistent":

> We think that the regulatory debate is germane to the larger debate over a phase-out because almost everybody is in agreement that land that can't be reclaimed shouldn't be mined.
>
> But it's only through debate on what reclamation is that we can ultimately reach agreement on where stripping should be prohibited.[17]

Countering the coal industry's contention that it was more than willing to embrace strip-mining regulations, she explained at the Senate surface mining hearings that:

> There has been a great deal of rhetoric on the part of the industry that where the land cannot be reclaimed then strip mining should not be continued. Yet, in the 92nd Congress, and at this early date in the 93rd Congress, it is evident that the mining industry remains highly resistant to any legislation which includes specificity.
>
> While it is argued by the industry that specificity in Federal criteria is "punitive" or "arbitrary" rather than "corrective" due to "the diversity in terrain climate, biologic, chemical and other physical conditions," it may also be argued that detail in the criteria facilitate the promulgation of Federal regulations and the development of State programs. This has certainly been the case in Pennsylvania, which has the Nation's most stringent State regulatory law. . . .[18]

About two and a half months after the Senate committee finished its hearings on surface mining, it began markup sessions on S. 425, Jackson's substitute for the committee bill reported to the full Senate at the end of the Ninety-second Congress. At the second markup session, June 25, Alan Bible introduced an amendment to limit the bill to regulating the strip mining of coal and not of other minerals. Not only would a bill limited to coal be more specific than an all-minerals bill, but most members of the committee also assumed that it would be easier to get through the House-Senate conference, especially since the bill the House had passed at the end of the previous Congress (H.R. 6482) had also been limited to coal.

Though Jackson preferred an all-minerals bill, he favored the amendment "in the interests of getting a bill out."[19] But Fannin, Haskell, and James McClure (R., Idaho) insisted that S. 425 remain an all-minerals bill. Haskell claimed that limiting the bill to coal would make it seem as if Congress were "putting the gun to the head of Appalachia."[20] But despite the determined lobbying of the coal industry and the stolid efforts of a considerable and influential minority on the committee, the Bible Amendment was incorporated in the bill, thus changing its character considerably.

The next crucial amendment was proposed on September 10, at the last markup session, by Gaylord Nelson. The Nelson amendment would require that land that was stripped for mining be restored to its original contour. When introducing the amendment Nelson said that it was supported by Pennsylvania's Democratic governor and the state's two Republican senators, the United Mine Workers, and the Council on Environmental Quality. Jackson urged that the amendment be passed because "if Pennsylvania can live with this program, so can other states."[21] In spite of Jackson's influence, the Nelson amendment met with even more opposition than had the Bible amendment. Senator Hansen reminded his fellow committee members that the amendment was opposed by Democratic Senator Jennings Randolph from West Virginia, the Appalachian state which has suffered the most from strip mining. Senator Fannin mentioned that the senator from another Appalachian strip mining state, Kentucky's Marlow W. Cook, a Republican, also staunchly opposed the original contour requirement. Fannin urged that the amendment be rejected. Federal bills should set minimum, not maximum, standards, he said.

The industry's lobbyists had been hustling through the halls of

Congress for days trying to prevent passage of the Nelson amendment. Though they had claimed in the committee's hearings that thorough reclamation was technologically possible and that they were eager to do it, their intense lobbying belied their public protestations. One lobbyist from Bethlehem Steel Company, for example, insisted that reclamation was impossible on a slope steeper than 22 degrees because oil would run out of the crankcases of the bulldozers. He persisted in these arguments until he was thrown out of the staff offices of the Senate Interior Committee. (The staff knew quite well that at least two large West Virginia mining companies have strict policies to restore the mined land to its approximate original contour regardless of the slopes.) Such lobbying and such outrageously fallacious arguments were almost effective. The vote at the markup session was tied 6 to 6. Since the amendment was crucial, the committee agreed that those members not present would be permitted to vote. Once every member had been tallied, the tie was broken, and the amendment passed 8 to 6.*

The vote was split along party lines, except that Republicans Buckley and McClure voted for the amendment and Democrats Metcalf and Johnston sided with the opposition. Thus six out of eight Democrats voted for the Nelson Amendment and four out of six Republicans against it.

Shortly after the bill was released to the full Senate, Senator Randolph protested to Jackson that it would discriminate against "mountaintop mining." Since mountaintop mining often leaves a broad, flat plateau in place of a previously steep slope, the land is more useful if it is not restored to its original contours. For three days, members of Senator Randolph's staff and of the Interior Committee's staff argued, coddled, and coaxed their way toward a

* The eight members voting for the Nelson amendment were Jackson, Bible, Church, Abourezk, Haskell, Nelson, Buckley, and McClure. Those opposed were Metcalf, Johnston, Fannin, Hansen, Hatfield, Bartlett. The two senators not present at the September 10 markup session were Bible and Church.

satisfactory compromise. On October 9, 1973, the day after debate on S. 425 began, Senator Jackson introduced a "mountaintop" amendment:

> Subsequent to committee action on this bill, it came to our attention that there was some ambiguity in the bill with regard to the continuation of certain mining techniques. Of particular concern is the practice of mountaintop mining . . . We are aware that in some instances responsible mining operators have demonstrated that mountaintop mining operations can be carried out in a self-contained area with little damage to the surrounding areas creating in the process level or gently rolling land that can be used for a number of socially beneficial uses. In particular, we have spoken with such men as the head of Cannelton Coal Co., who conducts a large mountaintop operation in West Virginia. In an area where flat land is scarce, his surface mining and reclamation operation has produced land to be used for housing developments and a local school . . . It has never been the intent . . . to prohibit responsible surface mining operations, and I do not believe that such is the result . . . we do not want to shut down operations as those of Cannelton Coal, particularly in the face of an impending energy crisis, and this amendment is designed to prevent such problems.[22]

The rest of the Senate must have been impressed with the Cannelton operations, too, since it accepted Jackson's amendment with hardly a dissent.

The other strategic floor amendment concerned the rights of surface owners when the mineral rights and the surface rights were owned by different persons. In the original draft of the bill, the applicant for a surface mining permit needed either to obtain the written consent of the surface owner or to post a bond to pay the surface owner for any damage to the surface, crops, or improvements on the land caused by the mining. For months, environmentalists had been lobbying to persuade Senate Majority

Leader Mike Mansfield (D., Mont.) to introduce an amendment requiring only the written consent of the surface owner. If this were accepted by the Senate, then the coal companies would not have the option of posting a bond against damages. But as Mansfield began to realize the implications of the environmentalists' proposal, he "began to have second thoughts when it occurred to him that this gave the surface owners control over a resource that actually belongs to all the people," according to a Senate staff member. "So he concluded that the only fair thing to do was to close off stripping in these areas completely," and he phrased his amendment accordingly to prohibit strip mining on publicly owned lands.

Opposition to this amendment was led by the two ranking minority members on the Interior Committee, Fannin and Hansen. Immediately after Mansfield introduced his amendment on October 8, Fannin claimed that he supported Mansfield's efforts to protect Montana and the rest of the country, but he protested:

> We are proposing to change our basic law, as far as getting consent is concerned. The existing law protects the surface only. Each state has responded to that problem by passing its own laws. If we pass national legislation, we, in fact, abrogate all those State laws . . .
>
> Federal lands are owned by all the people; they are not owned merely by the people in a State. If we pass this bill, we will cause a reversal of the ownership of property . . . What we are talking about is giving the surface owner a windfall. We are giving him a veto power never intended by law or equality . . .[23]

Fannin had already indicated his opposition to any provision in S. 425 that would absolutely prohibit mining in any part of the country: "We just cannot afford to manacle our potential short-term source of energy by allowing lands to be set aside and restricted from mining."[24] The next day Senator Hansen was "deeply concerned about some of the actions undertaken by the

Senate. The Mansfield amendment . . . threatens the availability of a significant amount of America's most readily available low sulfur coal."[25]

That Hansen and Fannin were responding to the coal interests' intensive lobbying against the Mansfield amendment is likely but, of course, cannot be proved. The president of the American Mining Congress, J. Allen Overton, Jr., confessed that the industry's "most grievous difficulty" with S. 425 was the Mansfield amendment.[26] National Coal Association president Bagge told the annual meeting of the Geological Society of America that:

> The theory behind the Mansfield Amendment is that the strippable coal it freezes in place could be replaced by coal from underground mines . . . [but] 85% of the [lands of the federal government] and most of the leases granted are for strippable coal. To acquire deep coal reserves could entail new leases. . . . Even if the freeze on leasing were ended today, and supposing that a coal company had some geological geniuses who could locate suitable reserves of deep coal by tomorrow morning, it takes three or four years to develop a deep mine. That would still leave some power plants waiting a long time for coal to arrive.[27]

Mansfield denied all these allegations and maintained that the amendment's sole purpose and effect would be to protect the rights and livelihood of the ranchers in his state who own the surface rights, but not the mineral rights, on their grazing lands. He proclaimed that he did

> not want to see any portion of the population, no matter how small, or how Republican—and these [ranchers] are mostly Republican—deprived of their rights. They should be allowed to maintain the lands they have developed, and on which they have lived for generations. . . . They are not going to be able, unless this protection is provided, to stand up against the big—and I mean big—coal companies which are moving into that part of the Union.[28]

After Mansfield and Fannin had wrangled verbally on the Senate floor for about ten minutes, Lee Metcalf jumped into the breach on Mansfield's side. Metcalf advised his colleagues that they

> must remember that there is so much coal and so many thousands of acres and so many billions of tons of coal that can be mined that it is a pretty good idea that the Federal Government reserve some of the coal for future activity. And if we need this coal in another decade, or in another two decades or so, there it is. It is not under the control of the rancher or that land owner that acquired surface rights in a grazing homestead a half century ago. It is still under the control of Congress.[29]

Metcalf's and Mansfield's logic, plus the power of the majority leader, were more effective than the homilies of Fannin and Hansen about the energy crisis and the rights of the coal operator. Half an hour after Mansfield introduced his amendment, it was passed by a solid margin of 53 to 33. The Interior Committee was evenly split on the amendment: 6 members voted for it, 6 opposed it. Two members were not present for the vote.*

The amendment's success destroyed many illusory hopes of the coal industry, just as it bolstered the confidence of the environmental movement. William E. Hynan, the National Coal Association's vice-president for law, was stunned: "We felt on the Senate side there were some realistic people. But to have the Mansfield amendment pass at the last minute like that was really unbelievable."[30] Charles A. Robinson, corporate counsel for the National Rural Electric Cooperative Association (a nonprofit association representing nonprofit rural electoral cooperatives throughout the country), groaned that the Mansfield amendment could affect

* Those who voted for the Mansfield amendment were Abourezk, Haskell, Hatfield, Jackson, Johnston, and Metcalf. Those from the Interior Committee opposing the measure were Bartlett, Bible, Buckley, Fannin, Hansen, and McClure. Church and Nelson were absent.

power companies and electric cooperatives "as far south as Texas and Louisiana and all along the Upper Missouri Valley." And Alex Radin, the general manager of the American Public Power Association (a nonprofit organization representing 1,400 publicly owned electrical companies), warned that the Mansfield measure "could well preclude some of our members from going ahead with planned projects."[31] But while the coal industry and utilities were becoming progressively more alarmed about the Mansfield amendment, Louise Dunlap was exultant:

> The industry outrage in response to the bill just documents the fact that they don't want a bill that would regulate them at all.
> [The Mansfield Amendment is] . . . the first major step in recognizing that because of our widespread availability of coal there are certain areas in the country that can be declared as off limits to stripping.[32]

On the morning of the vote (October 9, 1973) on S. 425, Carl Bagge and American Mining Congress president J. Allen Overton, Jr., sent a joint letter to each senator urging the bill's defeat. The bête noire of the industry was the Mansfield amendment, which Bagge and Overton criticized as the provision "most devastating to the satisfaction of the Nation's immediate energy needs." They predicted that the Mansfield amendment would remove about six billion tons of low-sulphur coal from production. "To needlessly bar the mining of the urgently needed coal," they advised three days after the Arab oil embargo had begun, "would be arbitrary and short-sighted in the best of times. To do so now, when the only other ready alternative supply of additional fuel is Middle East oil, is an incredible gamble."[33]

But the lobbying pressure of the mining industry was not enough to prevent the overwhelming passage of S. 425. Eighty-two senators were willing to make the "gamble" that Bagge and Overton warned against. Even those who had opposed the Mansfield amendment voted for the entire bill on the assumption that the amendment would be deleted in the House-Senate conference.

The lone member of the Interior Committee to join the bill's eight-member opposition was Dewey Bartlett (D., Okla.), who said that his vote was "one of the toughest . . . that I have had to cast." Though the senator "fully supported regulations that would require land that was surface mined to be fully and completely reclaimed," he was opposing the bill once the Mansfield amendment was added because, he said, it would remove too much coal from potential production. He urged that rather than "arbitrarily exclude" from production over 42 million acres, they should be made "available for mining in an environmentally acceptable way to help prevent a severe crisis in energy supplies."[34]

Having lost one battle, the coal and utility lobbyists began to focus on the House Interior Committee. They had a better chance to affect some of the major provisions of the House bill because of the lack of organization and cohesion in the House committee, which was still trying to establish a new identity under the chairmanship of Jim Haley. While the situation on the House side could not be described as chaotic, it could hardly be considered disciplined. It seemed to take more time to perform less work than in previous years, and its work schedule on the surface mining bill lagged far behind that of the Senate. For example, the full Senate Interior Committee held four days of hearings and five markup sessions on S. 425. But in the House Interior Committee the subcommittees on the Environment and on Mines and Mining held joint hearings for six days and then twenty-four joint markup sessions that stretched from July 9 to November 12. The House bill, H.R. 11500, then went to the full committee, which held sixteen markup sessions from February 28 to May 14.

There were three major arguments during the five-month joint subcommittees' markup, and all occurred in the last month, November.* One was over an amendment introduced by John F.

---

* Some of the more crucial and thorny amendments were resolved at that point only because of a deal worked out by the committee's majority and minority members on November 6. The majority leaders then agreed that the bill would not be debated by the full committee until January 27. In

Seiberling (D., Ohio) to impose a $2.50 per ton fee on all mined coal and to use the money to establish a fund for reclaiming "orphan lands," lands that had never been restored after they were mined. Two similar amendments, one introduced by John Melcher and the other by Teno Roncalio (D., Wyo.), sought to include a more moderate version of the Mansfield amendment in the House bill.

Strongly supported by the United Mine Workers of America and the environmentalists, the Seiberling amendment was introduced and adopted on November 8. The amendment had a dual purpose: ostensibly to help salvage orphan lands; actually to make deep mining more attractive. It would offset the difference of 75 cents to $2.50 a ton between stripped coal and deep-mined coal by giving the mining operator up to 90 percent of the fee's total for credit for reclamation activities, equipment required by the Coal Mine Health and Safety Act of 1969, and payment of black-lung benefits as required by the Coal Mine Health and Safety Act. Members of Seiberling's staff and of the House Interior Committee freely admitted that the clause was carefully structured to give relatively easy credit gains for activities associated with underground mining. During debate in the markup, Seiberling estimated that deep mining operations would be taxed about 15 cents and strip mining about $1.50. This would produce a reclamation fund of some $400 million that would provide for the reclamation of all orphan lands within twenty to twenty-five years. A member of the committee staff confessed that "the

exchange the minority leaders agreed to drop their opposition to votes being taken at the joint committee's markups without a quorum present.

Louise Dunlap, the environmentalists' leader, charged that the committees' minority members, especially Sam Steiger, deliberately manipulated the calendar to delay the full committee's consideration of the bill until the winter, when potential fuel shortages could undermine support for a strong surface mining bill. Steiger replied that the charges were "nonsense." He explained that he had called for a quorum several times in the markup sessions, not to delay the bill but to insure that more subcommittee members would be involved in developing the legislation. See "Environment Reporter," Bureau of National Affairs, p. 1152.

amendment tends to equalize the cost of underground mining." He added that "Every underground miner in the country could hit $2.25 a ton in credits, but not so with the strippers. The most they could get would be around $1.50 a ton."[35]

The Nixon administration and the coal industry mounted a two-front attack against Seiberling's proposal. The National Coal Association's vice-president for congressional relations, John B. Howerton, said, "Seiberling himself said the purpose of his amendment was to make underground mining more attractive. I don't think a reclamation bill is the place for a provision like that." He added, "Anything not having to do with reclamation is prohibitory . . ."[36]

The industry's chief ally, the Nixon administration, joined the fight with letters couched in official language and lobbying fraught with official muscle. On November 9, Interior Secretary Rogers Morton wrote Interior Committee Chairman Haley asking him to correct the "deficiencies" of S. 425. Foremost among these was the "hasty and ill-advised" Mansfield amendment:

> Despite the increasingly difficult energy future we face, legislation insuring full reclamation of surface mined land has my strongest support. But there is no room in it for arbitrary provisions which needlessly undermine the energy base of the country, such as the . . . [Mansfield amendment].[37]

Three days later William E. Simon, then director of the Federal Energy Office, told Haley he was "greatly alarmed" at the Seiberling amendment. He charged that it "would undoubtedly result in less coal being mined" and would impede efforts to substitute low-sulphur coal for oil and gas. He feared that it would double the costs for western strip-mined coal and would cause a 50 percent boost in the national average cost of mined coal.[38]*

---

* Though the Seiberling amendment was opposed by one branch of the Nixon administration, it was implicitly supported by another, the Environmental Protection Agency. On September 27 Russell E. Train, EPA director, noted that only 3 percent of the nation's total coal supply lies near the surface, where it can be stripped. With such a minute amount of strippable

The Simon letter was denounced by one member of the House Interior Committee, who said it seemed to have been written "by one of the more vocal members of the National Coal Association."[39] Eight days after Simon complained to Haley, Seiberling himself refuted the energy czar's allegations which, Seiberling charged, were based "in part . . . on an erroneous reading of the amendment."[40] Seiberling contended that the coal costs resulting from the tax would not approach those estimated by Simon because credit provisions would lower the total tax liability. "Far from resulting in less coal being mined," Seiberling said,

> the amendment will make possible an immediate as well as long-range increase in coal production. By making deep mining competitive with strip mining, it will be possible, with a minimum of capital involved and in a minimum of time, to reopen hundreds of deep mines which have been closed because of their inability to compete with strip mines.[41]

Even after the amendment was accepted by the joint subcommittees,* the administration was still hoping to have it deleted during the markup sessions of the full committee. On February 6, 1974, Undersecretary of the Interior John C. Whitaker, a geologist and a former White House energy aide, wrote to Chairman Haley that the Seiberling tax was "particularly objectionable." "The fee," he warned,

> will unreasonably raise current coal costs and penalize current coal consumers for damages caused by other operations and, to the extent that credits for past expenditures are pro-

---

coal, Train maintained that "the underground reserves are by all odds the predominant sources that we have. We're going to have to get at this in any event. The sooner we can make underground [mining] more economically attractive, more technologically feasible and more socially acceptable as a way of life, way of employment, the better off we're going to be." ("Deep-Mined Coal Termed Essential for Clean Energy," George C. Wilson, Washington Post, Sept. 27, 1973, p. A35.)

* The November 8 vote on the Seiberling amendment was a voice vote, so it is impossible to determine who favored and who opposed it.

vided, could operate as a barrier to market entry and cause dislocations in the economic factors bearing on mine operations.[42]

The other major fight during the joint committees' markup was over inserting some provision in the bill that would be roughly comparable to the Senate's Mansfield amendment. On November 12, John Melcher introduced a provision to delete the option given a surface miner, when the surface rights and the subsurface rights are owned by different parties, either to post a bond against surface damages or to solicit the surface owner's permission to mine. Melcher's amendment would require the surface miner to obtain the explicit permission of the surface owner, since a bond for damages would not satisfactorily compensate an owner whose buildings were destroyed or who might not be able to plant crops for five to ten years after mining.

Arizona's Sam Steiger objected strenuously to the Melcher amendment. He claimed that, like the Mansfield amendment, it would arbitrarily preclude surface mining, rather than protect against its abuse.

Morris Udall, in one of the rare moments when he and Sam Steiger agree, also opposed Melcher's amendment. Udall said he was trying to avoid two qualities in the mining bill: 1) absolutes, such as those embodied in the Mansfield amendment to the Senate bill; and 2) windfalls to those not entitled to them, such as would result from the Melcher amendment. One of the "vices" of the Melcher amendment, Udall said, was that the surface owner would be given the unilateral right to determine whether federal coal is to be removed; a coal company might have to buy coal twice, once from the federal government and once from the surface owner.

Melcher insisted that his amendment would not curtail mining operations or deliver windfall profits. Instead, it would simply give the surface owner the prerogative of protecting the value of his own lands and property. But despite Melcher's insistence, the infrequent team of Steiger and Udall triumphed after twenty-five minutes of debate. On a hand vote the Melcher amendment was defeated 11 to 19.

With an eye toward the House-Senate conference on the two houses' surface mining bills, Teno Roncalio then offered an amendment that would place on the mine operator who does not own surface rights the burden of convincing the surface owner that the surface will be rehabilitated after mining and the owner given fair compensation. But Steiger opposed Roncalio's amendment as vigorously as Melcher's. He predicted that if this amendment passed, the surface owner would find that he had no alternative except a partnership with the coal operator. This would invite all sorts of "chicanery"—phony alliances, phony stock deals, and phony titles.

Again, Steiger's arguments were more persuasive than those which proposed to give the surface owner some measure of security. The Roncalio amendment was as soundly defeated as the Melcher amendment.* Unless the environmentalists and their sympathizers on the Interior Committee could slip a surface-owner-protection clause into 11500 in the full committee's markup or on the floor of the House, the House-Senate conferees would have to eliminate the Mansfield amendment or so emasculate it that it would be barely recognizable.

The Melcher and Roncalio amendments were the last amendments any member of the joint committees wanted to introduce. Now there was nothing to do but vote the bill out of the joint committees to the full committees for another series of markup sessions. These threatened to proceed as slowly and lugubriously as the joint committees' markup sessions.

Once the full committee met on 11500,† it was apparent that

---

* Those voting for the Roncalio amendment were Bingham, Burke, Burton, de Luge, Kastenmeier, Melcher, O'Hara, Owens, Roncalio, Seiberling, and Mink. The opposition consisted of Bauman, Camp, Cronin, Foley, Hosmer, Jones, Kazen, Ketchum, Martin, Runnels, Ruppe, Sebelius, Skubitz, Steelman, Steiger, Towell, Vigorite, Young, and Udall.

† Of the 39 members of the full committee during the first half of the

the bill was in more trouble than it had been since its inception. On the first day of the markup session, February 20, the committee agreed to postpone action until the next day as a courtesy to ranking minority member Craig Hosmer, who was preparing a substitute bill. Another ominous portent came from another Republican, William Ketchum (Calif.). Observing that H.R. 11500 was a "highly controversial bill," Ketchum warned the committee that he intended to ask for a quorum call whenever necessary because the bill warranted the attention of the full committee. Although Ketchum advised the members that he was not threatening to delay the bill, Sam Steiger, who had been one of its major opponents, told Ketchum that it sounded like a threat to him.

The next day Hosmer introduced his substitute, H.R. 12898. Both H.R. 11500 and S. 425 were inordinately weighted with environmental safeguards, he said, and did not offer the coal industry sufficient incentive to increase its output. These bills were inappropriate to the times, they

> were born in a climate of abundant energy supply. [Then] alternatives to coal as an energy source were cheap and plentiful. The situation [since the enforcement of the Arab oil embargo on October 6] has changed drastically. The facts are that there no longer is an abundance of energy resources to meet our requirements, and there is a severe shortage in our country today. The need for access to our coal resources by surface mining is now critical. . . .
> . . . Whether you like them or not, and whatever their motives, the National Coal Association, the American Mining Congress and the National Association of Electric Companies have pointed out that H.R. 11500 will stifle coal production at the very moment that as a Nation our national interest requires that it be increased. Millions of people have never seen a strip mine but over a hundred million in the last week have seen a gasoline line at their neighborhood filling station.[43]

Ninety-third Congress, only nine did not sit on one of the two subcommittees that handled 11500.

Most of the debate over the Hosmer substitute focused on two areas. The first was the deletion of the requirement that stripped land be restored to its original contour. Hosmer maintained that his bill

> sensibly says that you have to protect streams against silta-
> tion and acid runoff, insure the stability of slopes, and
> guarantee that revegetation does occur—but it also sensibly
> says that you don't have to go to all the trouble and expense
> of returning to original approximate contour in cases where,
> after mining, the land can be put to an equal or better use
> without doing so.[44]

But the chairmen of the two subcommittees that had produced H.R. 11500 contended that restoring stripped land to its approximate original contour was standard procedure in Pennsylvania and had been accomplished in mountainous terrain in both West Virginia and eastern Kentucky. Also, they said, engineering studies indicated that regrading to the original contour significantly reduced the major environmental impact of surface mining in the Appalachian coal fields.[45]

The second point for debate was the enforcement time for the bills' regulations. H.R. 11500 provided for both a ninety-day phase-in period for the interim program and an eighteen-month phase-in period for permanent programs. Representatives Udall and Mink noted that this was sufficient time "to allow operators to adjust their mining and reclamation practices *without a loss of production.*"[46] The Hosmer substitute also implemented its interim standards within ninety days, but, unlike H.R. 11500, it did not prevent the licensing and opening of new mines on federal lands during this period. In a memo to the full committee Hosmer reminded his colleagues that "the nation's need for coal to replace petroleum is not ignored" by his substitute. He also blithely ignored the ninety-day standards of H.R. 11500 and just mentioned the eighteen-month permanent standards. If, as Hosmer claimed, the original bill had included only the latter, it would have been accurate to contend that "By the time impact standards are drafted and circulated, administrative hearings and court actions concluded and leases issued, 2½ to 3 years could go by before anyone could get a license to open a new surface mine on public land."[47]

In their refutation of Hosmer's allegation, Udall and Mink noted that some discussions between the Interior Committee staff and Interior Department officials had revealed that the department's apprehension was due to a similar misunderstanding. The department had incorrectly believed that H.R. 11500 did not contain a ninety-day phase-in period and had thus considered it a threat to coal production.[48]

Though the members of the House Interior Committee are excessively genteel and scrupulously respect the parliamentary procedures of the House, Hosmer's move to shelve H.R. 11500 after it had crawled for eight months through two subcommittees and their markup sessions aroused the ire of both Democrat John Melcher and Republican Philip Ruppe. When Hosmer finished extolling the virtues of his bill, Ruppe labeled it "an industry bill," and Melcher roared that it was "watered-down."[49] He charged that Hosmer was turning "a petroleum shortage and a gasoline imbalance into an issue to create a climate to pass a bill which would be a rip-off of the Western states."[50]

Hosmer denied that the industry had inspired H. R. 12898. It was a bill, he said, that had originated mostly at the White House. As for Melcher, Hosmer charged that he had not even read the substitute, which Hosmer had just finished writing the previous morning. He warned the Montana Democrat that "there is no reason for that kind of language except perhaps a response to some knee-jerk environmentalist."*[51]

After tempers had cooled and a modicum of reason had re-

* Later, Melcher laughed about his shouting match with Hosmer. He said that he relished Hosmer's comment that he was fronting for some "knee-jerk environmentalist" because he could use it in his home state, where he is not highly regarded by environmentalists.

turned, the committee unanimously accepted Udall's suggestion to study the Hosmer substitute until the next committee meeting, Wednesday, February 27, when it would debate both bills for thirty minutes and then vote to determine which would be the mark-up vehicle. This extra week gave interests from outside Congress time to pressure, wheedle, and coerce committee members. One Interior Committee staff member said that Capitol Hill was swarming with more lobbyists than he had ever seen before. Louise Dunlap steadily maintained that "The argument that they have to gut the strip-mining bill of its environmental safeguards to keep the lights on is a bogus argument. . . . Tough standards in a strip-mining bill will not interfere with coal production and could not be fairly blamed for shortages in other fuels."[52] With equal fervor Carl Bagge praised the Hosmer substitute for representing "reason and rationality" and condemned H.R. 11500 as "designed to force coal underground."[53]

On February 26, the morning before the committee was to vote on which bill would be its markup vehicle, the *New York Times* pleaded editorially with the committee members to reject the "enfeebled and shadowy" Hosmer substitute.* The substitute, said the *Times*, "would allow operators to go on dumping earth

---

* An earlier *Times* editorial had also urged the quick enactment of a strong surface mining bill. On September 18, 1973, the *Times* condemned the strip mining that has ruined the streams and land of such eastern states as West Virginia and Kentucky. "Now these 'badlands,' " the *Times* mourned, "are moving westward at a sickening rate as strippable coal deposits are exploited from New Mexico to Montana." The newspaper accurately predicted then that both the House and the Senate bills "will be opposed on the ground that more coal than ever is needed to meet an imminent energy crisis. The argument in this case is more fallacious than usual. The more conservative estimate is that well over 90 percent of this country's coal reserves can be taken by deep mining, a ratio that applies to the low-sulphur variety as well. The fierce concentration on strippable coal is explainable solely by the quick, huge profit that it yields.

"Strip mining has already done damage to the country far out of proportion to the value of its production, even taking into account the desirability of low-sulphur coal in reducing air pollution. The House bill would not only minimize that damage but would stimulate a deep-mine industry now suffering from lost personnel and lagging in technical advances. The

down mountainsides, would make no serious demand on them for survival and growth of replanted vegetation and do no more to protect Western water resources than subject them to further study." The *Times* admitted that the nation must draw on its coal supplies, especially during the present energy crisis, but

> it needs its land, too. It cannot afford to have it raped and abandoned at the rate of 1,000 acres a week for coal alone, as it did last year. The Senate bill and the original House bill would yield the coal and then reclaim the land.
>
> The substitute would yield perhaps more coal and surely more profits—but at the certain cost of a devastated countryside.

The next morning, the very day of the vote on the Hosmer substitute, the *Times* published the results of an engineering study commissioned by the Appalachian Regional Commission and the State of Kentucky that contradicted the coal industry's forecasts that H.R. 11500 would be a catastrophe for the industry. The report concluded that "complete contour restoration methods are generally desirable and feasible using existing equipment" and that the most effective ways to prevent landslides "are roughly comparable in profitability to existing conventional contour methods and can be practiced using equipment."[54]*

Meanwhile, the Nixon administration was jockeying for a bill that would completely satisfy it. On February 6 it had unequivocally rejected H.R. 11500 with the allegation that it would "result in serious losses in coal supplies [for the nation]."[55]†

---

price of these setbacks can be high when, the last greedy dollar having been extracted from the strip-mines, the nation is forced to turn back to its real coal reserves." See Editorial: "Stripping the Land," *NY Times*, September 18, 1973, p. 47.

* This study, by Mathematica, Inc., of Princeton, New Jersey, and Ford, Bacon and Davis, of New York City, was actually released in Kentucky on February 6, 1974. But Udall and Mink used this as their reserve ammunition and did not circulate a memo with the study's conclusions until the day before the vote on the Hosmer substitute.

† The February 6 letter from Interior Department Undersecretary John C.

Though the administration had totally rejected the original strip-mining bill, it also had serious reservations about the Hosmer bill. On February 22 it advised Hosmer that it would support his bill only if he altered it to satisfy the administration's requirements. Among the twelve alterations that the administration requested Hosmer to make in his bill were:

—that the Environmental Protection Agency have the authority to ensure complete compatibility between the programs initiated by the bill and those already under EPA authority. This would replace Hosmer's "clearly inadequate" proposal that the EPA's Administrator merely be consulted about the regulations that would emerge from the bill,[56]

—that Hosmer delete his provision that citizens' suits could be initiated only if the person whose interests might be adversely affected could show that actions of the Interior Secretary or of the bill's regulatory authority had caused such effects. This provision, the administration insisted, "would create confusion and could insulate mining operators,"

—and that the bill's definition of open-pit mining be altered to eliminate its "unjustifiable exception from regulation of bituminous mining."[57] This loophole would exempt from regulation the giant strip mines of the West and surface mines that were scheduled to soon open in Montana, Wyoming, and the Dakotas.[58]

By the next committee meeting, the battle lines were clearly drawn outside the committee, but no one was certain where they lay on the inside. Hosmer was rallying his forces; Udall, Mink,

---

Whitaker elaborated on this theme of H.R. 11500's severely retarding coal production: "Preliminary estimates show that demand in 1974 will exceed 1973 production by upwards of 15 percent for these oil substitution uses [of coal] and other demands. In addition, such estimates show that coal production losses might amount to five to fifteen percent of 1973 production other things being equal, if H.R. 11500 is enacted. The country simply cannot afford this 20 percent to 30 percent shortfall in view of the current energy situation."

and Ruppee were rallying theirs. Hosmer, though, had more reason to be optimistic, because despite the months of hearings and markups on H.R. 11500 its main proponents were still not certain the day before the vote whether they had definitely recruited the necessary 21 votes for the bill's passage.

The debate on the Hosmer substitute began ominously. The day before the committee met, the Rules Committee had voted 9 to 4 to kill the land use bill that Udall and environmentalists had been shepherding through Congress for three years.* Hosmer, who had already exploited the worsening energy crisis as a *raison d'être* for his bill, now used the Rules Committee's action for all it was worth. At the beginning of the Ninety-third Congress, Hosmer told his colleagues, the committee was confronted with "a very, very strict environmentally oriented land use policy bill." The bill's orientation created much opposition to it, both in the full House and in the Interior Committee. The committee finally amended the bill until it was what Hosmer called "a good bill": "It did not give the environmentalists every damn thing they wanted, but that is not possible. That is not in the book. Yet because that bill started the way it did, it generated so much opposition that it just got shot down in flames in the Rules Committee." Hosmer cautioned committee members that if they wanted the strip mining bill to go through the same experience, then they should vote for H.R. 11500, which was "doomed, because of the opposition that it has already generated. No matter what you do with it, it will be like the land use bill, they [the Rules Committee] will still think it is a bad bill and they will vote it down . . ." North Carolina's Roy Taylor, admitting that he was torn between the members of the subcommittees "who worked long and hard on this bill" and his constituents in North Carolina

---

* The bill, similar to one that the Senate had passed by a 64 to 21 margin in June 1973, would have provided $800 million over the next eight years for states to develop comprehensive plans for regulating the use of land, especially for such projects as power plants and airports with severe environmental impact.

who greatly relied on Appalachian coal, confessed that the major factor for his siding with Hosmer was the previous day's decision by the Rules Committee. He urged the committee "to take the conservative approach and mark up a bill which is not too objectionable to the people of our nation who need coal."

The first member to speak against the Hosmer substitute was Udall, who proclaimed that the purpose of his bill was to have coal mined "in an environmentally sound manner and to put the land back so we will not disgrace this generation or future generations." To buttress his position, Udall referred to the support he had received from the governors of Illinois and Pennsylvania and from Pennsylvania's assistant deputy secretary for mines, Walter N. Heine, who had called Hosmer's substitute a measure that

> would seriously undercut the decades of support effort by states like Pennsylvania to regulate surface mining.
>
> Not only is it regressive, but it would unfairly discriminate at a most inappropriate time against eastern coal-producing states by, in effect, not only permitting but encouraging the unregulated development of Western coal fields through the exemption of open pit coal mining.[59]

Patsy Mink, who had endorsed the complete prohibition of surface mining, challenged the Hosmer bill on the grounds that its chief defect was "the wide-open loophole which permits the Federal agencies that will supervise the interim period to come out with all sorts of exemptions and discretionary exemptions [from the regulations] which we [the joint subcommittees] have worked out so carefully." These exemptions, she said, would "create havoc, inequity, and injustice."

The last person to speak against the Hosmer substitute was John Melcher, whom Hosmer had shouted down the previous week when the Montanan called his substitute a "rip-off for the West." This week Melcher said that his comment had been "really an understatement."

The sole judges of whether Hosmer's substitute was really a

"rip-off for the West" were now the members of the committee. As the committee's clerk went through the roll call for a record vote on whether to substitute Hosmer's bill for H.R. 11500, the tally constantly seesawed—first in favor of the Hosmer substitute, then in favor of the Udall-Mink bill. One bill would lead for a few votes, then the other would catch up and lead for another few votes. But by the end of the tally, and to the relief of the environmentalists and the members of the committee who had carefully nurtured H.R. 11500 for so many months, it was apparent that the coal industry's all-out effort to defeat the bill had failed by two votes, 21 to 19. Five Republicans had defected from their ranking minority member to join the sixteen Democrats who wanted H.R. 11500 as the markup vehicle (see Table 3).

Patsy Mink was clearly relieved. The vote, she said, represented a "vindication of our effort to set up federal standards for protecting land to be stripped of its coal." But she was also bothered by the slim margin that had saved H.R. 11500 and realistically predicted that it would be a nip-and-tuck effort during the bill's markup to preserve the bill's strong nation-wide standards.[60]

After four months of work, the strip mining bill was finally reported by the Interior Committee to the full House on May 14, 1974, by a 26–15 vote. Ten of the dissenting members filed separate views on the bill in which they used such language as "ill-conceived" and "shortsighted and dangerous." The bill's key provisions eliminated "highwalls," the vertical banks remaining after coal has been scraped from a mountainside, and "spoil banks," the coal covering of rock and dirt that is spilled down the mountainside; topsoil over the coal had to be preserved, protected, and replaced after the completion of mining; mine operators would be responsible for replacing vegetation for five years after the initial reclamation effort; and mining companies had to have the written consent for mining from the owners of surface properties in areas where the federal government has retained the mineral rights.

TABLE 3.

House Interior Committee Vote on February 27, 1974, to Substitute the
Hosmer Proposal (H.R. 12898) for the Udall-Mink Bill (H.R. 11500)

	Republicans	*Democrats**	*Total Vote*
NAY	28% (5 members)	73% (16 members)	52% (21 members)
YEA	72% (13 members)	27% (6 members)	48% (19 members)

YEA	NAY
Bauman	Bingham
Camp	Burke
Clausen	Burton
Hosmer	Cronin
Johnson	de Luge
Jones	Dellenback
Kazen	Foley
Ketchum	Kastenmeier
Lujan	Meeds
Martin	Melcher
Runnels	Mink
Sebelius	O'Hara
Skubitz	Owens
Steiger	Regula
Stephens	Roncalio
Symms	Ruppe
Taylor	Seiberling
Towell	Steelman
Young	Udall
	Vigorite
	Won Pat

* The percentages for the Democrats are based on 22 voting members rather
than the 23 Democrats that are on the committee, since Chairman Haley
usually refrains from voting unless there is a tie vote.

On July 25, the House approved the bill by a 298–81 vote. But
the conference to reconcile the differences between the House and
Senate strip mining bills did not meet until August 7—and then
did not finally adjourn until December 3. One member of the conference sighed that its eighty-seven hours were "inordinately long
and unnecessarily frustrating." After sweating through compromises on regulating mining in national forests, national grasslands,
Indian lands, and areas where there are extensive underground
waters, and to provide funds for reclamation, the conferees spent

their last five grueling sessions arguing over the rights of surface owners. The Senate bill contained the Mansfield amendment, which would ban strip mining completely where the surface rights above federal coal were privately owned. The House bill's Melcher amendment gave the surface owner a veto over any mining for federal coal beneath his property. By the time the Senate bill reached conference, though, virtually all the senators who had supported it had abandoned it, after confessing that they had not realized it would have removed from production about 80 percent of the federally owned coal in the nation. After debating some twenty proposals, the conferees eventually settled on a proposal made by Sen. J. Bennett Johnston, Jr., on December 3 that combined elements of earlier compromises offered by Senator Jackson and Representatives Udall and Melcher. This proposal limited veto power to surface owners who three years before their consent was requested had 1) owned the land; and 2) used it as a principal place of residence or occasionally farmed or ranched on it; or directly received a significant portion of their income from the use of the land for farming or ranching. The Johnston compromise would also have limited financial compensation to the surface owner from the coal operator to the fair market value of his property plus any damages to his surface property or crops caused by the mining. An additional amount was assured surface owners equal to the damages or $100 an acre, whichever was less.

On December 13 the House approved the conference report by a voice vote. Within minutes after it cleared the House, Frank G. Zarb, director of the Federal Energy Administration, told a White House press briefing that President Ford would definitely veto the measure. In language reminiscent of the propaganda of the National Coal Association, Zarb said that he had recommended a veto because the bill would exacerbate the energy shortage and would reduce coal by as much as 141 million tons from the projected production levels for 1977. Two other participants at the White House briefing—Interior Department Undersecretary John C. Whitaker and John R. Quarles, Jr., deputy administrator of the

Environmental Protection Agency—said that they had urged Ford to sign the bill.

Undeterred by the veto announcement, the Senate approved the conference report by voice vote on December 16 and sent it to President Ford for signature.

Since Congress was adjourning on December 20, the President had the option of either vetoing the bill before that date, which would give Congress an opportunity to override the veto, or letting it languish unsigned for ten days, which would then kill the bill through a pocket veto. There was no mention of the bill from the White House before Congress adjourned. On December 30—in a statement issued from his skiing White House at Vail, Colorado—Ford announced that the bill's "unnecessary restrictions on coal production would limit our nation's freedoms to adopt the best energy policies," and that S. 425 would never be law.

4

This Land Was Their Land:
Little White Lies,
Great White Father

Once upon a time, as stories with morals often start out, there was a broad land filled with forests, game, and a people who treasured and honored all that came from the land and lived on it. In those days the people were almost as one, the land was seemingly without end, and the game was fecund and plentiful. One lived in the grain and tenor of the land; as a people, the inhabitants felt the communion of life and the commonalty of their shared existence. In the west of this land, the people hunted for their meat and they killed their chief supply, the buffalo, only as needed, for they loved their land and all that lived on it.

Now the buffalo are gone. But the white man—who came in numbers far greater than that of the mighty beast who tramped the dusty plains—is still around. And for the Indian he represents not only the death of the buffalo but also the near-death of the Indian spirit. The white man's rapacity has not diminished since his rampages of the eighteenth and nineteenth centuries. He still covets the Indian's land, and he still molests the Indian people. But his methods for decimating the native Americans have become more sophisticated, and in their sophistication, more deadly. Instead of wiping out Indian tribes, the Bureau of Indian Affairs now encourages Indians to migrate to cities, where they may easily lose their Indian identity and join the urban poor. Instead of directly stealing Indian lands to exploit the minerals on them, Congress passes resolutions allowing whites access to the minerals. And as a fitting denouement to the nineteenth-century reservation policies that crowded Indians onto useless lands, the federal government until recently preferred to announce that the tribe no longer existed, that there was no longer a reservation, and that the ex-Indians were no longer entitled to federal benefits. From the beginning of Caucasian settlement in North America the Indian-white man melodrama followed a scenario that went something like this: recognize an Indian not as a man but as a savage unfit to live among whites; relegate him to the worst patches of land, land where no white man would live; deprive him of his dignity and livelihood; and finally, strip him of his ethnic pride by officially terminating his tribe.

The success of the white man's depredations against the Indians is substantially dependent upon the members of the Interior committees and their attitudes. Often forgotten among what are usually considered more important subcommittees are the Indian Affairs subcommittees. While subcommittees such as Public Lands or Minerals, Materials and Fuels deal with issues that affect all 200,000,000 Americans, the Indian Affairs subcommittees deal only with the nation's 700,000 Indians. Because the jurisdiction of the subcommittees is necessarily limited and their political clout minimal, their members most often serve on them in lieu of better assignments. Very few are there because of an interest in Indian issues. Even those who serve as the subcommittees' chairmen are often there only because of seniority and circumstance. They would rather chair other, more powerful subcommittees, but consent to head Indian Affairs because no matter how impotent or insignificant a subcommittee is, being a chairman offers an opportunity to garner more staff, more authority and more power.

Fortunately for the Indians, two of the rare exceptions to this rule are the present chairmen of the Indian Affairs subcommittees —Senator James Abourezk (D., S. Dak.) and Representative Lloyd Meeds (D., Wash.). According to *Race Relations Reporter* magazine, when these men became chairmen they "were well known for their incisive and intelligent approach to Indian matters and they began to clear out the many pieces of legislation that had lingered in the committees for several Congresses."[1] As one long-time Indian activist said, "For the first time, we have friends heading the subcommittees." Rarely does an Indian dissent from this view.

Neither Abourezk nor Meeds can reap local political benefits from the Indian Affairs chairmanship. The existing anti-Indian hostility in Abourezk's South Dakota was exacerbated by the 1972 takeover of Wounded Knee. Both Washington State and the city of Tacoma have been trying for the past few years to evict fourteen tribes from fishing along the rivers of Washington, even though they were granted this right by treaty in 1854 and 1855.

The attitudes of the Indian Affairs subcommittees toward Indians, the extent of their desire to help or to eliminate them as a cultural and ethnic entity, is largely contingent upon the philosophies of the chairmen of the full committees, of the Indian Affairs subcommittee members, and—although this may seem ancillary—of the staff directors of the subcommittees and the full committees.

The staffs for the committees and their subcommittees are generally a reflection of the chairmen and subcommittee chairmen. For instance, Wayne Aspinall was never known as a friend of the

Indians. One Indian intimately familiar with the mechanics of the House Indian Affairs Subcommittee called Aspinall a "bastard," and since he was the chairman of the House committee for years, he was an especially potent bastard. Aspinall appointed as the committee's general counsel Lewis Sigler, a man whose views closely conformed to his own. Sigler's career included long stints as assistant legislative counsel in the Interior Department and associate chief counsel in the Bureau of Indian Affairs. Since he joined the Interior Committee staff in 1968, Sigler's facility and expertise with laws relating to Indians has been recognized and respected, but as one of the chief architects of the terminationist policies of the 1950s he has also been widely criticized for refusing to recognize the adverse sociological and cultural factors that affect Indians. As one Indian who is knowledgeable about Capitol Hill said, "Damn few people know so much about Indian law as he does. He is very competent in technical matters. But he feels that Indians should get off their asses; they should get off the dole. That doesn't go down very well with my people."

After Aspinall was defeated in the 1972 primary and James A. Haley became House Interior Committee chairman, Sigler's power and influence declined and the more humane attitudes of Haley (D., Fla.) and of the new chairman of the subcommittee dominated. Haley had chaired the Indian Affairs Subcommittee for nearly eighteen years. While many Indians consider him paternalistic, he was at least sympathetic to their cause, although his sympathies had been blunted by the Aspinall autocracy. Haley indicated his concern for the Indians in a 1970 interview:

> The Indian people are the most harassed, pushed around folks in the history of our nation. We put the Indian off in remote areas. We killed his initiative, tried to make a farmer out of a hunter. We signed treaties and broke them. The Indian people are really a second nation within us, but we have treated them as second class citizens of our own. The blackest pages in our history concern our dealings with them.[2]

Haley has been praised by Indians as a good counterforce to Henry Jackson, who has been chairman of the full Senate committee for the past decade. While Jackson and others were advocating the termination of Indian tribes during the 1950s and 1960s, Haley fought for their continuation under the Bureau of Indian Affairs and for other federal help. The leader of one national Indian group praised Haley for his "good harassing tactics" against his foes in this long battle. But Haley's instincts are basically conservative, fiscally and socially. So not only did Indians have to contend with the not-so-benign neglect of Aspinall, they also had to cope with the innate conservatism of Haley, which prevented him from championing the Indian cause that extra bit that might have made the difference between success and failure.

Now, with Aspinall gone, with Haley sitting in the chairman's seat of the full committee, and with Meeds ruling the Indian Affairs Subcommittee, Indians are not only relieved, they are even hopeful. One Indian leader praised Meeds as "sensitive, imaginative." Another says he is "open, receptive, concerned." Unlike Haley, his instincts are basically liberal, which automatically makes him a more natural champion for the Indians. Although Haley cared, he did not care enough. Meeds places a high priority on civil rights and prides himself on his involvement with the 1968 Indian Bill of Rights that defined the civil rights of Indians. Meeds is convinced of the necessity for large federal programs and for an equitable distribution of benefits and funds. His first priority when he became Indian Affairs Subcommittee chairman, as we will see later in this chapter, was to restore federal benefits to the Menominee Tribe of Wisconsin, which had been terminated as a tribe in 1954.

Until very recently the Indians have traditionally had fewer friends in the Senate than in the House. In fact, even with Aspinall riding herd on the House committee, it was possible to say that the House Indian Affairs Subcommittee was more favorably disposed toward Indians than the Senate subcommittee. During the 1950s the chairman of the Senate Subcommittee was Arthur

Watkins (R., Utah), the nation's major advocate of termination. When Watkins began his crusade, he concentrated on some small Paiute tribes in his home state. A senator, he seemed to imply, should first prove his mettle with his own constituents. Though Watkins made one nominal concession when negotiating with the Paiutes—federal recognition of their tribal marriages—he recanted on even this provision on the final legislation. He managed to "free" the Indians from federal supervision by placing them under a private trusteeship that rarely communicated with the tribe and that was more restrictive than federal guardianship had been.

Watkins' patron during the terminationist phase was the chairman of the full committee, Clinton Anderson (D., N.M.). Anderson, in turn, was supported by the full committee's staff man for Indian Affairs, James Gamble, one of the Indians' worst nemeses since the days of General Custer. Both used pressure. Custer's was armed and military; Gamble's was cultural and legalistic. But both aimed to eliminate the Indian from the face of the United States.

Gamble's authority over the Indian Affairs Subcommittee was almost as great as that of the subcommittee or full committee chairmen, if not greater. In a 1968 *New Republic* article, "Lo, the Poor Indian," Ralph Nader reported that Gamble, "with the apparent knowledge of Senator Jackson and Clinton Anderson, has long been the chief congressional worker for termination of Indian reservations and assimilation of the Indian into the mainstream of American life.[3]

And in his powerful 1969 indictment of America's modern Indian warfare, *Custer Died for Your Sins,* Vine Deloria, Jr., portrayed Jackson as the pawn of Gamble. Gamble, Deloria said,

> has remained in the background while Henry Jackson . . . has had to accept public responsibility for Gamble's moves against the tribes.
> Rarely does a judgment bill [for Indian claims] come

before the committee but what Gamble tries to have a termination rider attached. So powerful is Gamble that Jackson might be characterized as his front man. But Jackson is busy with his work on the Foreign Relations and other important committees and so he accepts Gamble's recommendations without much consideration of alternatives.[4]

One section of a termination bill drafted by Gamble in the late 1960s revealed what Deloria called a "typical Gamble gambit."[5] In exchange for the return of some of their original reservation lands, the Colville tribe of eastern Washington had to agree to be terminated. Gamble inserted a provision into the termination bill stating that the Interior Secretary can determine whether any of the tribe's members are so incompetent that they cannot vote after termination on whether to sell the reservation's lands. If a member is incompetent, then the Interior Secretary can appoint a guardian for him. Yet as Deloria points out:

> Incompetency is never mentioned as a requirement for voting in the first part of the bill. But hidden in the middle is a provision giving the Secretary of the Interior unlimited discretionary power over Indian people. Theoretically the Secretary could declare all of the Colvilles incompetent and place them under a private trustee. They would then be judged too incompetent to handle their own money, but competent enough to vote to sell their reservation. Is it any wonder that Indians distrust white men?[6]

Gamble's decline began with Senator George McGovern's chairmanship of the Indian Affairs Subcommittee. Though even McGovern's staff will admit that the senator was more concerned with the affairs of his Select Committee on Nutrition and Human Needs, he was substantially more concerned about Indians than his immediate predecessor, Lee Metcalf, had been. Gamble constantly tried to coopt McGovern, to advocate legislation that the senator abhorred, even to schedule hearings without his knowledge so that the senator was ill prepared to question the witnesses. (McGovern left the Interior Committee in 1973, when he joined the Foreign Relations Committee.)

The Indian community has been very much disappointed in Forrest Gerard, the committee's present staff specialist on Indian affairs. A Blackfoot Indian, Gerrard seems to be more concerned with Jackson's presidential campaign than with the social and economic needs of his people. The staff member of an Indian group based in Washington dismissed Gerrard as a man "who's forgotten who he's serving" and who fits "the image of a government Indian," which is not a compliment whether it comes from a white or a fellow Indian. Gerrard has earned the Indian epithet "apple": one who is red on the outside but white on the inside.

Though the Indians still have to contend with Henry Jackson and Forrest Gerard, their greatest hope on the Interior Committee and in the entire Senate is a small, unimposing senator of Lebanese descent, James Abourezk from South Dakota. One Indian leader called Abourezk "a tremendous advocate." He is a man who seems to have the respect and confidence of virtually the entire Indian community, ranging from moderate groups like the National Congress of American Indians to more radical federations like the American Indian Movement. Because of his spontaneous approach, Abourezk has more respect among Indians than he does among fellow senators. After years of subcommittee scorn and neglect of Indians, perhaps it is better that the man who chairs the subcommittee have the respect of the people for whom the subcommittee is responsible, since at least with respect comes hope.

There are two crucial factors in Abourezk's deep concern for the Indians. One is that he grew up on an Indian reservation in South Dakota, where his father had a trading post—what is now euphemistically called a "general store." There he witnessed the plight and desolation of the Indians. The second factor is his sympathy for the Palestinean refugees. He relates their expulsion from their lands now in Israeli hands to the theft of the Indians' lands by the white man.

Abourezk's respect for Indians is indicated by his reluctance to hold hearings on any subject related to Indians without first assessing their reactions to such hearings. His empathy is apparent in a joint resolution (Senate Joint Resolution 133) that he introduced in mid-July 1973. This would establish an American Indian Policy Review Commission to investigate the fulfillment of the treaties and agreements between the United States and all the Indian tribes, to review the policies, practices, and structures of the federal agencies dealing with Indians, and to collect and compile the data necessary to understand present and future Indian needs. The resolution was prompted by what Abourezk called the "despair, frustration and alienation among young and older Indians alike" that was caused by the "failure of governmental institutions to enable individual Indians to enjoy good health, to receive meaningful academic and vocational training, to find satisfying employment, to live in decent and acceptable housing, and to enjoy fundamental civil rights. . . ."[7]

The resolution was passed by the Congress in 1974.

Abourezk's affinity for the Indians' cause and his intuitive grasp of their natural preferences was also apparent in a March 1971 statement urging the Justice Department to investigate the death of Raymond Yellow Thunder, a fifty-one-year-old Oglala Sioux. Yellow Thunder had allegedly been accosted in the streets of Gordon, Nebraska, by five whites and forced into an American Legion hall, where he was stripped and made to dance for the pleasure of the Legionnaires. A few days later Yellow Thunder died of a delayed hemorrhage caused by blows to the head. Abourezk warned Richard Kleindienst, who was then Attorney General, that

> the Indian people involved in this cause fear that the whole affair may be whitewashed. The situation has threatened to explode into violence and may do so again unless the Federal government makes clear that it is willing to step in to assure the full and complete investigation and possible execution of those responsible for Yellow Thunder's death.[8]

But the Justice Department failed to take Abourezk's advice seriously; the state and local governments failed to prosecute; and the Indians' frustration and despair over the unsolved murder of Yellow Thunder slowly fermented. Finally, in 1972 the American Indian Movement seized the town of Wounded Knee, South Dakota, seeking justice for the killing of Yellow Thunder and publicity for the more radical elements in the Indian movement.

TERMINATION POLICY AND THE MENOMINEES

The harm the Indian Affairs subcommittees can do to the Indians was typified by the misguided and cruel policy of termination, whose chief advocate was the chairman of the Senate Indian Affairs Subcommittee for most of the 1950s. This policy was intended to end the federal government's responsibility for the Indians, to make the process of their assimilation into white society virtually moot. There would no longer be Indians because their entire cultural and ethnic identity would be erased. As a spokesman for the Blackfeet Tribe put it, "In our Indian language, the only translation for termination is 'to wipe out' or 'to kill off.' We have no words for termination . . ."[9]

Long before this lament, the Five-County Cherokees of the Southwest issued a declaration that paralleled it:

> In these days, we are losing our homes and our children's homes. When our homeland is protected, for ourselves and for the generations to follow, we shall rest.
>
> In the vision of our creator, we declare ourselves ready to stand proudly among the nationalities of these United States of America.[10]

But the United States government was apparently not ready to let the Indian stand proudly on his own land. A 1953 concurrent resolution in the House of Representatives (H. Con. Res. 108) officially established terminationist policy. It proclaimed that Congress intended to make the American Indians subject to the same laws and entitled to the same privileges and responsibilities as are applicable to other citizens of the United States, to end their status as wards of the United States, and to grant them all of the rights and prerogatives pertaining to American citizenship. . . .

. . . [and that they] should assume their full responsibilities as American citizens. . . .[11]

One of the tribes most severely affected by termination was the Menominee Tribe of Wisconsin. The Menominee were a small woodland tribe that had lived in the region around what is now Green Bay, Wisconsin, before the white man's coming. Their ancestors, a peaceful Algonquin people, once occupied nearly one and a half million acres in northeastern Wisconsin and the Upper Peninsula of Michigan. After a series of treaties culminating in the Wolf River Treaty of 1854, they were confined to about 234,000 acres along the Wolf River and in northeastern Wisconsin. In exchange for ceding their land, the federal government promised that it would act as their trustee and would provide them with government services through the Bureau of Indian Affairs.

The Menominee were relatively prosperous by Indian standards. They were one of three tribes in the nation that could pay for the cost of most of their federal services. According to a Wisconsin newspaper, "the Menominees were a relatively self-sufficient people with good schools, one of the best Indian hospitals in the nation, community services, and a tribal-owned sawmill."[12] But almost all the individual Menominee were poor, their federal services were not of the highest standards, and their health, housing and education fell far below the national (white) norms.[13]

The Menominee forest was valued at $36 million. In 1951 the tribe was awarded $8.5 million by the United States Court of Claims because of BIA mismanagement of the forests.[14] The award was put into the federal treasury to await a congressional bill authorizing its distribution. By 1953 the Menominee expected to have a portion of the settlement—about $5 million—distributed among them on a $1,500 per capita basis.[15]

But in 1953 the Republicans assumed control of Congress for the first time in twenty-one years. In what Kirke Kickingbird, the director of the Institute for the Development of Indian Law, called the Republicans' "first overt act against the Indian community," the new Congress passed its now infamous joint resolution declaring its intent to terminate every tribe in the nation. The new chairman of the Senate Interior Committee, Arthur Watkins of Utah, was especially insistent that he had the cure for the age-old "Indian problem." He demanded that the Menominee accept immediate termination in exchange for the money the United States owed them.

Since neither the Menominee nor any other tribe realized the implications of termination, they invited Watkins to explain the concept to them.* On June 20, 1953, he spoke for forty-five minutes to the Menominee Greater Council, advising them that Congress had already decided to terminate the tribe, although the one bill that had been passed relating to the Menominee had come through the House and this related only to the distribution of their settlement.

After Watkins left the council, it voted, 169 to 5, to accept termination—but only five percent of the 3,200 Menominee participated in the vote. A Menominee group later said:

> Most of our people chose to be absent from the meeting in order to express their negative reaction to termination. Many who did vote affirmatively that day believed that Congress would impose termination regardless of their vote. Others thought they were voting *only* in favor of receiving their per capitas.[16]

* Watkins' attitude toward the Menominee is clear from his recollections of his trip to their reservation: "It was a very interesting experience. I appreciated . . . the opportunity to see how they lived, how they felt about it. That was one of the most interesting experiences of the whole trip. I had the same experiences visiting Europe, *the refugee camps of the Near East* [emphasis added]." (*Freedom with Reservation*, p. 13.)

While the Menominee were preparing their own termination plan, they learned that Watkins was pushing hard for his bill in Washington. Another council meeting immediately convened and defeated the pro-termination decision of the previous meeting by 179 to 0.

This second vote had no effect on Watkins. He introduced his termination bill in 1953, when it was defeated on a technicality, then reintroduced it in 1954. The day after President Eisenhower signed the bill into law on June 17, 1954, Watkins predicted that

> this measure could well mark the beginning of an epoch—an epoch which will provide a greater and better future for the Indian citizens of the United States. . . .
>
> It is my sincere belief that better days lie ahead for these people who have been so sadly neglected in many ways in the past. I believe a glorious future lies ahead for them.[17]

Eisenhower, too, held similar hopes for the effect of termination on the Menominees:

> I extend my warmest commendations to the members of the tribe for the impressive progress they have achieved and for the cooperation they have given the Congress in the development of this legislation. In a real sense, they have opened up a new era in Indian affairs—an era of growing self-reliance which is the logical culmination and fulfillment of more than a hundred years of activity by the Federal Government.[18]

The termination plan finally took effect in 1961. The Menominee tribe immediately came under the jurisdiction of all state laws and regulations and no longer had a land base protected by federal laws. It became Wisconsin's twenty-second county—its smallest, poorest, worst educated, unhealthiest and least developed. Termination had been strongly opposed by the state, which feared that the only result would be not "freedom" for the Indians but a poverty pocket that would burden welfare rolls. As an official of the Wisconsin Tax Commission warned, if the Menominee

> have to go to heavy taxation of their timberlands, that means they have to cut on some other basis than their present substained-yield method.* And as soon as that happens, the forests will eventually deplete, and we may have a substantial welfare problem. That is a problem the State of Wisconsin now has with the Indians in the Bad River reservation, where the lands are alloted, and the Indians sold their lands, and now they are on relief, in prosperous times as well as poor times. It is a continuing problem. And the State doesn't want anything like that to happen in this instance.[19]

The minimal security the Indians did receive was a $3,000 bond for each member on the tribal rolls as of 1961. The bond would mature in the year 2000, would pay 4 percent interest, and could be sold. The bond would divide the capital assets of the reservation into a corporation structure. In addition, each Menominee received 100 shares of stock in Menominee Enterprises, Incorporated, a corporation established to operate the sawmill. The First Wisconsin Trust Company was given the voting rights and shares for minors and incompetents and thus had total control over the corporation. A majority of its board of directors were non-Menominees.

As the termination deadline approached, the chances of Menominee self-sufficiency grew increasingly slim. The tribal hospital was closed for lack of funds and inability to conform to state health standards. The utilities had been sold because the tribe could not afford to maintain them. Between these losses and the

---

* The sustained-yield method of timber cutting, pioneered by the Menominee, guarantees that there will be approximately equal acres of timber to be cut each year. Rather than sweeping clear swaths through the forests, the Menominee cut just those trees above a certain height from one end of their forest to the other. They continue the process the following year, starting at the perimeter of the forest where they finished the previous cutting season.

structure of Menominee Enterprises Incorporated, the deck was well stacked against the Menominee in the new experiment known as termination.

The next decade was disastrous. The sawmill was saddled with 90 percent of the taxes levied by Menominee County. With rising taxes, the corporation that ran the mill did not have enough current income to pay interest on the corporate bonds issued to the tribe's members. The corporation had to dip into the capital reserved from the original amount that had been on deposit in the federal treasury before termination and that was transferred by the law ending federal recognition of the tribe. In four years, $239,000 was taken from the reserve. This depleted the reserve to $864,000.*

Because of its increased tax burden, the sawmill had to modernize to increase its efficiency. Before termination it had employed 410 Menominee. After modernization, employment dropped to 230 people, with additional seasonal employment ranging between 65 and 130.[20]

To provide a measure of solvency, the tribe finally leased its beloved Wolf River to the state for $250,000 a year. Menominee Enterprises then decided to lease summer cottage sites to whites to procure extra income. In resigned desperation, the tribe next decided to sell the land. In 1967 Menominee Enterprises formed a partnership with a land developer to develop Legend Lake, a series of small lakes artificially linked together with approximately 5,000 acres adjacent to the lake. They projected that 2,500 lots would be sold to whites.[21]

By 1970 the Menominee were caught in a malevolent cycle. The sawmill's losses forced the tribe to sell the lands at Legend Lake for revenue, and these sales also further depleted the timber supply, which in turn increased the sawmill's losses. Finally the sawmill burned down.

---

* It had been conservatively estimated before termination that a minimum of $2 million in reserve funds was needed to make the sawmill economically feasible. (*One Hundred Million Acres*, p. 152.)

While the Menominee were waiting for the sawmill to be rebuilt, they were almost completely dependent on the sales of the Legend Lake lots. As they watched more and more whites moving into their county, they realized that eventually the whites would be in the majority.

In the spring of 1970 a demonstration against the Legend Lake development erupted after the new white owners of the land forced some Menominee to leave a traditional picnic spot. The Menominee were furious that whites had the power to prohibit Indians from using ancestral tribal lands. Resolved to bring an end to termination and to the humiliating history of the previous decade, the Menominee formed a new organization called DRUMS (Determination of Rights and Unity for Menominee Stockholders).

For once, the Menominee were favored by circumstances. The creation of DRUMS coincided with several important changes in the American consciousness of Indians. This was caused in part by books such as Vine Deloria, Jr.'s *Custer Died for Your Sins* and Dee Brown's *Bury My Heart At Wounded Knee*, and by the sympathy of white youth for the Indians. Long neglected and long ignored, Indians suddenly became models for the nation. Their attitude toward the land was in tune with the new ecology and organic food movements; their reverence toward his gods was accorded new respect because of white fascination with religion and mysticism. These new attitudes cast the Indians not as aliens, but as precursors and paradigms.

Even more important was the July 8, 1970, statement by President Nixon officially reversing termination as a policy of the federal government. Nixon stated that the Indians "are the most deprived and most isolated minority group in our nation" because the federal-Indian relationship had "oscillated between two equally harsh and unacceptable extremes"—excessive paternalism and termination.[22]

The President deplored termination as "wrong" for several reasons. One was that its basic premise was wrong.

Termination implies that the Federal government has taken on a trusteeship responsibility for Indian communities as an act of generosity toward a disadvantaged people and that it can therefore discontinue this responsibility on a unilateral basis whenever it sees fit. But the unique status of Indian tribes does not rest on any premise such as this. The special relationship between Indians and the Federal government is the result instead of solemn obligations which have been entered into by the United States Government . . .

. . . To terminate this relationship would be no more appropriate than to terminate the citizenship rights of any other American.

Another reason was that its

practical results have been clearly harmful in the few instances in which . . . [it] actually has been tried. The removal of Federal trusteeship responsibility has produced considerable disorientation among the affected Indians and has left them unable to relate to a myriad of Federal, State, and local assistance efforts. Their economic and social condition has often been worse after termination than it was before.

The final grounds for dismissing termination were the debilitating effect it had had on those Indians who had not been terminated:

The very threat that . . . [the Federal-Indian] relationship may someday be ended has created a great deal of apprehension among Indian groups and this apprehension, in turn, has had a blighting effect on tribal progress. Any step that might result in greater social, economic or political autonomy is regarded with suspicion by many Indians who fear that it will only bring them closer to the day when the Federal government will disavow its responsibility and cut them adrift.

This new consciousness and the new political atmosphere indicated by President Nixon were reflected in the 1972 platforms of the Republican and Democratic parties, which both included pro-Indian planks. The Democrats pledged that they

> . . . support [the] rights of American Indians to full rights of citizenship. . . . We strongly oppose the policy of termination and we urge the government to provide unequivocal advocacy for the protection of the remaining Indian land and water resources. . . .[23]

And the GOP convention, held about a month after the Democratic convention, praised President Nixon for having "evolved a totally new Indian policy which we fully support." But it damned the Democrats for the failure of the new policy and blamed the "opposition Congress [which] by inaction on most of the President's proposals, has thwarted Indian rights and opportunities." The Republicans also stated their awareness "of the severe problems facing the Menominee Indians in seeking to have Federal recognition restored to their tribe and promise a complete and sympathetic examination of their pleas."[24] Forgotten, apparently, was the fact that it was a Republican senator in a Republican administration who had successfully advocated the Menominee termination.

Along with the new consciousness and the new platitudes came a new Congress. The new chairmen of the Indian Affairs subcommittees were determined to help the Indian people and reverse the depredations of the past decades. The Menominees saw their opportunity and began the most intense congressional lobbying ever initiated by an Indian group. DRUMS leader Ada Deer mounted a one-woman siege, haranguing members of Congress in the halls of the Capitol and debating with them in their offices. She was later credited by many members with conducting the most effective lobbying campaign they had ever witnessed.

On May 2, 1973, Menominee de-termination bills were introduced in both the House and the Senate by members of the Wisconsin delegation, Senators William Proxmire and Gaylord Nelson and Representative David Obey, whose district included

Menominee County. As Obey introduced the House bill (H.R. 7421) he condemned the termination as "a grave mistake." It had been initiated during the 1950s, he recalled, because it was assumed that

> Indian lands, culture and identity would slowly fade away, and with it a national responsibility to a people who occupied our land before most of our ancestors ever arrived here.
>
> Now I think the country knows better. We know that Indians want and deserve a measure of self-determination, to manage the natural and human resources of their people. But self-determination is a far cry from termination. . . .
>
> When termination became final, it was clear that the termination act was not a measure for distributing aid to the Menominee people, but a vehicle for potential destruction of the tribe as a whole.[25]

As Senator Nelson introduced the Senate bill (S. 1687), he stressed the economic depression of the Menominees:

> The present situation in Menominee County is bleak. Average unemployment is 26%, as opposed to 5% for the state of Wisconsin as a whole. According to the 1970 census, the average per capita income for the Menominee County Indians was $1,028 compared with the $3,158 for the state of Wisconsin as a whole. Almost 40% had incomes below the poverty level compared with Wisconsin's 7%, and 25% of those families reported receiving income from public assistance welfare as against 3% for the state.
>
> The prospects for the future of Menominee County are even bleaker . . . Economic stagnation is probable . . . At this time, it is thus imperative that additional public funds be funnelled into Menominee County or its tax burden be lessened if the Menominees are to meet their financial obligations. Restoration of Indian status is their only hope for cultural survival.[26]

Within a few weeks the Menominee bill was warmly embraced by the Nixon administration and the congressional leadership.

Representative Meeds called it a "symbolic" piece of legislation whose passage would be "just and fair and show this government is big enough to admit a mistake." Meeds warned that the bill's defeat would be "disastrous—a signal to the Indians that we are only engaging in rhetoric . . ."[27]

At an awards dinner of the National Congress of American Indians, Senator Jackson attacked termination as "a morally reprehensible policy. It has also proved to be just plain bad policy, unworkable as it is unjust," he said. "I am firmly convinced that the Menominees have a valid claim for corrective action. Their claim cannot, in equity and good conscience, be ignored."[28]

At the end of June, Interior Secretary Rogers Morton joined Jackson and assailed termination as a policy that had "long since been discredited . . ."[29] On July 11, 1973, HEW Secretary Casper Weinberger proclaimed his support for the bill if minor alterations were made.[30] And on August 31, the President's counselor for domestic affairs, Melvin Laird, a former congressman whose district had included the Menominee reservation and who had opposed termination, announced his support for de-terminating the Menominee. Though he had "always believed the Menominees made a mistake voting for termination," he praised them for their tenacious efforts to survive since their traditional status with the federal government had been severed:

> Formidable odds notwithstanding, they have managed to maintain a workable governing structure, a tribal constitution, and the firm cohesion of their basic social institutions. They have struggled to preserve a rich heritage. The Menominee tribe . . . attempted to make the best of a deplorable situation. . . .[31]

As support continued to multiply for the Menominee bill, the Indians grew increasingly confident that the government's policy was changing and that they would win their fight. Ada Deer announced that the nation was witnessing an historic reversal of government policy. This government has tried for 200 years to eliminate the Indians. They tried wars, they tried disease, they tried putting us on reservations. They tried acculturization, shipping us off to cities. Termination was the ultimate expression of that. We're going to continue to survive.[32]

And survive they did. On October 16, when the House voted on the Menominee bill, Lloyd Meeds pleaded with the House to pass the bill and revive Indian pride and dignity:

> . . . this body can most effectively terminate the policy of termination by the passage of the legislation, which will restore to the Menominee Indians those Government Services to which other Indian tribes are entitled, and remove the fear of termination from them and other Indians, so that they can make progress and may have, indeed, their self-dignity and their tribal dignity restored.[33]

James Haley was contrite over having introduced the original Menominee termination bill on the floor of the House. He admitted that a year and a half after the bill's passage he had discovered how Senator Watkins had coerced the Indians into voting for termination:

> Had I known what I know now, or what I knew a little later, I certainly would never have brought a termination bill to the floor of the House and asked that it be passed.
> I think the truly real justice that we could do here is to receive our brethren back into the many benefits that they are entitled to as Indians.[34]

Wisconsin's Kastenmeier severely castigated termination as "a senseless policy, that is abhorrent, not only to the Menominee, but to the majority of the Indian people."[35]

And John Saylor, in one of his last House speeches before his death, tagged the Menominee de-termination bill the "final chapter of a tragedy": it was not a perfect bill, he said, but it was "a better bill than the monstrosity that was rammed through this House in 1954 as part of the mistaken termination policy . . ." Saylor expected it to "permit [the Menominee] to save their tribe from extinction and salvage their own personal identities."[36]

The only member of the House who spoke against the bill was Representative James Collins (R., Tex.). Defending the bill that had instituted termination, Collins used precisely the same archaic arguments that had been used by such terminationist stalwarts as Senator Watkins:

> By re-establishing the Menominee Indian Reservation, we would be encouraging an environment that has a proved record as a loser . . .
> Why send the Menominee Indians down to a reservation? Give them the square break and opportunity of an Irishman. Let them be a full-time American.[37]

But Collins was able to garner only two allies to help him resist the bill. Opposing them were 404 representatives who favored restoring to the Menominee their legal and cultural status as Indians, restoring to them what was left of their ancient lands, reviving some lost and almost irretrievable sense of dignity and worth.*

At this point the bill had to be rushed through the Senate and signed by the President before the end of the year. If the Menominees were not returned to reservation status by the beginning of 1974, Menominee Enterprises would be forced to pay another $600,000 in property taxes and $350,000 in interest and other outstanding bills that would force it into bankruptcy.[38]

On December 7 the Senate unanimously passed the Menominee bill on a voice vote. Fifteen days later the President signed the bill into law as "a clear reversal of a policy which was wrong, the policy of forcibly terminating Indian tribal status . . ."[39]

---

* Joining Collins in his opposition to the bill were Robert P. Hanrahan (R., Ill.) and Earl F. Landgrebe (R., Ind.). The one member of the House Interior Committee not present for the vote was New York's Jonathan Bingham.

The new law received hosannas from various Indian leaders. LaDonna Harris, wife of former Senator Fred Harris (D., Okla.) and director of Americans for Indian Opportunity, hailed the act for eliminating "the fear of termination that has haunted all tribes since the Menominee were terminated." Charles Trimble, executive director of the National Congress of American Indians, praised the Menominee de-termination as the "bright light in this administration's treatment of Indians." Vine Deloria, Jr., called the act the most constructive piece of Indian-related legislation since the 1934 BIA Reorganization Act which decelerated the sale of Indian lands to non-Indians.[40]

The Menominees finally got back their land and are presently going through the throes of again becoming a people, a nation within a nation. With their own labors and the assistance of the federal government, perhaps they will regain the self-respect and dignity they enjoyed before termination.

In a January 1974 editorial the *Wall Street Journal* called the whole termination policy a disaster, not

> because self-reliance and individual initiative are unworthy goals. On the contrary. It was disastrous because Washington did not understand that it is virtually impossible to successfully impose alien values on people with vastly different traditions and culture. From dealing with American Indians to formulating foreign aid programs, Congress has too often failed to take into account the very values and traditions that distinguish effective reform from ineffective intrusion. The short-lived Menominee experiment will stand as a conspicuous monument to this lack of understanding.[41]

If Congress is to cease such experiments, it must develop a rational compassion. For virtually the entire span of white settlement of the North American continent, the Indian has been decimated, exterminated, physically evicted from his lands, and morally condemned for his alleged savagery and heathenism. It is only in the past few years that the new awareness of Indian values and traditions has begun to change that pattern. It is only very recently that the Indian Affairs subcommittees have begun to reflect and expand this new awareness.

The attitudes of the subcommittees should not be dependent upon whether Meeds, Abourezk, Haley, or Watkins chairs them, but upon the justice and decencies that are due the Indians. The subcommittees should not consider how the rights of the Indians might conflict with the pecuniary desires of strip miners, oil companies, or ranchers who want Indian lands. They should deal only with what is due the Indian and what is rightfully his. Without these standards, the Indian Affairs subcommittees will be ineffectual and insulated, severed from the true reality of the Indian situation. Let us reason together, as Lyndon Johnson was fond of saying, and let us live together also, in the respect and harmony that can be fostered by sympathetic and knowledgeable Indian Affairs subcommittees.

5

Blueprint for a New Landscape: Are the Times A-Changin'?

For years the cry for congressional reform has been rising. While the nation has experienced the agonies of assassinations, bombings, and marches for a myriad of humane causes and psychotic rationalizations, while the national psyche has been forced to bend in the winds of a new consciousness, Congress has been sitting on its haunches, stolid and distant, removed from the forces swaying and rocking about it. As Bob Dylan sang at the opening of the sixties, "the times they are a-changin'."

But how fast the times change for Congress, and whether they change at all, is largely dependent upon its own desire for reform.

The present American constitutional system implies a faith in the innate virtue of man, the man who comprises the broad American constituency and the man who sits in Congress, frequently somnolent, often insulated from the concerns and vicissitudes of society. Perhaps the faith of the founding fathers was justified. Perhaps our governmental institutions do have the potential for substantially changing themselves, transforming their deficiencies into dynamic vigor, their weakness into strength. The history of congressional reform indicates, however, that the influence of Rousseau on Washington, Madison, and Jefferson was appropriate for their times, when men still lived in villages and on farms. It appears to be less effective today, when the majority are urban dwellers. If the founding fathers are to be vindicated, then Congress must first vindicate itself.

Land reform has been the slogan of some of the most crucial revolutions of the twentieth century. Though true land reform may be impractical and revolution unlikely in this country, any new attitudes toward the land, either its use or its preservation, must eventually come from or be reflected by the Interior committees. Basic changes in the mechanics of the committees, in the quality and quantity of their work, must accompany these new attitudes. The previous chapters have detailed both some of the committees' more glaring and more subtle handicaps. Among these are a lack of coherent philosophical direction, dominance by the chairman and impotence of the subcommittees, overrepresentation from certain geographical and ideological sectors, lack of concern for the public interest as evidenced by poor attendance at subcommittee and committee meetings, and excessive sympathy for private interests. If Congress, and especially the members of the Interior committees, is truly concerned about effectively administering the nation's lands and resources, then it should consider the following reforms for the committees, reforms that could change not only the quality of the Interior committees, but of the American land as well.

One of the most necessary changes would be to give the committees a sense of ideological and geographical balance, to distribute their membership more equitably across the political and geographical spectrum of the nation. The committees have traditionally been dominated by the West, primarily because their jurisdiction has traditionally been the administration of federal lands, the bulk of which are west of the Mississippi. But the concept of sectionalism, of East versus West, North versus South, is a bankrupt one. It divides the nation rather than uniting it. It is a concept based on sectarianism and parochialism rather than a sense of domestic nationalism that transcends localities.

In this age of ecological concerns and dwindling energy resources, membership on the Interior committees should no longer appeal just to those interested in exploiting the federal lands for private ends. It should no longer be the haven of the westerner concerned with scalping national forests or for southwesterners who reflect their constituents' drive to make money from oil. Instead, under contemporary conditions, the committees that are responsible for the nation's land should represent all the regions and reflect all the concerns of the country.

This may be done in one of three ways, or possibly a combination of all three. First, the committees' jurisdiction could be altered to make service more appealing to a broader group of congressmen. This is the tack of the present House Select Committee on Committees, an *ad hoc* committee established in January 1973 to propose reforms for the House committee structure. Headed by Representative Richard Bolling (D., Mo.), the Select Committee has suggested that the Interior committees be retitled the Committees on Energy and Environment. Rather than having such diverse jurisdictions as Indians, public lands, territories, wildlife refuges, and mining, the new committees' responsibilities would be more limited and more clearly defined. They would include matters relating strictly to the environment and energy, such as water and power resources, clean air and drinking water, noise pollution, radiation, and solid waste. The areas over which the committees would lose their jurisdiction would be distributed to the Government Operations, Agriculture, and Natural Resources committees.

Second, the committees could acquire a more diverse membership by requiring that members of Congress serve on each committee for no more than ten years. This would enable each member to achieve expertise in a topical area, knowledge that he could relate to another committee's jurisdiction through a sort of crossfertilization.

If the rotation were done correctly, it would also prevent the committees from being dominated by either one locality or one political attitude. The committee on committees (or whichever body would administer rotation) could assure that no one region or philosophy would dominate. While there is no guarantee that such a practice would be followed, at least the appointing group would have the options to prevent the Interior committees from becoming pawns of special interests.

A third route to alteration of the committees' composition would be to sensitize the congressional leadership and the committees on committees, which appoint members to committees, to the need for the Interior committees to reflect the makeup of the country, not merely of a few regions. This last suggestion, though, is contingent upon the predispositions and sympathies of the leadership and the members of the committees on committees. It could very well be less effective than either compulsory rotation or changing the committees' jurisdiction.

One of the major problems of the Interior committees, as well as most other congressional committees, is that they have no comprehensive legislative program, no sense of priorities or cohesion in the legislation they produce. Members introduce bills, hearings are held on them, and they are reported to the floor of either chamber, but there is little, if any, philosophical or ideological link among them. This could be dramatically altered by creating a Committee on Legislative Flow for each chamber. The new committee would be composed of the leadership of both parties, the chairmen of each committee, and, in the Senate, the vice-president. By November 1 of the first session of each Congress, each regular committee would submit to the Committee on Legislative Flow its legislative and oversight schedule for the rest of the first session and the entire second session. The Legislative Flow Committee would then set a priority schedule for the legislative committees by mid-December. This would not only mesh the legislation produced by individual committees, but would also provide an organized direction for the legislation produced by the entire Congress.

To increase the attendance of members at markup sessions there should be a limit placed on the use of proxies, or, even better, proxies could be completely prohibited. This would increase attendance and also provide more intelligent voting.

Furthermore, to improve attendance at committee hearings as well, absenteeism could be limited to no more than 25 percent of the committee's hearings and markup sessions per session. If a member's absenteeism exceeded 25 percent, he would no longer be a voting member of the committee.

Since the House Interior Committee lacks a special oversight subcommittee, it should immediately form one. The Senate Interior Committee does have such a subcommittee, but its members are three of the committee's most senior members, Jackson, Bible, and Fannin. Both committees' oversight subcommittees should draw one-third of their members from the most senior committee members and the remaining two-thirds from the most junior members. For the younger members this would be an excellent introduction to the work of the committee, and they could draw upon the experience and knowledge of the more senior members. As one representative has said,

> oversight activities are an ideal way to involve the junior Members. They can be delegated major responsibility for reviewing the performance of the executive branch by otherwise occupied subcommittee chairmen, thus making better use of their considerable talents and energies, involving them

in committee work, and acquainting them with the programs and processes of government for which they bear responsibility.[1]

In addition, to assure that the strategic oversight function is accomplished, each oversight subcommittee would have to meet at least as often as the committees' most active legislative subcommittee. Such regular meetings would force more active oversight.

The number of subcommittees that each Interior committee member can serve on should be reduced to two. This would give each member an opportunity to develop greater expertise in a subcommittee's jurisdiction, rather than simply having his name appear on the roster of three or four subcommittees about whose jurisdictions he knows virtually nothing. A long, winding trail of subcommittee memberships may look impressive on campaign brochures, but it does nothing to aid the qualified and knowledgeable review of pending legislation.

If public financing of congressional campaigns is not legislated, incumbent committee members should be prohibited from accepting campaign contributions from any group, commercial firm, or individual with a vested interest in the committees' work.

Committee members should also be prohibited from engaging in any commercial activity that is regulated by the Interior committees, such as ranching, strip mining, or oil drilling. Most of the committees' members have severed their past ties with such activities, but others, particularly Senator Hansen, have not.

The subcommittees of the Senate Interior Committee should have their authority expanded so that they are not dominated by the committee chairman. And most importantly, each subcommittee chairman should have the sole right, with the approval of a majority of his subcommittee's members, to appoint the staff of the subcommittee.

Finally, the Indian Affairs and the Territorial Affairs Subcommittees should be moved to the Government Operations Committee. This is necessary for two major reasons. First, territories and Indian lands are not technically public lands, but rather lands held in trust by the federal government. They do not quite mesh with the general jurisdiction of the Interior committees. Second, it is the rare member of Congress who joins the Interior committees because he is interested in Indians or in territories. He is there because he is concerned about utilizing the land and its resources or about preserving them. The rights of Indians and the administration of territories invariably conflict with the broader jurisdictional responsibilities of the Interior committees. Indians and territories would be better served if each were either given a separate committee or placed in the Government Operations Committee, which oversees the functions of the executive branch —which in turn administers territories and Indian lands.

*   *   *

Woody Guthrie sang feelingly that "This land is your land." He was right. This land does belong to the people in the broadest sense. The public lands, water and air, nonreplaceable mineral resources, are everyone's concern, because they affect the quality of life for everyone in the nation. The people must see that the land is tenderly preserved and properly maintained.

Technically, all this is the direct responsibility of the members of the Interior committees, and it is to the people that they are ultimately responsible. If America is to have clean streams, broad forests, and clear air, then it must first have responsible and responsive Interior committees with members who care for the land, both rural and urban. Even before that we must have a concerned and informed electorate, one that places the national environment above sectional greed, one that values nature and knows that man is not necessarily above nature, but *in* it as well. Only then will this land truly be ours.

Members of the Interior Committees

Majority:

Henry M. Jackson, Chm. (Wash.)

Clinton P. Anderson (N. Mex.)

Alan Bible (Nev.)

Frank Church (Idaho)

Frank E. Moss (Utah)

Quentin N. Burdick (N. Dak.)

George S. McGovern (S. Dak.)

Lee Metcalf (Mont.)

Mike Gravel (Alaska)

Minority:

Gordon Allott (Colo.)

Len B. Jordan (Idaho)

Paul J. Fannin (Ariz.)

Clifford P. Hansen (Wyo.)

Mark O. Hatfield (Ore.)

Ted Stevens (Alaska)

Henry Bellmon (Okla.)

James Buckley (N.Y.)

Subcommittee on Indian Affairs

Majority:	*Minority*:
McGovern, Chm.	Fannin
Jackson	Hansen
Anderson	Bellmon
Burdick	Allott
Metcalf	Buckley
Gravel	

Subcommittee on Minerals, Materials and Fuels

Majority:	*Minority*:
Moss, Chm.	Jordan
Jackson	Bellmon
Bible	Allott
McGovern	Buckley
Gravel	

Subcommittee on Parks and Recreation

Majority:	*Minority*:
Bible, Chm.	Hansen
Jackson	Fannin
Anderson	Hatfield
Church	Bellmon
Moss	

Subcommittee on Public Lands

Majority:	*Minority*:
Church, Chm.	Hatfield
Jackson	Allott

Majority:

Bible
Metcalf
Gravel

Minority:

Fannin
Buckley

Subcommittee on Territories and Insular Affairs

Majority:

Burdick, Chm.
Jackson
McGovern
Metcalf

Minority:

Bellmon
Jordan
Hansen

Subcommittee on Water and Power Resources

Majority:

Anderson, Chm.
Jackson
Church
Moss
Burdick
Metcalf

Minority:

Allott
Jordan
Fannin
Hansen
Hatfield

Special Subcommittee on Legislative Oversight ·

Majority:

Jackson, Chm.
Anderson

Minority:

Allott

SENATE COMMITTEE ON INTERIOR AND INSULAR AFFAIRS, NINETY-THIRD CONGRESS

Majority:

Henry M. Jackson, Chm.
 (Wash.)
Alan Bible (Nev.)
Frank Church (Idaho)
Lee Metcalf (Mont.)
J. Bennett Johnston, Jr. (La.)
James Abourezk (S. Dak.)
Floyd K. Haskell (Colo.)
Gaylord Nelson (Wis.)
Howard M. Metzenbaum
 (Ohio)

Minority:

Paul J. Fannin (Ariz.)
Clifford P. Hansen (Wyo.)
Mark O. Hatfield (Ore.)
James L. Buckley (N.Y.)
James A. McClure (Idaho)
Dewey F. Bartlett (Okla.)

Subcommittee on Indian Affairs

Majority:

Abourezk, Chm.
Jackson
Metcalf
Haskell
Metzenbaum

Minority:

Bartlett
McClure
Fannin

Subcommittee on Minerals, Materials and Fuels

Majority:

Metcalf, Chm.
Jackson
Bible
Johnston
Nelson
Metzenbaum

Minority:

Buckley
Hansen
Bartlett

Subcommittee on Parks and Recreation

Majority: *Minority*:
Bible, Chm.   Hansen
Jackson   Hatfield
Church   McClure
Johnston
Nelson
Metzenbaum

Subcommittee on Public Lands

Majority: *Minority*:
Haskell, Chm.   McClure
Jackson   Hatfield
Church   Buckley
Abourezk
Nelson

Subcommittee on Territories and Insular Affairs

Majority: *Minority*:
Johnston, Chm.   Fannin
Jackson   Buckley
Metcalf   Bartlett
Abourezk

Subcommittee on Water and Power Resources

Majority: *Minority*:
Church, Chm.   Hatfield
Jackson   Hansen

Majority:	*Minority*:
Metcalf	Fannin
Haskell	
Metzenbaum	

Special Subcommittee on Legislative Oversight

Majority:	*Minority*:
Jackson, Chm.	Fannin
Bible	

Special Subcommittee on Integrated Oil Companies

Majority:	*Minority*:
Haskell, Chm.	Buckley
Johnston	Bartlett
Nelson	

HOUSE COMMITTEE ON INTERIOR AND INSULAR AFFAIRS, NINETY-SECOND CONGRESS

Majority:	*Minority*:
Wayne N. Aspinall, Chm. (Colo.)	John P. Saylor (Pa.)
	Craig Hosmer (Calif.)
James A. Haley (Fla.)	Joe Skubitz (Kans.)
Ed Edmondson (Okla.)	John H. Kyl (Iowa)
Walter S. Baring (Nev.)	Sam Steiger (Ariz.)
Roy A. Taylor (N.C.)	James A. McClure (Idaho)
Harold T. Johnson (Calif.)	Don H. Clausen (Calif.)
Morris K. Udall (Ariz.)	Philip E. Ruppe (Mich.)
Phillip Burton (Calif.)	John N. Happy Camp (Okla.)
Thomas S. Foley (Wash.)	Manuel Lujan (N. Mex.)
Robert W. Kastenmeier (Wis.)	Sherman P. Lloyd (Utah)

Majority:

James G. O'Hara (Mich.)
William F. Ryan (N.Y.)
Patsy T. Mink (Hawaii)
James Kee (W. Va.)
Lloyd Meeds (Wash.)
Abraham Kazen (Tex.)
Bill D. Burlison (Mo.)
Robert G. Stephens, Jr. (Ga.)
Joseph P. Vigorito (Pa.)
John Melcher (Mont.)
Teno Roncalio (Wyo.)
N. J. (Nick) Begich (Alaska)
James Abourezk (S. Dak.)

Minority:

John Dellenback (Ore.)
Keith G. Sebelius (Kans.)
James D. (Mike) McKevitt
  (Colo.)
John H. Terry (N.Y.)
Jorge L. Cordova (Puerto Rico)

Subcommittee on Environment

Majority:

Aspinall, Chm.
Haley
Edmondson
Baring
Taylor
Johnson
Udall
Kastenmeier
O'Hara
Ryan
Kee
Burlison
Vigorito
Melcher
Roncalio

Minority:

Saylor
Hosmer
Kyl
Steiger
McClure
Lloyd
Dellenback
Sebelius
Terry

Subcommittee on Indian Affairs

Majority:	*Minority*:
Haley, Chm.	Steiger
Edmondson	Kyl
Taylor	Camp
Mink	Lujan
Meeds	Sebelius
Stephens	Terry
Melcher
Begich
Abourezk

Subcommittee on Irrigation and Reclamation

Majority:	*Minority*:
Johnson, Chm.	Hosmer
Haley	McClure
Edmondson	Clausen
Baring	Camp
Udall	Lujan
Foley	Dellenback
Meeds	McKevitt
Kazen
Stephens
Roncalio
Abourezk

Subcommittee on Mines and Mining

Majority:	*Minority*:
Edmondson, Chm.	McClure
Baring	Hosmer

Majority:	Minority:
Burton	Skubitz
Foley	Steiger
Kastenmeier	Camp
Kee	McKevitt
Kazen	Cordova
Burlison	
Vigorito	
Melcher	

Subcommittee on National Parks and Recreation

Majority:	Minority:
Taylor, Chm.	Skubitz
Johnson	Kyl
Udall	McClure
Kastenmeier	Clausen
O'Hara	Ruppe
Ryan	Lloyd
Mink	Sebelius
Meeds	McKevitt
Kazen	Terry
Burlison	Cordova
Stephens	
Melcher	
Roncalio	
Begich	
Abourezk	

Subcommittee on Public Lands

Majority:	Minority:
Baring, Chm.	Kyl
Edmondson	Steiger

Majority:	*Minority*:
Johnson	Clausen
Udall	Ruppe
Burton	Camp
Kastenmeier	Lujan
O'Hara	Lloyd
Kee	Dellenback
Melcher	
Roncalio	
Begich	
Abourezk	

Subcommittee on Territorial and Insular Affairs

Majority:	*Minority*:
Burton, Chm.	Clausen
Haley	Hosmer
Taylor	Skubitz
Foley	Ruppe
Ryan	Lujan
Mink	Sebelius
Meeds	McKevitt
Burlison	Cordova
Stephens	
Vigorito	
Roncalio	
Begich	

HOUSE COMMITTEE ON INTERIOR AND INSULAR AFFAIRS, NINETY-THIRD CONGRESS

Majority:	*Minority*:
James A. Haley, Chm. (Fla.)	Craig Hosmer (Calif.)
Roy A. Taylor (N.C.)	Joe Skubitz (Kans.)

Majority:

Harold T. Johnson (Calif.)
Morris K. Udall (Ariz.)
Phillip Burton (Calif.)
Thomas S. Foley (Wash.)
Robert W. Kastenmeier (Wis.)
James G. O'Hara (Mich.)
Patsy T. Mink (Hawaii)
Lloyd Meeds (Wash.)
Abraham Kazen, Jr. (Tex.)
Robert G. Stephens, Jr. (Ga.)
Joseph P. Vigorito (Pa.)
John Melcher (Mont.)
Teno Roncalio (Wyo.)
Jonathan B. Bingham (N.Y.)
John F. Seiberling (Ohio)
Harold Runnels (N. Mex.)
Yvonne Brathwaite Burke
    (Calif.)
Antonio Borja Won Pat
    (Guam)
Wayne Owens (Utah)
Ron de Lugo (Virgin Islands)
James R. Jones (Okla.)

Minority:

Sam Steiger (Ariz.)
Don H. Clausen (Calif.)
Philip F. Ruppe (Mich.)
John N. Happy Camp (Okla.)
Manual Lujan, Jr. (N. Mex.)
John Dellenback (Ore.)
Keith G. Sebelius (Kans.)
Ralph S. Regula (Ohio)
Alan Steelman (Tex.)
Joseph J. Maraziti (N.J.)
David Towell (Nev.)
James G. Martin (N.C.)
William M. Ketchum (Calif.)
Paul W. Cronin (Mass.)
Don Young (Alaska)
Robert E. Bauman (Md.)
Steven D. Symms (Idaho)

Subcommittee on Environment

Majority:

Udall, Chm.
Foley
Kastenmeier
O'Hara
Vigorito
Melcher

Minority:

Ruppe
Hosmer
Steiger
Dellenback
Sebelius
Steelman

Majority:	*Minority:*
Roncalio	Towell
Bingham	Martin
Seiberling	Cronin
Burke	Bauman
Owens	Symms
de Lugo	
Jones	

Subcommittee on Indian Affairs

Majority:	*Minority:*
Meeds, Chm.	Regula
Taylor	Hosmer
Stephens	Lujan
Melcher	Steiger
Burke	Camp
Owens	Towell
de Lugo	Young
Jones	

Subcommittee on Water and Power Resources

Majority:	*Minority:*
Johnson, Chm.	Lujan
Udall	Hosmer
Foley	Clausen
Meeds	Camp
Kazen	Dellenback
Stephens	Steelman
Roncalio	Towell
Runnels	Ketchum
Burke	Symms
Jones	

Subcommittee on Mines and Mining

Majority:

Mink, Chm.
Udall
Burton
Foley
Kastenmeier
O'Hara
Kazen
Vigorito
Melcher
Seiberling
Runnels
Owens
Jones

Minority:

Camp
Hosmer
Skubitz
Steiger
Ruppe
Steelman
Martin
Ketchum
Cronin
Young
Bauman

Subcommittee on National Parks and Recreation

Majority:

Taylor, Chm.
Johnson
Kastenmeier
O'Hara
Mink
Meeds
Kazen
Stephens
Roncalio
Bingham
Seiberling
Won Pat
Owens
de Lugo

Minority:

Skubitz
Hosmer
Clausen
Ruppe
Camp
Sebelius
Regula
Steelman
Martin
Ketchum
Cronin
Bauman

Subcommittee on Public Lands

Majority:	*Minority*:
Melcher, Chm.	Steiger
Johnson	Hosmer
Udall	Clausen
Burton	Dellenback
Runnels	Regula
Won Pat	Towell
Owens	Young
Jones	

Subcommittee on Territorial and Insular Affairs

Majority:	*Minority*:
Burton, Chm.	Clausen
Taylor	Hosmer
Foley	Skubitz
Kastenmeier	Ruppe
Mink	Lujan
Meeds	Sebelius
Stephens	Regula
Vigorito	Martin
Bingham	Bauman
Burke	Symms
Won Pat	Ketchum
de Lugo	

II

THE HOUSE AGRICULTURE COMMITTEE AND THE SENATE AGRICULTURE AND FORESTRY COMMITTEE

6

The Agriculture
Committees
of Congress

. . . there are in this country, three interests, the agricultural, commercial, and manufacturing. And how happens it, sir, that the agricultural, the great leading and substantial interest in this country, has no committee—no organized tribunal in this House to hear and determine on their grievances? If the commercial or manufacturing interests are affected, the cry resounds throughout the country; remonstrances flow in upon us; they are referred to committees appointed for the purpose of guarding them, and adequate remedies are provided. But, sir, when agriculture is oppressed, and makes

NOTE: Research on this chapter was completed in 1972 and therefore does not take into acount changes in committee membership since that time.

complaint, what tribunal is in this House to hear and determine on the grievances?[1]

When Congressman Lewis Williams (D., N.C.) made this plea on behalf of agriculture in 1820, agriculture was the dominant industry in the young American nation. Congress, which is now a collection of lawyers, was then a convocation of farmers. The committees on agriculture, when they were established in the House in 1820 and the Senate in 1825, were a microcosm of Congress as a whole.[2] From the beginning the committees were imbued with the aim of service to farmers, idealized in Jeffersonian doctrine as the backbone of the nation's democratic virtue.[3]

In the 1970s agriculture (now more properly termed agribusiness) remains a vital if not dominant industry, but the farmer, at least Jefferson's version, is a dwindling anachronism. The committees who claim to represent him, far from being a microcosm of Congress, have become highly unrepresentative of the economic, political, and regional interests prevailing on Capitol Hill. The committees' single-minded advocacy of producers' and processors' interests, appropriate perhaps when the majority of citizens were employed in farming, is now intensely criticized for its neglect of consumers and the urban poor, as well as the poor farmer and sharecropper.[4]

The committees are now at a watershed in their history. After decades of restricting production to protect farmers from the economic adversity of superabundance, they now find themselves advocating increased production to protect world food trade from the adversity of scarcity. With the food crisis now center stage the world over, Congress as a whole increasingly seems to think agriculture is too important to be left to the farmers, or at least too important to be left to the parochial, rural-based congressmen who traditionally serve on the farm committees. Indeed, there is little in the committees' history to indicate that they have the vision and flexibility to respond to world food shortages with the imaginative and innovative leadership required. It is these committees, nevertheless, that will make the decisions which will largely determine the price and availability of food in the world of the 1970s and 1980s.

JURISDICTION

The jurisdiction of the Agriculture committees is full of anomalies. Their conservative membership[5] presides over one of the nation's largest welfare systems—the food stamp and commodity programs, and warmly embraces its largest foreign aid program, Food for Peace. Although fiscally as well as ideologically conservative, committee members created a vast system of subsidies to compensate wealthy farmers for not producing food, even in areas where malnutrition has been a national disgrace. While high world prices for most farm commodities have put most of the subsidy programs in abeyance in 1973–74, the committees continue to have a stranglehold on virtually all programs that affect the economy, living conditions, nutrition, and recreation of rural America. The blame for the national neglect that has tolerated rural squalor in many parts of the nation is more properly laid at the door of these committees than anywhere else. But if the committees bear responsibility for these social failures, they must also receive some of the credit for the astonishing economic success of American agriculture. However inequitably they may have been distributed, the benefits lavished on American agribusiness have helped make it the most productive and innovative food machine in the world.

The jurisdiction of the House committee, as defined in the Rules of the House of Representatives, specifies the following categories:

1. Agriculture generally.
2. Inspection of livestock and meat products.
3. Animal industry and diseases of animals.
4. Adulteration of seeds; insect pests; and protection of birds and animals in forest reserves.
5. Agricultural colleges and experiment stations.

6. Forestry in general and forest reserves other than those created from the public domain.
7. Agricultural economics and research.
8. Agricultural and industrial chemistry.
9. Dairy industry.
10. Entomology and plant quarantine.
11. Human nutrition and home economics.
12. Plant industry, soils, and agricultural engineering.
13. Agricultural educational extension services.
14. Extension of farm credit and farm security.
15. Rural electrification.
16. Agricultural production and marketing and stabilization of prices of agricultural products.
17. Crop insurance and soil conservation.[6]

The jurisdiction of the House and Senate Agriculture committees differs slightly. The School Lunch Program is in the Agriculture Committee in the Senate, and in Education and Labor in the House. Sugar legislation is controlled by the Finance Committee in the Senate, and in the Agriculture Committee in the House. Pesticide legislation is shared by the Environment Subcommittee of the Senate Commerce Committee and the Senate Agriculture Committee. The investigative work of the Senate Select Committee on Nutrition overlaps with that of the Senate Agriculture Committee, although the Select Committee has no legislative authority.

In the past, the byzantine complexity of farm legislation shielded it from outside scrutiny. David Bell, chief of the Budget Bureau under President John F. Kennedy, considered the farm program the most difficult legislative package he ever tried to understand, and Samuel Lubell, a respected pollster and political commentator, has called it a "conspiracy against public understanding."[7] It is said of the milk marketing legislation that it has the familiarity of Sanskrit and the logic of Catch-22. It is only in the past six years that interest in problems of hunger, subsidy payments, and rising food prices has pierced the shield of ennui behind which the farm committees have traditionally operated.

Agriculture's friends are still in control of the committees, but they no longer have unchallenged control over farm policy. A decade ago the only suspense in farm legislation was which commodity group—cotton, wheat, tobacco—was going to get a bigger piece of an ever increasing farm benefit pie. Now the suspense is whether there will be any pie to divide up at all. During the past decade two general changes in congressional agriculture politics have combined to make the passage of farm bills a more uncertain affair.

First, the Agriculture committees, especially the House committee, have become increasingly unrepresentative of the interests that have begun to take notice of agriculture bills. The fundamental causes of this increasing unrepresentativeness are shifts in the committees' jurisdiction, the birth of the consumer movement and the hunger lobby, and changes in personnel because of the seniority system.

Two decades ago the agribusiness industry was the only identifiable group (aside from taxpayers generally) that perceived itself to have any stake in the farm bills then being passed. The committees reflected this fact; all of their members were rural. Urban liberals and labor unions now care very much about farm bills, because they now contain all the nation's hunger legislation and have a major impact on food prices. Consumers have always had a stake in farm legislation (because of its effect on prices), but they never organized around their interests until the late sixties; so they, too, are new actors on the stage. Yet the makeup of the Agriculture committees has not changed accordingly. As in 1950, they are still largely composed of members representing no significant interest except agribusiness; members who are generally hostile to labor interests, consumer interests, urban interests generally, and to the interests of the poor clients of the food stamp program.* All the members of the House committee are from

---

* This study was completed in early 1973. Since then the rural conservatism of the committee has been diluted to some degree. In particular, the addition to the committee of Peter Peyser (R., N.Y.), an outspoken critic, added some balance in the 93rd Congress.

small-town-rural districts, 42 percent are from the South, and together they comprise what is probably the most antilabor, anti-consumer, and generally antiliberal committee in the House;[8] the average Americans for Democratic Action rating for the House committee members in 1971 was 29, compared with a rating of 41 for the House as a whole.[9] (The 1971 ratings for the committee leadership were even lower: 5 and 3 for the chairman and the ranking minority member respectively.)

The Senate committee, while not quite so unrepresentative nor so generally conservative, is much the same. In 1972 only five of the fourteen Senate committee members represented states containing a metropolitan area of as much as 500,000 people, and 29 percent are from southern states.[10]

Furthermore, until recently neither the House nor the Senate committee was even representative of the agribusiness sector itself. Until 1970 the strange workings of the seniority system had thrown almost all the leadership positions in both committees to members representing cotton constituencies. Both committees were chaired by cotton-based members—Representative W. R. Poage of Texas (who remained chairman in the Ninety-second and Ninety-third congresses) and Senator Allen E. Ellender of Louisiana—and most of the more senior members on both committees were from cotton-dependent regions. The 1972 elections further reduced the relative influence of cotton, especially in the Senate committee, but it remains high, with the corn and grain growers relatively short of influence.

The effect of this unrepresentative committee makeup is to jeopardize the integrity of farm committee bills. When they reach the House and Senate floors—especially that of the House—committee bills are rarely changed significantly through floor amendments.[11] When legislation is complex (as with tax bills or farm bills), the committee is simply presumed to know best how to write the kind of bill in question. The other members will feel free to vote the bill up or down on the floor, but are usually not successful in amending it in any major way. But the unrepresentativeness of the Agriculture committees has led to the writing of bills in committee that have increasingly dissatisfied interests not represented on the committees but with an important stake in agriculture policy. The committees' bills have sometimes favored farm interests over labor interests; farm interests over taxpayer interests; farm interests over consumer interests; farm interests over the interests of the poor; and, between farmers, rich interests over poor interests, and cotton interests over corn and grain interests.

All this has led to controversy over farm bills on the floor, where groups not on the committees or underrepresented on them have tried to alter the bills to include their perspectives through the clumsy floor-amendment process. This trend was carried to the ultimate extreme in 1973, as we shall see, when Chairman Poage completely lost control of his committee's bill on the House floor and the House changed it, through amendments, into what Poage (and many other Agriculture Committee members) regarded as an unacceptable bill.

The second important change in congressional agriculture politics grows from the drastic decline in the numerical strength of the farm-belt congressional contingent. Thirty years ago farmers comprised 25 percent of the nation's population. Today they make up only a fast-fading 5 percent.[12] The decline of farm political power in the sixties was drastic. The 1960 census designated 230 out of 435 districts (53 percent) as predominantly rural. The 1970 census found only 85 rural districts (20 percent). The trend continues in the seventies.[13] In 1970 there were only 35 congressional districts with more than 20 percent of its work force in agriculture. As reapportionment and urbanization continue to shrink rural influence on Capitol Hill, opposition to benefits for farmers continues to expand. According to the most optimistic estimates of the undersecretary of Agriculture, only 150 members of the House can now be counted on as reliable supporters of farm legislation.[14] Congress is more sensitive to consumer complaints about high food prices and urban complaints about farm subsidies than ever before.

THE CHAIRMEN

Herman Talmadge has been a senator from Georgia since 1957 and chairman of the Agriculture Committee since 1970. He is generally regarded as both more pragmatic and more progressive than his predecessor, Allen Ellender of Louisiana. A strong defender of rice and cotton interests in Louisiana, Ellender was less sensitive to the interests of food grain growers and livestock interests than Talmadge, who comes from a state with a more diversified agriculture.

Ellender ran the committee with an autocratic hand, husbanding power in the chairmanship and withholding staff resources that might have helped other members develop expertise to challenge the chairman's priorities. Talmadge, on the other hand, has gradually expanded the committee staff. In 1969, under Ellender, the committee was staffed by four professional and three clerical workers.[15] Talmadge, in 1973, had ten professional and six clerical staff members working for the committee.[16] In a break with the Ellender practice, Talmadge has also permitted some liberal members, such as Senator Hubert Humphrey (D., Minn.), to bring staff onto the committee, even when the staff's loyalty may flow more to the member than the committee chairman—something Ellender abhorred. Talmadge went a step further and, in 1970, created a new subcommittee on rural development and appointed Humphrey its chairman.

Generally, Talmadge has ruled with a lighter touch than Ellender, permitting committee members to develop independent positions on food policy issues, which are then integrated into committee legislation. In contrast to both his predecessor and Robert Poage, his counterpart in the House, Talmadge has proved particularly adept at building bridges to urban and liberal factions in the Senate. As a result, his committee's legislation continues to escape major attack on the Senate floor.

In another change since the days of Ellender's chairmanship, Talmadge has begun some oversight of the Department of Agriculture. According to Agriculture Committee staffer James Gilt-meier, whereas Ellender "thought it safe to believe the department," and the committee therefore did little oversight work, the committee under Talmadge is taking a closer look. Some initiatives under Talmadge have been: to investigate the Department of Agriculture's handling of the equine encephalitis outbreak in Texas in the summer of 1971; to initiate a General Accounting Office investigation of alleged discrimination in Farmers' Home Administration housing; and to press the Department to release authorized but impounded funds for such things as farm operating loans and summer feeding programs. Though oversight is still unjustifiably neglected, some progress is being made.[17]

Robert Poage, seventy-five, has been representing the eleventh district of Texas for thirty-eight years, which puts him fourth in seniority in the House. A cotton farmer himself, with a 1,900-acre spread, he has always identified closely with the relatively small cotton growers who farm the rolling "black land" prairie of north central Texas. Because the land is not irrigated and is marginal for cotton, the growers have been heavily dependent on the direct cotton subsidies that Poage has strenuously protected as chairman.[18]

With no children and no hobbies, Poage has devoted his life to the Agriculture Committee. By all accounts, he is one of the hardest workers in the House, regularly coming in on weekends to answer his own mail and prepare for hearings. Like his colleague, Jamie Whitten (D., Miss.), who is chairman of the House Appropriations Subcommittee on Agriculture, Consumer Protection and the Environment, Poage is a serious, almost fanatical student of agricultural policy, delighting in the minutiae of peanut allotments and marketing orders that less experienced members despair of mastering.

Agriculture is his life and woe to the member who gives less than his full attention to the committee's work. In Poage's committee, hearings start on time. A member who dawdles in after testimony has begun is sometimes forbidden to ask questions of the witness. Easily annoyed by absenteeism—viewed as routine in other committees—Poage has threatened to read the names of absent members on the floor as punishment.[19]

Poage's rigid standard of service has made committee life uncomfortable for members with less than the chairman's obsessive devotion to agriculture. This particularly applies to liberal or urban members with many outside interests. Vigorous, stubborn, abrasive, intelligent, fair—these are the adjectives most often applied to Poage in conversations with his committee colleagues. One of the last of the old-style committee bosses, he treats his members as a stern but just patriarch might treat mischievous sons in a state of prolonged adolescence. On the committee's trips abroad, for example, Poage insists that the American embassy give him the fifty-dollar per diem allowances granted to visiting congressmen to distribute to his flock as he sees fit.[20] Scrupulously honest and personally frugal, the chairman apparently feels he is the safest steward of public funds.

Poage controls his committee by force of personality and mastery of legislative detail as much as by the use of his considerable prerogatives as chairman. These powers include appointing members to subcommittees, assigning legislation to subcommittees, making and unmaking subcommittees, choosing the members of conference committees, recognizing members at hearings, and deciding who goes along on annual pilgrimages "on committee business."[21]

Although he is a fiscal and ideological conservative, Poage is generally admired for his fairness in the chair. But in hearings on social welfare issues, which offend his strict Spencerian ethic, his performance reveals little social imagination. His treatment of witnesses testifying on social problems such as malnutrition has often been hostile and even vituperative. In the past he has squandered opportunities to build political bridges to the labor-liberal faction in Congress by failing to cultivate the few urban liberals on his committee, such as Allard Lowenstein (D., N.Y., defeated 1972).[22] Lack of such bridges has hampered legislative trade-offs and thus hurt farm bills on the floor. In this behavior, of course, the chairman is reflecting the sentiment of the great majority of the members of his committee.

One of Poage's assets is that nearly everyone agrees that he is a great improvement over the former chairman, Harold Cooley. A congressman from North Carolina's tobacco belt, with a taste for high living, Cooley showed great interest in tobacco, whose farmers kept him elected, and sugar, whose lobbyists kept him solvent. On most other committee matters he delegated leadership to his first lieutenant, Bob Poage, then as now the real workhorse of the committee.

Cooley's operating style as chairman was imperious, overbearing. He was vindictive when crossed and used the powers of the chairmanship to punish his enemies. He was highly secretive, preferring to deal with people who were lobbying the committee behind the closed doors of his office. Poage, by contrast, is generally regarded as courteous, accommodating, and accessible to his members. He encourages new members to talk and is quick to offer advice. This attitude is a great departure from the Cooley days.

In 1965, at the first full committee meeting of a new Congress, Chairman Cooley addressed the freshman members. According to Congressman Thomas Foley (D., Wash.), who was present, Cooley "emphasized that freshman Representatives should not interrupt senior Representatives, that they should wait their turn to question witnesses, that they should listen and learn from the more experienced members, that they should generally keep their mouths shut, etc., etc., etc." After a few minutes of Cooley's condescending lecture, Representative Joseph Resnick (D., N.Y.), a liberal maverick on the committee, angrily exclaimed, in a voice heard clearly in the committee room: "No Southern reactionary bastard is going to shut me up."[23] Resnick paid for his outburst with ostracism by the chairman and, eventually, censure by the full committee.

Cooley also eschewed the bipartisan harmony that Poage has

worked so hard to bring to the committee. Cooley's partisanship was partly a reaction to his dislike for the ranking minority member, Congressman Charles Hoeven (R., Iowa), but it also reflects the fact that in the period of his chairmanship—1958–66—he did not need Republican votes to protect his committee's bills on the floor. Poage, operating in a Congress far less supportive of farm interests, has felt that he must rely on the Republican help to get his bills passed.

Unlike Cooley, Poage is extremely sensitive about maintaining his committee's prestige on the floor. It is a matter of personal ego for the chairman to get a bill through the House without significant amendments. In a recent committee print, "The Committee on Agriculture—Its Jurisdiction and Its Work," the committee notes proudly that "very seldom are there substantial changes made on the Floor of the House."[24] In recent years, as debate on farm bills has become increasingly stormy, Poage has made even greater efforts to reach a consensus in committee before taking a bill to the floor.

In building a consensus, Poage must contend with political and commodity factions on his committee. Conservative southern and southwestern congressmen from cotton, tobacco, peanut, and rice districts have traditionally provided his base of support. But with the defeat or retirement of Thomas Abernethy (D., Miss.), John McMillan (D., S.C.), Watkins Abbitt (D., Va.), and Graham Purcell (D., Texas) in 1972 this base has dwindled and Poage has had to seek support from other committee factions to maintain control.

On the chairman's political left is a moderate group of northwestern and midwestern congressmen led by Congressman Foley, an articulate and aggressive liberal who ranks third in seniority in the group. Foley works closely with Bob Bergland (D., Minn.), John Melcher (D., Mont.), and Frank Denholm (D., S. Dak.) in seeking labor, liberal, urban, and consumer support for foreign agricultural and food aid legislation.

Poage prefers to work with more conservative Republican

members to get the additional support he needs. Ideologically incompatible with Foley, he enjoyed a close relationship with the ranking minority member, Page Belcher (R., Okla.) until Belcher retired in 1972. Charles Teague (R., Calif.), the new ranking minority member, is a less secure ally, primarily because he embraces the Republican administration's policy of reducing payments to cotton farmers. Up to 1973, however, the coalition of southern Democrats and Republicans was solid enough to give Poage his way in committee and help protect his bills on the floor.

The factions in the Senate committee differ significantly. With Hubert Humphrey (D., Minn.), George McGovern (D., S. Dak.), and Dick Clark (D., Iowa) as committee members from farm states, both liberal Democrats and wheat and feed-grain farmers are in a stronger position than in the House committee. The Senate Committee on Agriculture and Forestry is more representative of the Senate than Poage's committee is of the House. Farmers are stronger in the Senate because many states with small populations are farm states and because virtually every senator, even those from states with the largest cities, has some vocal farming interest in his state that he does not want to offend.

THE SUBCOMMITTEES

The work of the House Agriculture Committee is divided among subcommittees whose members and chairmen are appointed by Bob Poage. Like the power of the full committees, both the number and the significance of the subcommittees have gradually declned over the last two decades. In 1958 there were eighteen subcommittees; ten years later, in 1968, there were fifteen; and in 1974 there were only ten. The decline of the subcommittee has been paralleled by a rise in the power of the chairman.

The subcommittees reflect the commodity orientation of the committee. The ten subcommittees are of two types. The six commodity subcommittees are those on cotton, chaired by B. F. Sisk (D., Calif.); dairy and poultry, chaired by Ed Jones (D., Tenn.);

forests, chaired by John Rarick (D., La.), livestock and grains, chaired by Foley; oil seeds and rice, chaired by Walter Jones (D., N.C.), and tobacco, chaired by Frank Stubblefield (D., Ky.). The functional or operational subcommittees are those on conservation and credit, chaired by Robert Poage himself; domestic marketing and consumer relations, chaired by Joseph Vigorito (D., Penna.), department operations, chaired by Kika de la Garza (D., Tex.), and family farm and rural development, chaired by Bill Alexander (D., Ark.). Each Democratic member has been assigned to at least one subcommittee of importance to producers in his district.

In many committees—the Senate Judiciary Committee and the House Appropriations and Government Operations committees, for example—the subcommittees become quasi-independent duchies whose rulers become respected and powerful figures in their own right.[25] This is not true of the House Committee on Agriculture. Poage's subcommittees have no separate budget, no staff, and less responsibility than those of other major committees in the House and Senate. Only about half the hearings are conducted through subcommittees; hearings on major bills such as general farm legislation and sugar legislation are held by the full committee.

In assigning committee members to subcommittees Poage consults the ranking minority leader but retains the final say on appointments. The authority to appoint subcommittee members and to make and unmake subcommittees is a major source of the chairman's power. Poage usually, but not always, observes seniority in exercising these powers. When Thomas Foley became chairman of the Subcommittee on Livestock and Grains, Poage, according to several committee members, saw Foley's position as a potential threat to his influence and proposed to divide the subcommittee into two parts, with John Melcher (D., Mont.) as chairman of a new subcommittee on livestock. Foley denies that Poage had any personal motive for this move, and eventually he persuaded Poage to change his mind. The fact is, though, that up to then Poage had advocated fewer subcommittees rather than more.

Poage has also used his position as ex officio member of all the subcommittees to turn around key votes that were going against him. In 1970, when the Subcommittee on Livestock and Grains, then chaired by Graham Purcell (D., Texas), voted to report a more expensive grains bill than Poage thought the administration would tolerate, he and Belcher, the ranking minority member and also an ex officio member of the subcommittees, made a rare appearance at Purcell's subcommittee and changed the outcome of a second vote.[26]

Although these incidents show the potential of the chairman's power, they are somewhat misleading because Poage does not generally throw his weight around as chairman. When he makes assignments he tries to be sure they match the interests of the members' districts. The Cotton Subcommittee, for example, is made up entirely of southerners from cotton districts. In the House Appropriations Committee, by contrast, congressmen are not generally assigned to subcommittees of special concern to their districts because such assignments might jeopardize the committee's mission of holding down public spending.[27] (Its Subcommittee on Agriculture is an exception to this practice because Whitten, the subcommittee chairman, closely identifies with southern cotton farmers and looks after their interests.) In the Committee on Agriculture, with its mission of service to producers, the subcommittees are not usually embarrassed by any fiscal restraints.

OVERSIGHT

Chairman Poage has discouraged his subcommittees from investigating U.S. Department of Agriculture (USDA) programs. He is content to leave the oversight function to Whitten's subcommittee and to the Government Operations Committee. When pressed in a recent hearing about his failure to review the implementation of the USDA programs his committee authorizes, Poage conceded that the committee has no systematic plan for program review. "Frankly," he said, "as I understand our Constitution, it doesn't contemplate that we should be the administrative body. I don't believe we have any right to control administrative agencies. I don't think it's any of our business how they run on a day-to-day basis."[28]

Poage's concept of oversight is basically very passive. He promises to investigate charges presented to the committee by outsiders but will not initiate investigations because, he says, they create "hard feelings, a loss of confidence on the part of our farmers" that would "destroy the effectiveness" of the department. Nearly all the major investigations of the Department of Agriculture have been conducted by other committees. The egregious record of USDA's Pesticide Regulation Division in the 1960s was revealed by the Intergovernmental Relations Subcommittee of the House Government Operations Committee,[29] and meat inspection failures have been exposed by the Public Health and Environment Subcommittee of the Interstate and Foreign Commerce Committee.[30]

Poage's paternal view of "his" Agriculture Department thwarts oversight, but even if the chairman burned with investigatory zeal, his committee lacks the staff to carry it out.

THE COMMITTEE STAFFS

The chairmen of the Agriculture committees, for reasons of thrift, power, and tradition, have kept their staffs to a minimum. In the first session of the Ninety-third Congress the House Agriculture Committee had only four professional staff members and one consultant. The Senate committee, until Ellender resigned as committee chairman in 1970, had a skeleton staff tightly under the chairman's control.

Recognizing that lack of staff has crippled Congress in its efforts to take back some initiative from the executive branch, Congress specifically authorized increased staffing for all committees in the Legislative Reorganization Act of 1971. However, when Senator Herman Talmadge (D., Ga.) succeeded to the Senate committee chairmanship, he took only modest advantage of this law by increasing the total committee staff to sixteen (1973 total). This left the Senate Agriculture Committee staff still the smallest among major Senate committees (see Table 4).

TABLE 4.
Staff and Budget for Senate Committees*

Committee	1973	1972	1971	Staff (1972)
Judiciary	$4,531,568	$4,171,668	$4,335,268	169
Labor and Public Welfare	2,490,640	2,298,640	2,330,640	78
Government Operations	2,239,288	2,155,260	2,031,168	66
Commerce	1,650,000	1,583,800	1,733,800	42
Foreign Relations	1,171,880	996,880	921,880	28
Banking, Housing and Urban Affairs	1,010,000	927,000	846,700	35
Public Works	975,000	975,000	950,000	30
Armed Services	870,000	845,000	790,000	24
Interior and Insular Affairs	825,000	765,000	770,000	28
Rules and Administration	713,912	709,912	573,912	15
Post Office and Civil Service	641,048	581,048	591,048	14
AGRICULTURE AND FORESTRY	562,000	530,000	567,500	11
District of Columbia	536,048	516,898	521,898	16
Veterans Affairs	450,000	400,000	360,000	14
Aeronautical and Space Sciences	413,548	366,048	366,048	9

* These figures include Maximum Gross Annual Compensation of $340,000 per committee for Regular Permanent Staff (Sec. 212(a) & (c) of Legislative Reorganization Act of 1946, Additional Permanent Staff Authorizations when approved by Senate, $10,000 Maximum Annual Increments for routine purposes of each standing committee (Sec. 134(a) Legislative Reorganization Act of 1946), Additional Funds for routine purposes as approved by the Senate, and Annual Expenditure Authorizations as reported by Senate Rules Committee and approved by the Senate.

SOURCE: U.S. Congress, Senate, Committee on Rules and Administration, *Legislative Calendar*, No. 2, 93rd Cong., 1st sess., July 1, 1973.

Over in the House, Chairman Poage has carried thrift even further, refusing to increase his committee's staff at all. As a result, the House Agriculture Committee has a smaller staff than even the House Administration Committee: smaller, in fact, than several House subcommittees (see Table 5). There are several explanations for Poage's staffing policy. First, the Agriculture

TABLE 5.

House Committee Staffs

Standing Committees	Staff
Government Operations	54
Banking and Currency	50
Public Works	49
Internal Security	44
Interstate and Foreign Commerce	40
Education and Labor	39
Foreign Affairs	36
Post Office and Civil Service	36
Appropriations	34
Armed Services	29
Ways and Means	29
Interior and Insular Affairs	24
Science and Astronautics	21
Merchant Marine and Fisheries	19
House Administration	17
AGRICULTURE	16
Veterans' Affairs	16
Judiciary	15
District of Columbia	14
Rules	7
Standards of Official Conduct	5

Select Committees	
Select Committee on Crime	20
Permanent Select Committee on Small Business	14
Select Committee on Committees	14
Select Committee on the House Restaurant	1
Select Committee to Regulate Parking	0

Senate Committee Staffs

Standing Committees	Staff
Judiciary	168
Labor and Public Welfare	86
Government Operations	74
Commerce	64
Foreign Relations	42
Appropriations	41
Public Works	38
Interior	35
Banking, Housing and Urban Affairs	31
Armed Services	25
Rules	22
Post Office	21
Finance	20
AGRICULTURE AND FORESTRY	16
District of Columbia	11
Aeronautical and Space Sciences	9
Veterans' Affairs	9

Select Committees

Select Committee on Small Business	21
Special Committee on Aging	15
Select Committee on Nutrition and Human Needs	12
Select Committee on Presidential Campaign Activities	-10
Special Committee on the Termination of the National Emergency	4
Select Committee on Standards and Conduct	2
Select Committee to Study Questions Related to Secret and Confidential Documents	0

SOURCE: Charles B. Brownson, *Congressional Staff Directory 1973*, Congressional Staff Directory (Alexandria, Va., 1973). This table represents staff sizes as of spring 1973.

committees have traditionally been more reactive than initiatory in developing farm policy. With the 1973 farm bill as an exception, the committee customarily waits for the administration to draft a bill rather than initiating major legislative changes itself.

In 1973 Poage allowed the Senate Committee on Agriculture to draft the bill, although he was prompted more by divisions on his committee than by any lack of staff to do the job. Similarly, the committee's investigative functions have remained mostly dormant. When it does investigate an issue, such as the Russian wheat deal in 1972, it relies heavily on the General Accounting Office to supplement its staff.

Several members of the Agriculture Committee would like to expand its investigative functions but are stymied by Poage's refusal to assign any staff to the subcommittees. Congressman John Melcher, for example, has long been concerned about the adequacy of USDA inspection of imported meat but finds it impossible to explore this subject in depth on his staffless subcommittee. Thomas Foley, the activist chairman of the Subcommittee on Livestock and Grains, asked Poage in 1973 to give him at least one staff lawyer to help him deal with the mushrooming crisis in feed grains, but Poage refused.[31] The chairman offers the aid of the committee staff to the subcommittees but this staff already has its hands full keeping track of legislation and has no time for major investigative work. The Republican members of the committee have even greater difficulty getting staff assistance. Both the House and Senate committees' staff have had a tradition of nonpartisanship, with staffers expected to serve all members equally. Some staff members, in interviews, used to claim ignorance of the political affiliation of their coworkers. Nonpartisanship and equal service continued to some extent during the early 1970s through the close cooperation between Democrats and Republicans based on Poage's alliance with Page Belcher. In 1973 this cooperation broke down and the philosophical uniformity of the committee members began to crack. As a result, Republican members began talking for the first time about demanding a minority staff.

By refusing to increase the staff, Poage exercises his prerogative over staff appointments to strengthen his position as chairman. Despite the professed traditions of nonpartisanship and equal service, staff members have always given their first loyalty to the chairman who appointed them and can fire them. Like other strong chairmen, such as Wright Patman and Wilbur Mills, Poage centralizes his power in the committee by having all committee information flow through him. Separate staff for the subcommittees would threaten this system.

Another, more prosaic reason for the staff's small size is Poage's sincere devotion to the ethic of thriftiness in government. Hyde Murray, associate counsel of the committee, notes that many rural congressmen on the committee share their constituents' belief that there are too many highly paid federal employees.[32] With Poage, they take great pride in not using their full quota of government-paid employees on their personal staffs and in paying those they do hire less than the authorized salaries. One of Poage's first acts as chairman was to cut the salaries of all committee staff members across the board. He prides himself on returning to the Treasury every year part of his committee's budget allocation. This practice is penny-wise and pound-foolish: money invested in committee staff to perform oversight duties would probably return itself many times over, in reduced USDA featherbedding and increased USDA efficiency. But Poage seems committed to his present policy.

Under Senator Ellender, the staff of the Senate Committee on Agriculture and Forestry operated on much the same principle that Poage continues to apply in the House. Ellender regarded staff as a necessary evil. He gave his aides clerical assignments, expecting them to act at the behest of senators only. As a result, the four professional staff members were relegated to a passive role, rarely initiating any action and responding to legislation only as it expired.[33] As in the House committee, bipartisanship was almost a mania with Ellender, a factor that mirrored the conservative philosophical harmony between Democrats and Republicans on the committee.

When Herman Talmadge took over as chairman he brought fresh blood into the staff, both by expanding it to eight professionals and by including for the first time staff people with moderate and even liberal views. James Thornton, a protege of Senator Humphrey; Michael McLeod, formerly on Talmadge's personal staff; and John Baker, a top USDA official under former Secretary of Agriculture Orville Freeman—all have worked, with Talmadge's blessing, to focus the committee on new issues such as rural economic development and child nutrition. The Rural Development Subcommittee, aggressively chaired by Senator Humphrey, had both Baker and Thornton as staff assistants during the period when the Rural Development Act was developed, although they are nominally assigned to the full committee.

As in the House, the bipartisan tradition has begun to break up in the Senate Agriculture Committee. In part this has happened because some committee members are at opposite political poles, with McGovern, Clark, and Humphrey in uneasy coexistence with ultraconservatives like Carl Curtis (R., Neb.) and Jesse Helms (R., N.C.). For the first time the Republicans have brought in minority staff. Curtis, for example, arranged for Forest Reece to join the staff to assist Republican members, a move which greatly disturbed older staffers such as Harker Stanton who served under Ellender when nonpartisanship was the rule.[34]

Staffs basically reflect their committees and it is therefore no surprise that the Senate staff is now divided into several factions: the old guard who are holdovers from the Ellender days; the activist moderate-liberals brought in by Talmadge; and the partisan conservative Republicans sponsored by Curtis and Robert Dole (R., Kans.). The resulting ferment and competition has pumped life into the committee. On the hunger programs, rural economic development, and forestry it is exercising investigative oversight that was unknown in Ellender's day.[35] The diversity of the Senate committee's staff, along with its increased size, helps make the committee more responsive to the shifting currents of farm politics, especially to the demands of new constituencies among the poor and the consumer movement. The staff is still smaller than such activist senators as Clark and Humphrey would like, but it is beginning to acquire the political flexibility and professional talent necessary to develop farm legislation acceptable to an increasingly hostile Congress.

The same cannot yet be said of the House committee. While Poage makes a point of frugality in food stamp expenditures and staff expenses, he is a frequent junketeer at public expense. The committee's jurisdiction over the billion-dollar Food for Peace Program gives its members a legitimate reason for travel abroad, but the scope of the travel, if not its style, might be questioned. In November of 1972 Poage took ten members of his committee, including Thomas Abernethy, a lame-duck congressman from Mississippi, on a round-the-world trip to study the food assistance program to Bangladesh.[36] In addition to visiting the Indian subcontinent, Poage's entourage also dropped in on Algeria, Sudan, Ethiopia, Bahrain, Muscat-Oman, Kuwait, Italy, and Spain. The itinerary was exotic, but Poage made sure his colleagues put business before pleasure. According to one of his traveling companions, he "ran the junket like a drill sergeant, doling out expense money personally in dribs and drabs and packing the schedule so tight that members, even if they had the money, had no time to spend it." As another member put it, "The chairman is the kind of man who even makes sinning seem like a duty."[37] The insensitivity that often marks his response to the social problems that come before his committee was painfully evident on the trip to Bangladesh. During an audience with Sheik Mujib, Poage sat impassively as the Bangladesh ruler praised the United States and India for coming to his country's aid. After a few minutes Poage interrupted with a tirade against both India and Prime Minister Indira Gandhi for their socialism, antiwar views, and above all ingratitude for American aid. An ashen State Department official tried to interrupt and explain that this was really not the time and place to attack the nation that had been Bangladesh's ally and savior, but the chairman plunged on, leaving a startled and confused Sheik Mujib in his wake.[38]

THE COMMITTEES AND THE LOBBYISTS

Like all committees in the House and Senate, the farm committees spend a large part of their time responding to proposals and complaints from lobbyists representing special economic interests. What is unique about the farm lobbyists is the legitimacy they derive from the committees' self-proclaimed mission of service to farmers. Because in the congressional system the agriculture committees have historically catered to agricultural producers, rather than to the public at large, committee members have enjoyed an intimacy with producer lobbyists that in other committees would be seen as improper. When the major farm lobbies were groups like the Grange, the National Farmers' Union, and the American Farm Bureau Federation—organizations with a large national membership of working farmers—this relationship had some Populist foundations. These groups still exist, but their influence has declined in direct proportion to the decline in farm population. Their place has been taken by lobbyists for the chemical industry, the food processors, and special commodity groups, who trade on the legitimacy of the traditional farm organizations although their interests may conflict with those of the family farmer the committees still claim to represent.[39]*

In addition to the national farm organizations, whose influence is primarily in their ability to control votes in rural districts, the lobbies with the greatest legitimacy in the Agriculture committees' view are those that represent specific commodity interests. These groups, such as the National Milk Producers Federation, or the American National Cattlemen's Association, tend to operate in the open, with financial contributions to political campaigns of-

---

* Central Soya and Continental Grain, for example, may lobby for increased production of feed grains to reduce the price they pay the farmers. Shell Chemical Company may lobby for reduced restrictions on pesticide use even though the restrictions were designed to ensure that the pesticides serve the farmers' interests by being effective and safe.

fered and accepted without embarrassment, even though the group making the contribution may have an interest in legislation pending before the recipient's committee. For example, Senator Humphrey (D., Minn.) accepted contributions from the Milk Producers while leading the fight in the Senate to increase milk price supports. Not all commodity lobbies have equal legitimacy before the committee, however. Milk money may be publicly acceptable; sugar money usually is not. The difference is in the membership of the lobbying groups. The milk producers represent thousands of dairy farmers, while the sugar lobbyists represent the Dominican Republic, South Africa, and other exporting nations seeking to increase or maintain their share of the sugar quotas.[40]*

A second distinctive feature of the farm lobbyists is that they have relatively little competition from consumer or citizen groups. Because the committees see themselves as advocates for the producers' interests, with the idea that what is good for the farmer is good for America, they see little need to seek out the consumer point of view. The committees' insularity has left them unprepared for the urban and consumer groups now demanding a voice in farm policy. Their insurgence on the House floor in 1973 signaled that these demands for a reordering of agricultural priorities are certain to intensify in the future.

The traditional lobbies still flex their muscles when major farm policy is pending, but their political leverage is gradually declining. One event marking the decline was the passage of the 1970 farm bill, which Chairman Poage designed and got through Congress despite the opposition of the American Farm Bureau Feder-

---

* The dairy lobby lost much of its prestige and influence following repeated disclosures from 1972 through 1974 of massive and/or illegal campaign contributions to the presidential campaigns of Richard M. Nixon and Hubert H. Humphrey and to numerous congressional campaigns. Two former dairy co-op officials were sentenced in 1974 to four-month prison terms and fined $10,000 each for violating campaign finance laws, and dairy contributions were sharply curtailed during the 1974 election campaign, lessening the impact of dairy money.

ation, the National Farmers' Union, and other farm organizations.

The influence of these general farm organizations on national farm policy depends to some extent on which party controls the White House. The Democrats tend to advocate high price-support levels with relatively rigid controls. Under a Democratic president, some of the major farm organizations tend to work directly with the Secretary of Agriculture in creating farm policy. This group includes the Grange, the National Farmers' Union, and the National Farmers' Organization, all of which support extensive federal farm aid. In contrast, the largest farm organization, the American Farm Bureau Federation, advocates a gradual abolition of the farm program and a return to the free market economy. It therefore has little influence with a Democratic administration.[41]

Under a Republican administration a more complex situation develops. The Republican Party generally advocates a smaller farm program with less rigid governmental controls—a position between that of the Democratic Party and the several farm organizations on one hand and that of the Farm Bureau on the other. The working relationship between the House Agriculture Committee and the Department of Agriculture that developed during the Nixon era has produced strong opposition. In 1970 twenty-two farm organizations supporting high loan and payment levels formed a Coalition of Farm Organizations to work against the Poage–White House alliance. Prominent among the Coalition membership were the National Grange, the National Farmers' Union, and the National Farmers' Organization. Although the Coalition worked closely with sympathetic Agriculture committee members such as Thomas Foley (D., Wash.) and Bob Bergland (D., Minn.), they were unsuccessful in substituting their bill.

With the political influence of the general farm organizations on the wane, the influence of commodity lobbies with large funds for campaign contributions is rising steadily. The limestone, dairy, and sugar industries have the most effective commodity lobbies.

The Sugar Lobby

The most tightly controlled commodity regulated by Congress has been sugar. For forty years both domestic production and foreign imports were strictly limited by the Sugar Act to insure high prices for American sugar producers.* The result has been a high price for domestic sugar, costing American consumers approximately $600 million per year. Foreign producers with an import quota could sell their sugar in the United States at a much higher price than on the world market. The Sugar Act also provided for direct payments to domestic sugar growers based on production. These payments totaled $92 million in 1970. Because the quota for foreign sugar was divided up and doled out to sugar-producing countries by the members of the Agriculture committees, the committees were besieged by lobbyists hired by sugar exporting countries trying to increase their share of the quota. These sugar lobbyists were known for their high salaries and connections in high places. Thirty-eight lobbyists for foreign sugar interests take in over $700,000 annually. Heading the list in 1971 was Albert S. Nemir Associates, representing Brazil for $180,000 in fees and salaries. Arthur L. and Arthur Lee Quinn received an annual total fee of $84,000, including expenses, for representing the sugar interests of British Honduras, Ecuador, Panama, and the West Indies. The late Harold Cooley, former chairman of the House Agriculture Committee, represented Liberia and Thailand, while former Republican Senate Whip Tom Kuchel was registered on behalf of Colombian sugar interests. Former Missouri Representative Charles H. Brown registered to represent the Colonial Sugar Refining Company Ltd. of Australia and Thomas Hale Boggs, Jr., son of the late House Democratic Leader Hale Boggs (D., La.) represented Central America sugar interests.[42]

In 1972 Poage assigned the task of considering modifications

* In 1974, over the opposition of the House Agriculture Committee, Congress refused to renew the sugar program, but it remains an instructive example of lobbying politics in the committee.

in the foreign quotas to a five-man drafting subcommittee chaired by Representative Thomas Abernethy (D., Miss.). The criteria the subcommittee used included United States relations with foreign countries, the balance of trade, and the participation of the foreign sugar workers in social benefits, but according to Julius L. Katz, Deputy Assistant Secretary of State for International Resources and Food, these criteria were of little relevance: "Were there some objective standard or formula by which quotas could be allocated, we would be spared the task of choosing among so many worthy claims. Unfortunately, however, there is no such standard or formula which would be commonly agreed or accepted."[43]

Consumer interest in lower sugar prices is rarely expressed. When it is, it is ignored. Richard A. Frank, of the Consumer Association of the District of Columbia, was the first consumer advocate to testify—in 1971—in favor of lower sugar prices. Committee members spent as much time questioning his legitimacy to represent the consumer as they did examining the substance of his criticisms.

Sugar lobbying has become much more open under Poage's chairmanship. Unlike the committee's former chairman, who saw lobbyists privately and wrote much of the sugar industry legislation himself—amid allegations of improper influence—Bob Poage refuses to hold private discussions with lobbyists, and goes so far as to have all contacts with them at open hearings. Poage also leaves the drafting of legislation to other members of the committee. As one committee member summarized the situation: "Poage was obviously attempting to dispel the bad publicity generated by his predecessor's handling of the sugar bill." But whether sugar quotas were distributed in secret or in the open, the results were the same—high prices for consumers and high retainers for the sugar lobbyists.

The flaw in the sugar lobbyists' technique became apparent in 1973, when world consumption of sugar reached the point where both world and domestic prices began to soar. In nine months of that year the world price exceeded the domestic price, according to the Department of Agriculture, thus lessening the supposed value of the Sugar Act.[44] Even in view of this situation, Chairman Poage opened Sugar Act hearings in February 1974 with the statement that "basically the act is working extremely well."[45] Committee members supported Poage's assertion, and amid claims that the Sugar Act was obsolete since there was no longer a world surplus of sugar, the Agriculture Committee voted thirty to five to extend the Act for another five years with some modification from previous extensions.[46] As the consumer paid more each month for a sack of sugar during 1974, the House surprised lobbyists and committee members alike by rejecting the Sugar Act extension by a 175–209 vote in June.[47] After forty years, the influence of foreign sugar lobbyists on the Agriculture Committee failed to carry the day.

Sour Milk—The Dairy Lobby

Though the dairy lobby, like the sugar lobby, has lost much of its influence in recent years, the case of dairy industry lobbying is mostly a clear and simple example of how money buys votes. The primary objective of the dairy lobby is to raise milk support prices. Whenever the market price of "manufacturing milk" (used for butter, cheese, and nonfat powdered milk) drops below the support price, the government begins buying, thereby guaranteeing that the farmers, who are co-op members, will be able to sell their milk at the support price. The higher the support price, the better the guarantee to the farmer.

The total amount of money shelled out to political candidates by the five major national political committees representing dairy and agricultural interests* was almost $3.4 million during the 1972 campaign.[48] To a great extent the dairy industry spreads its

---

* The major political committees are the Committee for Thorough Agricultural Political Education (C-TAPE) and the Trust for Agricultural Political Education (TAPE), both of the Associated Milk Producers, Inc.; The

money to congressional races aboveboard. According to Frank Wright in the *Washington Monthly*, "These men [members of Congress] would never be found doing the same thing for oil that they have done for milk, but perhaps milk money is thought to enjoy the sanctity of the product from which it is made."[49] (Dairy contributions to presidential campaigns have been of a much more clandestine nature). Whatever the reasons or methods of the distribution of campaign funds by the dairy industry, the result is clear. For every million the industry spends in campaign funds, a $300 million return is expected.[50]

By no strange coincidence, the dairy interests favored members of the House Agriculture Committee when the time came for campaign gifts. Committee Chairman Poage received $5,000 from political fund-raising arms of the dairy interests for his 1970 campaign, though he had no opposition that year. Representative Ed Jones (D., Tenn.), chairman of the Subcommittee on Dairy and Poultry, received $7,500—Jones had no opposition either. Representative Watkins Abbitt (D., Va.), a member of the same subcommittee, received $8,000 to fight nominal opposition.[51] In the 1972 campaign the top three House recipients of farm money were all members of the House Agriculture Committee: Graham Purcell (D., Tex., defeated), $11,500; Ed Jones (D., Tenn.), $10,000; and Jerry Litton (D., Mo.), $10,000.[52]

According to A. L. McWilliams, associate general manager of the Associated Milk Producers Inc., the contributions made to candidates in the 1972 campaign were made on the basis of support for "friends of dairy farmers and supporters of agricultural legislation. . . . We try to keep our friends in office and elect those who are our friends."[53] The industry seems to have excellent judgement: of the seventy House members who sponsored price

---

Agricultural and Dairy Educational Political Trust (ADEPT) of the Mid-American Dairymen, Inc.; the Trust for Special Political Agricultural Community Education (SPACE) of the Dairymen, Inc.; and the Political Action for Cooperative Effectiveness (PACE) of the National Council of Farmer Co-ops.

support hikes in 1970, more than thirty had received dairy money during 1969 and 1970.

The power and influence of the dairy industry is formidable. The Associated Milk Producers, Inc. (AMPI) claimed to have generated more than 50,000 pieces of mail from dairy farmers to lawmakers during a one-week period of a recent milk support price battle.[54] AMPI gained even more attention in September 1971 by holding the "largest dinner under one roof" for its members. Press agents for AMPI chartered a fifth of the nation's commercial air fleet to fly 38,000 members and their families to Chicago to devour 18,750 pounds of roast beef in the McCormick Place exposition hall.[55] It was power (votes) like this, plus campaign funds, that allowed AMPI and other dairy groups to plead their case for one hour with President Richard Nixon in 1971.

7

Benefits for Farmers:
A Review of
Committee Priorities*

Since the Depression, support for farm legislation has depended to a significant degree on the sympathy of the nonfarm sector for "family farmers," who were presumed, in a mixture of fact and agrarian sentimentalism, to be unfairly treated by other sectors of the economy. Public concern for the plight of the farm sector has

* This chapter is largely based on work by Ruth Glushien, whose research was completed before the farm bill of 1973 was passed. It provides a historical overview of committee priorities, as reflected in the distribution of benefits in the commodity programs. It does not take into account changes made in the commodity programs since 1972.

Between 1973 and 1975 the use of commodity programs to restrict production greatly diminished, as shrinking world food supplies and extraordinary exports to the Soviet Union made production expansion a major priority of the Nixon and Ford administrations. The failure of the smaller farmer to

176

been based on the vaguest of information about which "farmers" actually require aid.

Despite the obvious heavy costs of commodity price support programs, not much was done before 1965 to alert the public to their failure to assure parity of income to low-income farmers. Even with the "rediscovery" of poverty in the early 1960s, public attention focused more on the apparent waste of storing surplus commodities than on the inequitable distribution of benefits. One of the causes of this inattention might be called "the dullness of institutional sin." The disproportion of benefits to need is the simple consequence of using a price mechanism to distribute aid in an industry where the factors of production—land, labor, and capital—are unevenly distributed. Hence there was no manipulatory or administrative scandal to rival the Billie Sol Estes case that might focus headlines on the problem of low-income farmers.[1]

A second cause of neglect was the apparent complexity of farm loan programs. Few congressmen or newspapermen from non-farm areas could maneuver easily enough among the formulas for calculating crop allotment size and support prices to raise the basic issue of need against benefits. Subsidization through the nonrecourse loan method provided "its own blanket of obscurity as to who gets how much and who pays for it."[2] If one has to be subsidized, the economist John Kenneth Galbraith quips, "how much more seemly to have it out of sight."[3]

The ideology of economic independence surrounding the commodity loans has also tended to obscure whose interest they serve. Congressional farm spokesmen extol self-help, family enterprise, and free competition; this ideology has been a "vehicle to carry

---

get an equal share of the benefits of the old farm program, when production limitation was the goal, made him less able to take advantage of the higher prices and demands for full production in the 1970s. The continuance of rural poverty and the increasing substitution of corporate agribusiness for the small or family farmer—indeed, the financial and corporate structure of agriculture in the 1970s—was significantly shaped by the operation of the commodity programs between 1950 and 1970 described in this chapter.

the particular interests of their segment without clearly revealing the nature of these interests to non-farm supporters."[4] The entire price support system was scrapped in 1973 and replaced with a new "target price" (or guaranteed price) system. The machinery of this system is entirely new, but the pro-rich bias of the payment schedules remains the same; subsidy payments are now hitched to the total production of a farmer, growing as his production grows, which means that the gravy still flows mainly to the largest producers.

The first quantitative studies of how much Agriculture Soil Conservation Service subsidy aid goes to small farmers were made in the 1960s by James T. Bonnen, professor of agricultural economics at Michigan State University, who attempted to measure the degree of concentration in distribution of program benefits.[5]

Bonnen constructed Lorenz curves and Gini coefficients for a number of the commodity programs under the Agriculture Soil Conservation Service, estimating the proportion of program benefits going to each class (the classes are based on size) of farm acreage allotments (see Table 1, p. 17). If farm program benefits were distributed on an equal per capita basis, every 1 percent of the allotment holders would receive 1 percent of program aid. But in every ASCS program Bonnen examined, equality of per capita aid was nonexistent. In all cases program aid disproportionately benefited the larger growers. In the 1964 cotton program, the owners of the largest 20 percent of cotton allotments received 69.2 percent of ASCS cotton payments. The smallest 20 percent received only 1.8 percent of the benefits. In feed grains, the owners of the smallest 20 percent of allotments received only 1 percent of total program money. An even worse offender of equity was the sugar cane program, in which the top 20 percent of cane allotments received 83.1 percent of the benefits and the owners of the smallest 20 percent received only 1 percent. The Agricultural Conservation Program distributed its benefits most nearly equally: the largest 20 percent took a relatively modest

36.6 percent of benefits, while the smallest 20 percent received as much as 10.5 percent of the aid.

Bonnen concluded:

> . . . all of the commodity programs are fairly highly concentrated, some of them greatly so . . . The 40 percent of the smallest farmers [allotment holders] receive much less than a proportionate share of the program benefits, even in the case of the programs with the least concentrated distribution of benefits.[6]

Most agricultural economists agree that ASCS benefits are distributed on a highly unequal per capita basis. The lowest income farmers, most in need of financial aid to increase their efficiency or ease their transition out of farming, receive the least aid. The question remains whether the subsidy programs have increased the inequities of income distribution in farming (see Table 6). Some critics contend that the capital aid provided by the programs has allowed large farmers to invest in more machinery and increase their scale of operation, leaving the smaller farms even further behind in efficiency, but not all economists agree about this indirect effect. K. L. Robinson argues that price support and allotment programs have retarded the consolidation of farms into larger units.[7] There is no available way to estimate the rate of consolidation in the absence of government payments, but we can estimate the direct effect of government payments on income distribution in agriculture.

Bonnen has again laid much of the groundwork on this question.[8] Bonnen uses a mathematical device called a "Gini concentration ratio" to summarize, on a scale of 0 to 1, the extent to which program benefits are concentrated; that is, "how far a given distribution departs from a completely equal distribution of benefits among all beneficiaries."[9] If the Gini ratio is 0, each person in the program is receiving equal benefits. The closer the Gini ratio is to 1, the less equally distributed are the benefits. If program A has a ratio number higher than the ratio number of program B,

TABLE 6.

Distribution of Farm Income and Various Program Benefits
Proportion of Income and Benefits Received by
Various Percentiles of Farm Beneficiaries[1]

	Lower 20% of Farmers	Lower 40% of Farmers	Lower 60% of Farmers	Top 40% of Farmers	Top 20% of Farmers	Top 5% of Farmers
			Percent of Benefits Received by the			
Sugar cane, 1965[3]	1.0	2.9	6.3	93.7	83.1	63.2
Cotton, 1964[2]	1.8	6.6	15.1	84.9	69.2	41.2
Rice, 163[2]	1.0	5.5	15.1	84.9	65.3	34.6
Wheat, 1964						
Price Supports	3.4	8.3	20.7	79.3	62.3	30.5
Diversion Payments	6.9	14.2	26.4	73.6	57.3	27.8
Total Benefits[5]	3.3	8.1	20.4	79.6	62.4	30.5
Feed Grains, 1964						
Price Supports	0.5	3.2	15.3	84.7	57.3	24.4
Diversion Payments	4.4	16.1	31.8	68.2	46.8	28.7
Total Benefits[5]	1.0	4.9	17.3	82.7	56.1	23.9
Peanuts, 1964[2]	3.8	10.9	23.7	76.3	57.2	28.5
Tobacco, 1965[2]	3.9	13.2	26.5	73.5	52.8	24.9

Percent of Benefits Received by the

	Lower 20% of Farmers	Lower 40% of Farmers	Lower 60% of Farmers	Top 40% of Farmers	Top 20% of Farmers	Top 5% of Farmers
Farmer and Farm Manager Total Money Income, 1963[6]	3.2	11.7	26.4	73.6	50.5	20.8
Sugar Beets, 1965[3]	5.0	14.3	27.0	73.0	50.5	24.4
Ag. Conserv. Program, 1964[4]						
All Eligibles	7.9	15.8	34.7	65.3	39.2	(7)
Recipients	10.5	22.8	40.3	59.7	36.6	13.8

[1] This table presents portions of two Lorenz curves relating the cumulated percentage distribution of benefits of the cumulated percent of farmers receiving those benefits. Column 1 through 3 summarizes this relationship cumulated up from the lower (benefit per farmer) end of the curve, and columns 4 through 6 summarizes the relationship cumulated down from the top (highest benefit per recipient) end of the curve.

[2] For price support benefits.

[3] For price support benefits plus government payments.

[4] For total program payments. Computed from data in *Frequency Distribution of Farms and Farmland, Agricultural Conservation Program, 1964,* ASCS, U.S. Department of Agriculture, January 1966, Tables 3 and 8.

[5] Includes price support payments and wheat certificate payments as well.

[6] David Boyne, "Changes in the Income Distribution in Agriculture," *Journal of Farm Economics,* Vol. 47, No. 5, December 1965, pp. 1221–1222.

[7] Not available.

SOURCE: James T. Bonnen, "The Absence of Knowledge of Distribution Impacts: An Obstacle to Effective Public Program Analysis and Decisions," in U.S., Congress, Joint Economic Committee, *The Analysis and Evaluation of Public Expenditures: The PPB System.* Joint Committee Print. Washington: Government Printing Office, 1969. I: 440, Table 7.

then program A distributes its aid less equally. The same ratio device can be used to measure the distribution of gross income among farm families.

When Bonnen compared the Gini ratio of eleven ASCS programs to the Gini ratio of farmer's gross income (see Table 7), he found that eight out of eleven ASCS programs distributed their benefits less equally than existing income distribution. Only three

TABLE 7.
Gini Concentration Ratio for Benefits of ASCS Programs

Program	Gini Concentration Ratio
Sugar cane, 1965	0.799
Cotton, 1964	0.653
Rice, 1963	0.632
Wheat, 1964	
Price Supports	0.566
Diversion Payments	0.480
Total Benefits	0.569
Feed Grains, 1964	
Price Supports	0.588
Diversion Payments	0.405
Total Benefits	0.565
Peanuts, 1964	0.522
Tobacco, 1965	0.476
Farmer and Farm Manager	
Total Money Income, 1965	0.463
Sugar Beets, 1965	0.456
Agricultural Conservation Program, 1965	
All Eligible	0.343
Recipients	0.271

SOURCE: James T. Bonnen, "The Absence of Knowledge of Distribution Impacts: An Obstacle to Effective Public Program Analysis and Decisions," in U.S., Congress, Joint Economic Committee, *The Analysis and Evaluation of Public Expenditures: The PPB System.* Joint Committee Print. Washington: Government Printing Office, 1969. I: 440, Table 7.

programs—sugar beets, agricultural conservation, and wheat acreage diversion—reduced the gap in income between large and small farmers. In 1969 the funds spent on these three programs amounted to 14 percent of the ASCS budget. Most of the rest of an ASCS budget of $5 billion was spent even more regressively. Don Paarlberg, director of economics in the Department of Agriculture, acknowledged as early as 1964 that "The added purchasing power from farm programs should have the effect of reducing the income differential within agriculture . . . [yet] present farm policies, with a few notable exceptions, serve to widen rather than narrow the dispersion of income."[10]

According to the figures of Glen T. Barton, the commodity program also worked to increase the degree of regressiveness of the distribution of *net* income in agriculture.[11] From 1961 to 1967 the total income support of farm programs accounted for 45 percent of the net income of operators grossing over $10,000. It made up only 34 percent of net farm income for lower-income farmers with sales under $10,000. That families with gross sales (and an average higher net income) rely on government aid for a greater proportion of their net income than do farmers in lower gross sales classes implies that the distribution of net income would be less concentrated in the absence of government aid.

Why do the smaller farmers fare badly in the price and support programs? Part of the reason is the neglect of smaller operator problems in the Agriculture Department's discretionary administration of programs. Noteworthy is the Department's failure to distribute new cotton allotments progressively or to supervise adequately the division of payments between landlords and tenants.

But the major cause is the legislative design of farm programs: agricultural programs have traditionally been designed to generate income as a return on physical property, not as a return on labor inputs.

The basic aim of the farm program (until 1973) was to maintain agricultural prices by restricting farm output, which was achieved by paying farmers not to produce. Since both land and labor are required to produce commodities, this goal could theoretically have been achieved either by paying farmers to reduce their cultivated acreage, or by paying them to reduce their labor input. The design of the program, however, focused solely on restricting cultivated acreage, rather than labor input—much to the detriment of the poor farmer.

Eligibility for programs of any monetary consequence has centered on the ownership or control of land (excluding all farm wage workers from aid). Second, use of a price mechanism (the price support loans) to distribute aid automatically scales benefits to the size of commodity output and sales. In an industry where the nonlabor factors of production are highly concentrated, this funnels the bulk of aid to a few producers.

Third, the most lucrative source of return from farm programs has been the land itself, in the capitalization of program benefits into land values. Since 1950, though aggregate farm income has not risen, land values have doubled. Various factors account for the increase, but prominent among them are the allotments that entitle one to government aid. "The ability to collect a tobacco, wheat, cotton, corn, or other income or price support," notes agricultural economist Marion Clawson, "has been translated into higher land prices."[12] In a study of Pittsylvania County, Virginia, W. L. Gibson found that land worth $23 an acre for other uses brought as much as $1,695 with a tobacco allotment attached.[13] A more recent study suggests that a tobacco allotment may add $6,000 to the value of an acre.[14] In addition, farm supply control and acreage diversion payments have contributed to the rising price of farm land by creating an artificial scarcity of arable land; more than fifty million acres were kept out of production in 1970. The rewards of a boom in land prices accrue most heavily, of course, to farmers with large holdings, benefiting them as landowners rather than as farm operators. Farmers with little of value besides their own labor input have not shared in the gains.

The association of farm program aid with land ownership has

thus been the prime mechanism of the inequitable distribution of benefits. No account is taken of the income needs of a particular farmer's family, of how much farm work he himself performs, the length of time he has been in farming, or his employment opportunities elsewhere.

A secondary cause of the inequitable distribution of farm benefits is the failure of many landowning low-income farmers to *participate* in the price support programs. Department of Agriculture sources have estimated unofficially that up to one-half of small farmers with incomes under $3,000 do not participate in commodity programs. In some cases this is due to crop history; in the years used as a base for calculating allotments, the farmer may not have grown the particular crop. It is also due to limited information about the programs. The ASCS has never actively tried to enroll small farmers; it is generally up to the individual farmer to come to the county office and apply. But a greater limitation on small-farmer participation has actually been built directly into the commodity programs. To place a crop under loan, a farmer must have an available storage facility. He must build a barn or silo on his property or else pay a commercial warehouseman to store the crop. Although the Commodity Credit Corporation offers some assistance for the construction of on-farm storage facilities, the small farmer often does not have enough projected income to make construction possible or worthwhile. If his crop is small, the per unit costs of commercial storage would leave negligible net benefit in program participation.

There are of course a few program provisions designed especially to aid smaller farmers. In cotton, $31 million has been spent annually on a "double-dip" payment to farmers with cotton allotments under 10 acres or production under 3,600 pounds.[15] From 1963 until 1971 feed grain producers with allotments under twenty-five acres were able to divert their entire allotment for payment, even though the usual limit on diversion was one-half the allotment.[16] Until 1971 wheat producers with acreage of fifteen acres or less qualified for a special per bushel payment.[17] In the peanut program, an acre can be grown even without an allotment, allowing a small grower to benefit from any increase in free market prices induced by the supply limitation of the peanut price support program.[18] In cotton and tobacco, very small operators have been exempted from a cut in allotment in years when the total national allotment is reduced.[19]

But these special programs really have no significant effect against the farm price and income programs as a whole. First, some of the small farm programs are themselves unsuitably designed for the poorest of farm operators. The Agricultural Conservation Program, for instance, will not benefit those operators who have no assets besides their own labor. The ACP runs a cost-sharing plan that allows farmers to finance conservation practices such as planting trees or constructing a pond. The federal government pays one-half the cost of the project up to a total of $2,500.[20] If a half share is less than $200, the government increases its aid to somewhat more than 50 percent.[21] Despite this relatively progressive cost sharing, the program is of no use to farm operators who are not landowners, because ACP benefits accrue to land value, not labor. Former Deputy ASCS Administrator Raphael Fitzgerald says:

> Operators include many farmers who are tenants and share croppers and these latter farmers (regardless of race) are not generally willing or able to make the personal investment in carrying out a conservation practice, the major benefits from which will accrue to other persons.[22]

Few croppers or tenants can afford to finance conservation practices when the major benefits would go to the owner of the land.

A second problem is that these small-farm provisions are politically vulnerable. The extra small-farm payment in the wheat program and the small farm diversion provision of the feed grain program were terminated in the 1970 Agricultural Act. The conditions for qualifying for the small-farm cotton double-dip payment were restricted in that act to small farmers who live on the farm and derive their principal income from cotton production; no such residency or source of income requirement was placed on the cotton payments made to larger farmers.[23]

But the basic reason these small-farm provisions do not alleviate the regressive effect of farm programs as a whole is that they have little budget significance. The real obstacle to equitable payment distribution is the practice of assigning aid in the form of price supports paid in proportion to output. These are programs that cannot possibly be used efficiently to aid low-income farmers. According to Bonnen's study of the 1964 cotton program, to generate $1 more aid for the lowest fifth of farmers would have required spending an extra $55. Other crop programs are even less efficient for low-income aid. Since the lowest 20 percent of producers get only 1 percent of feed grain benefits, it would have taken $100 more in total expenditures in 1964 to generate $1 more aid for that group.[24] Setting up such costly machinery is not a sensible way to aid low-income farmers, if that is the objective. As one agriculture official acknowledged, "If the present supply adjustment and farm income programs are not sufficient, then you need some other program. This is beyond present farm programs. Present small farm provisions are minor to some of the other things that should be done."[25]

Proponents of the farm price and income support programs have offered a variety of reasons for continuing the programs unchanged despite their heavy cost and their general failure to help low-income farmers. One of the simplest arguments has been the contention that Congress never intended the program to redistribute income within farming. Kenneth L. Robinson of Cornell, although not necessarily an admirer of present ASCS programs, has phrased the argument well:

Nothing was said in the 1938 act, or in subsequent legislation so far as I can discover, about raising the incomes of the lowest third relative to those at the top. One cannot escape concluding that farm programs are now being condemned for not doing what Congress never intended for them to do, i.e., to bring about a substantial redistribution of income within the farm sector. They were adopted mainly for the purpose of pumping additional money into agriculture because of the conviction that some farmers were not receiving "fair incomes" under existing institutional arrangements.[26]

Congress, it may be argued, was only thinking of farmers' income deprivation relative to nonfarm groups, and expressed no intention to change income distribution within agriculture.

Nonetheless, the *expressed* purpose of the 1938 legislation was to restore "fair incomes" to farmers. The possibility that this rhetoric concealed an unspoken opposition to redistribution does not forbid taking the act's stated purpose at face value. Would it not then be consistent with *expressed* legislative intent to use our increased ability to target aid to the farmers with greatest relative deprivation of "fair incomes"? As Don Paarlberg, chief economist in the Department when Clifford Hardin was Secretary of Agriculture, has put it:

> If the welfare criterion [differential average levels of income as between the farm and nonfarm sector] is to be used as a basis of transferring purchasing power to the farm from the nonfarm group, the distribution of funds within agriculture should bear some relation to this criterion.[27]

In addition, there has been a major change in farm economy since the 1938 act was designed. Because differences in efficiency and output among farmers were somewhat less pronounced in the 1930s,[28] program benefits were probably more equally distributed in the early years of the program than they are now. It would not be unreasonable to consider redesign of farm legislation when its benefits have changed their pattern of distribution.

Finally, even if it is assumed that Congress intended to endorse the neglect of small farmers within the farm income programs, there is no reason we cannot deliberately change the standard of equity to be used. It may be that in 1938 the Congress foresaw and endorsed disproportionate aid to large farmers. Still, standards of merit and desert change, as do our notions of obligation and charity. Congressional intent may be a limiting mortmain for the courts, but it is not an inviolable prescription when we are proposing new legislation.

A second justification frequently offered for continuing the price support programs in their present form is that disproportionate aid to larger farmers is necessary compensation, whatever the income needs of small farmers. Large farmers deserve what they get, it is argued, because they receive a smaller return on their investment in farming than they would receive in a comparable investment in the nonagricultural sector. If additional aid is needed for smaller farmers, it should come from supplementary programs that leave unchanged the present price support program.

This argument is weakened by a 1967 Senate report that shows large farmers *are* presently getting comparable returns on investments in agriculture.[29] The Department of Agriculture measured by four different standards the so-called parity returns of farmers, "the equivalent that labor and capital employed in farming might get if they were employed elsewhere in the economy."[30] The study found that each commercial farmer with annual sales of $20,000 or more earned as much as or *more* than he would earn in the nonagricultural sector with the same resources. The smaller farmer, with sales under $20,000, earned less than parity of income by every standard of measurement used. Farmers in the lowest income group, with less than $5,000 sales, received less than one-half of parity income.

> For the larger farms—those with value of sales of $20,000 or more—returns from farming as a percentage of parity returns ranged from 61 to 128 percent in 1959 and from

> 107 to 167 percent in 1966 . . . In the case of farms with values of sales of $10,000 to $19,999, returns ranged from 54 to 83 percent in 1959 and from 81 to 98 percent in 1966. There was no instance in which these returns equaled or exceeded 100 percent . . . The pattern is even more striking for farms with value of sales less than $5,000 . . . Even in the generally good year of 1966, the highest percentage attained (for these farms) was 43 percent . . .[31]

It is likely that in the absence of farm program aid the parity returns of larger farms would be somewhat reduced, perhaps even more, proportionately, than the parity returns of low-income farmers. This estimate is made uncertain, however, by the role of program aid and allotments in inflating land values and encouraging heavy investment in equipment and fertilizer, which makes the rate of return achieved with any particular income smaller than it otherwise might be. In any event, if the criterion of "fair return for fair investment" is applied, it clearly justifies *some* redistribution of benefits toward the 1.8 million farmers with less than $5,000 gross sales who received only 43 percent of the return on comparable investment in nonfarm enterprises.

A third argument for retaining present programs contends that the price support programs are needed to attract more capital investment to agriculture than would otherwise be brought in by free market mechanisms. According to this premise, increased capital investment is needed to keep production costs down, to keep food prices low, and to develop larger production capacity to accommodate population increases. There are two obvious defects in this argument. So long as commodity programs are in operation specifically to keep food prices artificially high, one cannot justify the same programs on grounds of efficiency and low prices. A much simpler way to lower prices would be to end the commodity programs. It is equally misleading to justify subsidy programs on grounds of increasing capacity, so long as we are diverting fifty million acres a year under government contract to hold down production. Indeed the current problems of supply adjustment are the consequence of not limiting capital investment. The methods of production control designed in the 1930s limited only one of the factors of production—land. No attempt was made to limit capital or labor inputs or to restrain technological innovation. Average yields had been relatively stable prior to the 1930s, making limits on use of land a reasonable mechanism for controlling output. But new technology and the high prices of World War II triggered an increased investment in equipment and fertilizer that lasted throughout the 1940s, 1950s, and 1960s, boosting yields and the capacity for production in excess of demand.

A fourth contention in favor of the present system is that the distribution of benefits under farm and income support programs is an unavoidable by-product of the need to limit agricultural production. This view was aired in the 1969 House debate over farm subsidy appropriations, when Congressman Poage declared:

> We should not try to correct all the ills of agriculture through this one program. Take care of poverty and training needs and special credit needs, etc., through other means than by discrimination among farmers in payments which are merely program machinery, not welfare.[32]

Of course any payment made under any federal program can be labeled "program machinery." The non sequitur aside, Poage was contending that ASCS payments are a necessary mechanism for supply limitation. By the government's own figures this is not entirely true. Secretary Hardin testified in 1969 before the House Agriculture Committee that only $1.9 billion of the $2.9 billion spent under the cotton, feed grain, and wheat programs was needed to induce farmers to limit their plantings. Another $1 billion was used directly for income transfer. This situation is not "merely program machinery" and should be subject to equitable distribution (see Table 4). Furthermore, as noted in our discussion of indirect income support, the primary purpose of supply limitation is to increase the market price of commodities. This indirect income aid, like commodity loans, is prorated according to output and hence is unequally distributed among farmers. It is also seriously regressive with respect to consumers, for it amounts to an extra sales tax on food of close to 5 percent. This is, of course, especially burdensome to low-income families, who spend a relatively large proportion of their income on food. To exempt concentrated farm program payments from distributional scrutiny because they are necessary for supply limitation is therefore circular, for supply limitation itself has undesirable distributional effects.

The failure of the farm programs to distribute their benefits equitably helped fuel efforts in Congress outside the farm committees to restrict farm subsidies. This is the subject of the next chapter.

8

The Politics of
Subsidy Limitation

Subsidy limitation illustrates the shifting fortunes of farm power in Congress more clearly than any other issue. Every year from 1968 to 1973 either the House or the Senate voted to limit cash payments to farmers, but until 1973 the farm committees managed to keep the payments flowing with only modest changes, a considerable feat when one realizes that subsidy limitation has been endorsed by members of Congress from urban areas, the American Farm Bureau Federation, the Nixon administration (up to a point), and the majority of farmers.*

Large cash payments to wealthy farmers for not growing crops

NOTE: This chapter is based on the work of Ruth Glushien and Richard Guttman.

* In 1973-74, when prices for most crops were well above levels at which farmers could request subsidy payments, subsidy limitation was a less volatile issue in the House and Senate. The political struggle to limit subsidies

become the "scarlet letter" of the farm program in the 1960s. More than any other issue, it dramatized the inequities of farm policy and marshaled public opinion against all farm benefits. Americans pay twice for the farm subsidy program—first as taxpayers and later as consumers. Between 1956 and 1970, taxpayers contributed an average of $3.1 billion a year to price support programs and direct payment farm programs.[1] The major purpose of these programs has been to increase farm produce prices and thereby supplement farmers' incomes. By increasing the prices farmers receive for their agricultural products, however, the farm subsidy programs also increase the price consumers pay for their food. Charles L. Schultze, a Brookings Institution economist, estimates that between 1968 and 1970 the total annual cost to taxpayers and consumers of the farm subsidy program averaged $9 or $10 billion a year.[2]

In addition to the high costs of the program, the effort to limit farm payments has been motivated by a growing realization of the inequitable distribution of its benefits. Professor Schultze's calculations indicate that in 1969 the wealthiest 7.1 percent of farmers, producing over half of all agricultural produce, received more than 40 percent of all farm program benefits.[3] These large farmers would have an average annual net income of $13,400 without any farm program. Government price supports and direct payments served to more than double their income to $27,500. In contrast, the poorest 41.2 percent of the farmers, who raise only 2.7 percent of the crops, received a mere 5.3 percent of the farm program benefits. Government farm programs increased their average annual net income of $800 by only $300. Professor Schultze concluded:

> By their very nature, current farm programs tend to provide benefits—paid for by both consumers and taxpayers—

---

in 1970–72 remains important, however, because it graphically revealed the changing forces in farm politics that were to shape agricultural policy in the mid-1970s.

primarily to those larger farmers who produce the bulk of agricultural output. Conversely, the very large number of small farmers who in the aggregate produce only a modest fraction of total farm output are helped relatively little by these programs.[4]

In short, the majority of farm payments have gone to economically successful farmers who need no income supplements. As Senator John J. Williams of Delaware remarked, "Those collecting the money aren't cultivating farms. They're cultivating the treasury of the United States."[5]

Farm benefits, geared as they are to production rather than income considerations, have always been skewed in favor of the wealthy farmers, but until the 1960s, the public was relatively unaware of this fact because the benefits, as loans and price supports, were less visible than cash payments. The small family farmer was still seen by much of the public and Congress as the prime beneficiary and justification of the farm program.

Penetration of the fictions used to justify farm benefits was due mainly to a change in program design—the introduction of direct payments in the three major commodity programs during the 1960s. In the two decades after World War II, the major source of potential embarrassment to the Department of Agriculture in its price support programs was the apparent waste of storing large crop surpluses.[6] In 1954 criticism over the size of the government-owned surplus led the Eisenhower administration to attempt unsuccessfully to lower price supports, to bring them closer to world prices. By 1961, large surpluses had again accumulated and, as in 1954, the controversy over government storage induced a change of policy. Three events determined that the change would involve a system of direct payments to farmers.[7] In 1962 the House of Representatives failed to apply the usual mandatory acreage controls to feed grains, for fear that feed grain producers would no longer participate in any program of supply control that was not voluntary, and offered no incentive payments for compliance. In 1963 the wheat farmers voted in the local referenda run by the

Department of Agriculture to refuse mandatory acreage controls with penalties for overplanting. At about the same time cotton producers were faced with the fact that high cotton support prices kept American cotton from competing successfully on the foreign market. It appeared that a lower support price, coupled with an additional compensatory payment, might improve their competitive position yet maintain their traditional level of aid.

As a consequence, the use of direct payments began to win acceptance. In 1961 direct payments were applied as an emergency incentive for feed grain acreage reduction. In 1962 direct payments were incorporated into the wheat program; wheat processors were required to purchase certificates for every bushel of wheat processed. This payment was received by the farmer and appears to have been largely passed on to the consumer in higher bread and flour prices. In 1965 the cotton program incorporated a low support price to allow for world market competiton, supplemented by a direct income payment on the portion of the crop designated by the Agriculture Department as domestic consumption.[8]

The direct payments—paid in addition to the price support loans as simple cash grants—were a far more visible form of aid. Their budget cost was easily calculable, as was the amount of payment going to any particular farmer. Unlike the crop loans, direct payments were susceptible to ceilings or graduated limits, making it technically possible to gear aid to an income standard rather than total production.

The storm over subsidy programs broke in 1968 as the result of a decision by the Internal Revenue Service to begin a tax surveillance of the larger farmers receiving government aid. The IRS asked the Department of Agriculture for a list of all farmers receiving over $5,000 in direct program payments. Soon afterward the American Farm Bureau Federation, which had criticized price support legislation for years, heard of the list and through its Florida branch asked Senator Spessard Holland to secure a copy. Holland, who was chairman of the Senate Appropriations

Subcommittee on Agriculture, requested the tax listing from Secretary of Agriculture Orville Freeman on July 29, 1968. Walter Wilcox, Freeman's chief economist, advised against its release, fearing that the list would supply first-class ammunition to opponents of the farm program. But Freeman, who could not readily refuse Holland's request, agreed to provide a computer printout detailing the name, address, and size of payment of every farmer receiving over $5,000 annually in direct cash payments from the Agricultural Stabilization and Conservation Service.[9]

The list of bounties was published by Holland's subcommittee both in 1969 and in 1970. As predicted, it was a political windfall for farm program critics. Finally it could be shown that substantial farm payments were going to agribusinesses that did not deserve them on grounds of need. Though the list included only the direct cash payments, excluding the net cost of price support loans, the payments were large enough to arouse a good deal of ire among the public, newspaper editorialists, and nonfarm congressmen. The list showed, for instance, that the J. G. Boswell Company of Kings County, California, received a record high payment of $3.01 million in 1968. Second highest was Giffen, Inc., of Fresno County, California, with $2.77 million in 1968, followed by Southlake Farms of Kings County with $1.77 million.[10]

Dozens of other agribusinesses, chiefly in California, Arizona, Mississippi, and Arkansas, received payments in the hundreds of thousands of dollars. Several state prison farms received direct payments of over $10,000; Texas Department of Corrections Central Farm 520, in Sugarland, won $294,000. Banks also received aid for their agricultural ventures; a $170,000 payment to the Southern National Bank in Lumberton, North Carolina, was typical. The Reynolds Metal Company, in Henderson County, Kentucky, received $430,000; the Alabama Department of Mental Health, disguised as a farmer, received $17,000. A Mississippi farm called Hard Scrabble Plantation scrabbled for a direct payment of $17,000 annually. A less winsome payee for nationalists was the British-owned Delta Pine Land Company, in Scott, Mississippi, which received $605,000 in 1968. The beneficiary most often named in the press was Senator James O. Eastland, of Sunflower County, Mississippi, who received $116,000 in payments in 1968. In 1970 $40 million of the subsidies went to twenty-three farmers, and 40 percent of the money went to 5 percent of the farmers.[11]

Perhaps the most politically effective use of the list was to compare the payments for wealthy farmers with government stinginess toward hungry people in the same areas. Representative Paul Findley (R., Ill.) entered in the *Congressional Record* a list of 425 counties that participated in neither the food stamp nor the surplus food distribution program, yet received $2.4 billion in direct payments.[12] The list allowed calculation that the entire USDA migrant housing program was budgeted in 1967 for $100,000 less than the two largest direct subsidy payments. Less was spent on the school lunch, food stamp, commodity distribution, and cash grant food programs than on the direct payments to the largest 3 percent of farms. It became apparent also that the number of farms benefiting sumptuously from the price and income support programs had steadily increased. From 1966 to 1968 the number of farms receiving over $5,000 in aid rose by 23 percent, costing $1.33 billion in 1968.[13]

The statistics released to Senator Holland showing that 50 percent of the payments went to 9 percent of the farmers prompted the first congressional efforts to challenge the farm committees by introducing floor amendments to limit the size of payments. The committees' successful resistance to those efforts in 1970 provides a revealing profile of farm committee politics. The committees' battle that year was in retrospect a last rear-guard action by traditional farm politics against inexorable forces of change.

Two congressmen—John Findley (R., Ill.) and Silvio Conte (R., Mass.)—were first to propose a limit on the size of payments to any one producer. Their proposal was not essentially radical: though both professed distaste for the size of the sums going to the largest beneficiaries, they envisioned no phasing out of commodity price supports nor institution of any special programs for low-income farmers. Their attitude might be called enlightened conservatism—they meant to remove a high-visibility issue that might jeopardize the larger farm program. Findley, closely identified with the Farm Bureau, was philosophically in favor of a free market agriculture and therefore opposed to subsidies in principle. Conte was typical of those congressmen from urban industrialized states who were coming to see the farm program as wasting money that could better serve their constituents.

The idea of a ceiling on aid was not unprecedented. The Sugar Act of 1934 had reduced large payments on a sliding scale. Payment limits were specified in the Soil Bank program of the 1950s, in the Cropland Reserve Program, the Cropland Conservation Program, and the Agricultural Conservation Program. There had never been a limit, however, in the major ASCS price support and diversion programs.

Findley and Conte first proposed in 1968 to limit the size of ASCS direct payments to $20,000 per farmer. Liberal Republicans and Democrats joined forces in the House to pass the bill, but it died in the Senate and was eliminated in the House-Senate conference, where the conferees, appointed by Poage and Ellender, were hotly opposed to the concept of limitation.

In 1969 the issue of payment limitations again caught fire because of a leaked report from USDA favoring a ceiling. Sometime before the 1968 election, President Johnson commissioned Agriculture Undersecretary John A. Schnittker to make a study of whether a payment limitation was workable. On November 27, 1968, Schnittker completed his report with a favorable recommendation. Secretary Freeman promptly quashed the report, apparently because of his public stance against payment limitation on the basis that it would destroy the effectiveness of supply management in the major crop programs.[14] The White House lost its enthusiasm for the issue after the November election and made no attempt to circulate Schnittker's work. By early 1969, however, the report had leaked to various congressmen and had been placed in the *Congressional Record* by Representative Findley.[15] It had considerable impact, since Schnittker had defied Freeman's opposition to the payment limit and concluded a limit was feasible. Payments in the ASCS feed grain, wheat, cotton, and sugar programs, could be limited, Schnittker said, to $20,000 per farm or to $10,000 per program without serious adverse effects on production or on the effectiveness of supply adjustment programs. If administered firmly, such a limit, he estimated, could save from $200 to $300 million annually.

Most of the payments in the cotton program, his report revealed, were purely income supplements; only a fraction of the money was necessary to limit the size of cotton crops. The support price for cotton—about 20 cents per pound—was so low that production would not exceed market outlets even if all payments to growers and compulsory acreage allotments were eliminated. In the wheat program too payments were in large part income supplements, "set by law at substantially higher levels than would be required as incentives to assure enough participation by farmers to stabilize commodity carry-over."[16]

The report also revealed where most of the opposition to a payment limitation could be expected, supplying the first geographical and crop breakdown on producers getting $10,000 or more. The figures (see Table 8) showed that most farmers getting payments over $10,000 were cotton growers. Only 850 wheat growers and fewer than 4,600 feed grain farmers received $10,000, while in cotton almost 8,200 growers received payments of that magnitude or higher. The overall total of cotton payments in excess of $10,000 was $262 million, more than five times the "excess" for wheat and feed grains combined. Thus the fight over payment limitations was really a fight over the large payments in the cotton program. Therefore the western and southern states that supplied the farm committee leaders at the House and Senate would be hardest hit by a payment limitation.

In addition to the Schnittker report, a second survey, originally

TABLE 8.

Number of Payees Receiving $10,000 or More from Cotton,
Feed Grain, Wheat, or Wool Payments, by States, 1967

State	Cotton	Feed Grains	Wheat	Wool
Alabama	808	3	0	0
Alaska	0	0	0	0
Arizona	870	11	9	5
Arkansas	2,098	2	6	0
California	1,728	12	70	16
Colorado	11	26	449	17
Florida	10	0	0	0
Georgia	604	7	1	0
Idaho	0	4	290	18
Illinois	5	76	6	0
Indiana	0	50	1	0
Iowa	1	67	3	1
Kansas	4	47	647	0
Kentucky	22	2	2	0
Louisiana	814	3	1	0
Michigan	0	4	2	0
Minnesota	0	17	25	0
Mississippi	2,510	1	2	0
Missouri	330	54	6	0
Montana	1	11	613	7
Nebraska	1	72	55	0
Nevada	12	1	2	4
New Jersey	0	2	0	0
New Mexico	371	58	72	8
New York	0	0	1	0
North Carolina	217	10	0	0
North Dakota	0	2	262	0
Ohio	0	13	3	0
Oklahoma	200	9	226	0
Oregon	0	1	316	2
Pennsylvania	0	5	0	0
South Carolina	574	6	0	0
South Dakota	4	6	90	3
Tennessee	419	1	0	0
Texas	6,439	256	474	46
Utah	0	0	28	3
Virginia	1	2	0	0
Washington	0	2	905	3
Wisconsin	0	7	0	0
Wyoming	0	0	12	32
Total, United States	18,054	850	4,579	165

SOURCE: John A. Schnittker, *Limiting Farm Program Payments.* Unpublished U.S.D.A. study, November 27, 1968; printed in *Congressional Record* (91st Cong., 1st sess., April 30, 1969), p. H.10871.

released in 1968, added fuel to the fire for a payment limitation. *Doane's Agricultural Report* surveyed farmers about the proposed $20,000 limit and found that a large majority of them—85.5 percent—supported the idea.[17] Even in the cotton-specialized East South Central and West South Central states, over 75 percent voted in favor of the hypothetical limit (see Table 9).

TABLE 9.

Doane's Agricultural Report Survey: Should there be, or should there not be, a $20,000 per farm limit on payments for compliance with government programs?

	North Atlantic	South Atlantic
Yes	89.5	87.1
No	10.4	12.8
	East North Central	East South Central
Yes	89.7	78.8
No	10.2	21.1
	West North Central	West South Central
Yes	87.2	76.3
No	12.7	23.6
	West	United States
Yes	81.1	85.5
No	18.8	14.4

SOURCE: Doane Agricultural Service, Inc., "Agricultural Opinion Survey," *Doane's Agricultural Report* 31:30:10 (October 16, 1968).

In 1969 Findley and Conte resumed the legislative fight and again proposed a flat limit of $20,000 for each farmer, which would have saved $180 million, according to Charles Schultze's estimates.[18] Representative Conte finally proposed an even lower limit of $5,000 per crop, cutting payments of 85,000 farmers and saving approximately $493 million. Ninety-two percent of the cotton growers, 97 percent of the wheat farmers, and 98 percent of the grain producers would have been unaffected even by this lower limit.

During the Senate debate on Agriculture Department funds, Senator Charles Goodell (R., N.Y.) offered an amendment to limit subsidies to $10,000 for any given crop, which in 1968 would have affected 25,000 farmers, reducing their payments from $515 million to $265 million.[19]

The House again approved the Findley-Conte ceiling of $20,000, despite last minute maneuvering by the leadership to hold the tentative vote on a Monday, when eastern urban congressmen tend to be absent on visits to their home districts. On the final roll call, the $20,000 limit passed the House 224–142, a margin 12 votes larger than in 1968.

The Senate vote on the Findley-Conte floor amendment was the remaining question. If the President or the Agriculture Department applied some pressure, the ceiling might survive, since the seniority of the farm bloc senators was of no direct use. USDA's opposition to payment limits had changed little since the Freeman administration, despite Schnittker's report. "It is possible," Secretary Hardin conceded, "to design a sound farm program that limits the number of dollars that can be paid to any one farmer."[20] But he urged that any limit be delayed until after the 1970 crop year, not added as an appropriations amendment. "To make such a limitation effective," Hardin said, "legislative changes are needed . . . A simple amendment to the appropriations bill will not suffice."[21] The Senate killed the $20,000 limit by a vote of 53–34.

Hardin also tried to dampen prospects for a limit in 1970, when basic farm legislation was due to be rewritten. Initiative for a limit, he said, would have to come from the Congress. The USDA was ostensibly neutral toward the idea, but quite obviously hostile: "If there is a prevailing sentiment that something like this has to happen, and it is expressed by law, by Congress, of course we must adapt to it. But we are not taking a position of what ought to be."[22]

All these efforts to limit subsidies involved amendments from the floor, for there was virtually no support for curbs in the committees. In the House committee, even progressive Democrat Thomas Foley was lukewarm about limits, except as a bargaining tool to chip away opposition to the general farm program. While cotton farmers got the most benefits, almost all committee members had a few constituents with over $20,000 in payments whom they did not want to antagonize. And few members wanted to oppose Poage on a matter of such importance to his district.

Both the committees and the administration yielded ground in 1970, when they concluded that passage of the three-year farm price support bill depended on the enactment of some sort of ceiling. American public opinion had begun to demand reform of the subsidy program. In April 1970, for example, *Wallace's Farmer*, a leading farm journal, reported that 75 percent of farmers answering its questionnaire supported a limitation of $20,000 or less. Most of the remaining 25 percent, however, were concentrated in the cotton growing districts of the South and Southwest so powerfully represented on the farm committees. The administration, while it gave lip service to Republican policy in form of "uncontrolled" agriculture, did not want to antagonize the House Agriculture Committee, with whom it hoped to negotiate a less expensive farm program. Secretary of Agriculture Hardin therefore discussed with members of the House Agriculture Committee a "compromise limit" that provided for a graduated scale of payment reduction, with a $200,000 ceiling for each commodity program (ten times the Findley-Conte limit). Soon afterward, Hardin lowered his recommendation to a $110,000 limit per program. This was "a victory for the principle you have advocated," Hardin wrote to Conte.[23] It was hardly a victory in practice, for under Hardin's plan a single farmer could receive $110,000 in each of four crop programs, for a hypothetical total of $440,000.

Hardin's plan for compromise was challenged on July 8, 1970, when the Senate for the first time approved the $20,000 per farm limit on a vote of 40–37. A day later Hardin announced that he now favored a $55,000 ceiling on each crop.

> I have made it clear to Chairman Poage of the House Agriculture Committee and have stated publicly that we find the $55,000 payment limitation acceptable.
>
> I am continuing to work closely with Mr. Poage and the

senior members of the Agriculture Committee to try to find a satisfactory solution to the limitation issue. I think we understand each other.[24]

The $55,000 limit—designed to head off more stringent limits when the farm bill reached the House floor—was only reluctantly accepted by Chairman Poage of the House Agriculture Committee. Administration strategists had concluded there was little chance of winning House passage of the omnibus bill unless it carried some restriction on individual payments, but Poage, faithful to his cotton farmers, held out for no limits at all. At the last minute, when it appeared he would lose control of the bill on the floor without them, he finally agreed to the $55,000 limit for each crop program.

On August 3 the *Wall Street Journal* reported a rumor that the White House might be willing to accept a limit as low as $20,000.[25] Poage promptly pulled the farm bill off the weekly calendar as a warning to Nixon to abide by their understanding. On August 4 Nixon acceded, and circulated a letter of reassurance addressed to Page Belcher, ranking Republican on the House committee:

> The proper payment limitation would seem to me to be peculiarly within the province of Congress, and I will, of course, abide the Congressional judgment. For my part I subscribe to the analysis by your Committee and the Secretary of Agriculture. Both advise that too low a limitation would make it impossible for many farm producers to participate efficiently in the program . . .
>
> Secretary Hardin and a bipartisan majority of your Committee therefore recommend $55,000 as the limitation. I am aware of the widespread desire for a much lower figure, and it is easy to share that desire. However, I must agree with Secretary Hardin that in present circumstances this could be harmful to the constructive farm program which your Committee and the Department have so painstakingly evolved.

> You may therefore inform your colleagues that despite
> the obvious appeal of a lower limit, for these technical rea-
> sons I must prefer the limitation proposed by your Commit-
> tee.[26]

The Department has never published any study that rebuts the
Schnittker report's conclusion that the technical problems of a
payment limit were surmountable. Instead, the Nixon administration decided to yield to the still formidable political power of the
southern-dominated House Agriculture Committee.[27] With Nixon's letter in hand, Poage put the farm bill back on the calendar.

In his report on the bill Chairman Poage claimed that "the
amendment will preclude any farmer, whether an individual or a
corporation, to draw excessively large sums."[28] Poage further
noted that "the committee recognizes that many Members wish to
be 'on record' in favor of limitations. For this reason the limitations question was not presented as an integral part of the bill."[29]
The committee report predicted that the $55,000 payment limita-
tion would reduce farm payments by $58,300,000.[30]

In his analysis of the effects of the $55,000 payment limitation
Poage was being somewhat disingenuous, for simultaneous with
passage of the payment limitation the House Agriculture Committee had taken steps to insure its impotence. In a series of obscure
technical amendments to the cotton program, the committee had
created loopholes that allowed most farmers to evade the limits
legally. The cotton program was crucial because 89 percent of the
prospective savings resulting from the $55,000 payment limita-
tion were to come from the cotton program.[31] The Agriculture
Act of 1965 contained a provision authorizing the sale and lease
of cotton allotments but only under very restricted circumstances.[32] To insure that the payment limitation would result in
little if any decrease in federal payments to large farmers, the
House Agriculture Committee eliminated four restrictions on the
sale and lease of cotton allotments. Most important had been a
100-acre limit on allotments acquired by any one farm.[33] Second, a June 1 to December 31 transfer period limitation was

abolished.[34] Also eliminated was a ban on the sale of allotments to farms that had purchased cotton allotments during the past three years.[35] Finally, the former requirement of a referendum for out-of-county allotment transfers was eliminated.[36] In addition to dropping the previous restrictions on leasing and sale of cotton allotments, the House Agriculture Committee's bill also gave the Secretary of Agriculture discretion to define the term "person" as used in the bill. These two actions insured that, despite passage of the payment limitation, the great bulk of the farm payments would continue to be paid, although to a somewhat larger number of recipients.

Late in 1970 the Department of Agriculture adopted regulations that facilitated legal avoidance of the payment limit.[37] The regulations allowed each person in a fifty-fifty farming partnership to count as an "individual" for payment purposes; the partnership could thus collect up to $110,000 per program.[38] Each stockholder of a farming corporation could receive a separate payment up to $55,000 if he was "engaged in the production of the crop as a separate producer."[39] The Department also ruled that initial review of these changes in farming operations would occur at the county committee level.[40] In other words, the farmers themselves were charged with examining leasing, incorporation, and partnership arrangements to see if they were intended to evade the payment limit. The number of farms affected by the $55,000 payment limitation was so small that there was no reason why organizational changes could not have been examined by the Washington office, where a more stringent review would have been possible.

These changes did not escape the attention of the lower-subsidy forces in the House. Two weeks after the Agriculture Committee reported its bill to the House, Representative Findley submitted a substitute payment limitation.[41] His proposal differed from that of the House Agriculture Committee in three major aspects: it limited payments to $20,000 instead of $55,000; it included under its jurisdiction publicly owned land; most significantly, it required the Secretary of Agriculture to prevent evasion of the payment limitation by means of "subdivision of farms, production allotments, or bases thereof through sale or lease, or by other means." Conte, a cosponsor of the Findley amendment, submitted during debate a detailed draft of regulations expected by the authors of the $20,000 amendment to be employed in administering their proposal.[42] Representative Findley, commenting upon the Agriculture Committee's payment limitation, declared that "of course, there will be evasion [of the $55,000 limitation] because there is not tight language in the committee amendment to deal with that problem."[43]

After August 4, 1970, when the White House made clear its opposition to a $20,000 subsidy limit, the Findley amendment was a lost cause. Speaking against Findley on the floor were some of the most powerful figures in the House, including Agriculture Committee Chairman Poage, ranking minority member Belcher, Appropriations Committee Chairman George Mahon (D., Tex.) and Appropriations Subcommittee on Agriculture Chairman Whitten.[44] They argued that a $20,000 limitation would bankrupt many farmers or would drive farmers out of the voluntary commodity programs and thereby cause overproduction.

In reply, Representative Findley noted that the study made by former Undersecretary of Agriculture John A. Schnittker had concluded:

> Payments to producers under existing price support and acreage control programs for feed grains, wheat, cotton, wool, and sugar could be limited to around $20,000 per farm for all payments, or to $10,000 per program, without serious adverse effect on production or on the effectiveness of production adjustment programs.[45]

Shortly thereafter the House defeated the Findley amendment 134–161.[46] To escape personal accountability, the House members employed a nonrecorded teller vote whereby no record was made of how each representative voted. Later, in passing the Agriculture Committee-supported $55,000 payment limitation, individual votes were recorded, as is the normal procedure.[47]

After the House passed H.R. 18546, the Senate Committee on Agriculture and Forestry began deliberations on the bill.[48] In the Senate as in the House there was strong sentiment for a $20,000 limitation with tight enforcement provisions. Only a month earlier a $20,000 limitation proposed by Senator Ralph Smith (R., Ill.) had been added to the Senate Agriculture Appropriations bill by a vote of 40 to 35.[49] A major difficulty for opponents of the $20,000 limitation was the relative indifference of senators from feed grain and wheat producing states. The Department of Agriculture found that wheat and feed grains, unlike cotton, would be largely unaffected by a $20,000 limitation (see Table 10).

TABLE 10.

Number of Persons and Payments of Persons Receiving $20,000 or More from Cotton, Feed Grain, and Wheat Programs Payments in 1971

| | Persons | | Payments | |
| | | Percent of | Dollars | Percent of |
Program	Number	U.S. Total	(thous.)	U.S. Total
Cotton	8,742	2.6	308,117	37.7
Feed Grains	247	.1	7,186	.7
Wheat	1,112	.9	32,009	3.6
Total	10,012		347,312	

The subsidy limitation bill in the Senate was the victim of a logrolling maneuver between senators seeking higher payments for feed grains and southern senators seeking to preserve cotton payments at present levels. A group of northern Democrats, including Senators Walter Mondale (D., Minn.) and Quentin Burdick (D., N. Dak.), for example, offered to oppose the $20,000 payment limitation if the southern cotton senators would help their cause of high wheat and feed grain support levels.[50] Senators Eastland, Holland, and Ellender agreed and a deal was struck. In the ensuing vote on the Senate floor such northwestern farm state liberals as Mondale, Burdick, McGovern, Frank Church (D., Idaho) and Metcalf (D., Mont.) voted against a $20,000 limitation.[51] On September 15 the Senate passed a payment limitation identical to that ratified by the House.[52]

The $55,000 payment limitation was to become operative in 1971. It soon became evident that Conte's and Findley's warnings of evasion of the limitation were all too prophetic. As early as April 15, 1971, a prominent official of the Department of Agriculture acknowledged to Conte that "many producers who would otherwise be affected by the limitation are restructuring their farming operation so as to avoid the limitation."[53] On July 15, 1971, in response to growing criticism, the Senate passed a resolution proposed by Senator Humphrey requesting the Department of Agriculture to make a study of the effect of the $55,000 payment limitation on the farm program.[54] The department study, published March 16, 1972, reported:

> The 1971 payment limitation provisions of the Agriculture Act of 1970 resulted in the savings (actual reduction in payments) under the Upland Cotton, Feed Grain, and Wheat Set-Aside Program of $2,183,976. This represents 1.6 percent of $138.8 million paid to cotton, feed grain, and wheat producers who earned more than $55,000 in 1970.[55]

A month later the General Accounting Office published its study of the effect of the $55,000 payment limitation on government expenditures.[56] It concluded that "the $55,000 payment limitation caused no significant reduction in the total amount of 1971 cotton, wheat, and feed grain program expenditures."[57] Ninety-seven percent of the anticipated savings of $68,200,000 had failed to materialize.[58] Examining in detail the operation of ninety-eight producers, to discover their response to the payment limitation, the GAO investigators learned that the most common methods of avoiding the payment limitation included "leasing acreage allotments to spread payments to more persons, having payments made to individual partners in an existing partnership as an entity, and forming new partnerships to qualify more persons for payment."[59]

On June 29, 1972, Representative Conte revealed on the House floor how two well-known payment recipients managed to evade the intent of the $55,000 payment limitation.[60] Senator Eastland of Mississippi, third ranking member of the Senate Agriculture and Forestry Committee, had divided his 5,200-acre cotton plantation into eight business entities. Together they collected $160,000 in government subsidies, nearly the same as the amount received the previous year.

J. B. Boswell, the giant cotton farming corporation of Fresno, California, used a more complex method to collect its 1971 farm aid: 11,600 acres of cotton allotments were leased to five newly created organizations, qualifying fifty-three individuals for separate $55,000 payments. In addition, Boswell contracted to do the farming on the leased land. The fifty-three individual "business entities" then received payments of approximately $2,500,000 without having done any farming. Presumably the bulk of the $2,500,000 found its way back into Boswell's pockets.

Hyde H. Murray, associate counsel of the House Agriculture Committee, argues that payment limitation loopholes could be closed if Congress and the Department of Agriculture had the will to do so. Murray believes that the congressmen responsible for writing the $55,000 payment limitation knew that the bill would not accomplish its apparent goals.[61] But since the sale and lease of cotton allotments is specifically permitted by Section 344a of the Agriculture Act of 1970,[62] repeal of this provision would substantially reduce the ability of cotton farmers to evade a payment limitation.

Congressman Findley echoes Murray's belief that the $55,000 limitation "was drafted by people who do not believe in a payment limitation and who accepted one only as a way out of a deadlocked situation."[63]

Despite all the debate on subsidy limitation, the amount of federal money handed to large farms continued to escalate in 1971 (see Table 11).

TABLE 11.
Payments in Excess of $20,000

Year	Number of Farmers	Total Payments
1968	5,914	273,333,643
1969	7,795	366,779,945
1970	10,371	414,500,000
1971	13,751	486,339,509

This result is testimony to the influence of cotton congressmen in agricultural policy. In 1971, 89 percent of the money saved by a $20,000 limitation would have come from cotton farmers, as shown in Table 1. Yet almost without exception the most powerful congressmen on agricultural matters represent cotton-producing areas. In addition to Senator Ellender and Representative Poage, the chairman of the House Appropriations Committee in 1970 was George Mahon, from Lubbock, Texas; Whitten, the chairman of the House Appropriations Subcommittee on Agriculture, from Charleston, Mississippi. As long as representatives of cotton-producing areas retain their iron grip on agricultural matters, setting an enforceable farm payment limitation will be a tough battle.

In 1972, during House consideration of agriculture and environment appropriations, Representative Conte introduced the identical amendment he had introduced the year before—to limit annual subsidy payments to $20,000 per farmer. While Poage and Mahon praised the large farm operations that received much of the subsidy payments, Conte asked the House "to begin the task of restoring some measure of sanity and reason to a runaway farm program that has long been a scandal to the taxpayer and a disgrace to the legislative process."[64] The House defeated Conte's amendment 189–193.

The following year finally brought signs that Congress may

intend to control the subsidy giveaway. The effort was made without the assistance or concurrence of the Agriculture committees. The subsidy limits were lowered and attempts to close loopholes were initiated on the Senate and House floors, not in the committees.

In 1973 the Senate Agriculture and Forestry Committee retained the $55,000 subsidy limit in its farm bill. It was on the Senate floor that Birch Bayh (D., Ind.) introduced an amendment to lower the payment limitation to an individual farmer to $20,000. The Senate accepted the amendment with the approval of only four of the thirteen Senate Agriculture Committee members. An amendment by Senator Frank Moss (D., Utah) to prohibit large farmers from leasing farms to friends and relatives to collect additional subsidy payments was defeated by the Senate 42–44, with only two committee members voting in favor of closing this gaping loophole.

At the same time the Senate was acting on that farm bill, the House was considering its version. The House Agriculture Committee made only a minor change in the 1971 $55,000 subsidy limit, reducing the limit to $37,500 per farmer per crop. Representative Findley, still, with Conte leading the House effort to limit subsidies, promised that he would seek to further reduce the subsidy payments on the House floor.

In the meantime, Findley and Conte introduced complementary amendments to the Agriculture-Environment-Consumer appropriations bill. The Conte amendment, strengthened by the Findley substitute, provided for a $20,000 limit per person on farm subsidy payments and prohibited the selling or leasing of cotton acreage allotments to circumvent the payment ceiling. Findley stated that although the Agriculture Department had said the $55,000 limit would reduce program costs by $35 million, in fact only $2.2 million was saved during the first year of the program.[65] The House adopted the amendments.

When the Agriculture Committee's farm bill came to the House floor, Findley moved as he had promised to reduce the subsidy limit to $20,000 per farmer with a prohibition on selling or leasing cotton allotments to collect additional subsidy payments. Findley feared that his plan had been foiled, though, when Representative Bob Bergland (D., Minn.) first introduced, and the House adopted (303–89), an amendment pertaining only to the $20,000 limit and not closing the loophole. Findley feared that since the House had gone this far, it might not go far enough to support his amendment, which would also close the loophole. But Findley was wrong. After passing Bergland's amendment, the House passed Findley's stronger one, 246–163.[66]

As the Senate and House farm bills went to conference, each contained the $20,000 limit provision, but the Senate bill did not prohibit the leasing and selling of farms to circumvent the limit. The conferees agreed to retain the $20,000 limit but dropped the other provision, leaving the loophole in the law.

After the 1973 battle over the subsidy payments, it was apparent that the Senate and House had made some progress in limiting a program that was wasteful and discriminatory, but the major loophole remained. Farmers could still circumvent the limit by splitting up their land and collecting several payments for what was once a single plot. It is also noteworthy that the Agriculture committees in the Senate and the House, supposedly the bodies most familiar with agriculture issues, were of almost no assistance in the attempt to reform the subsidy provision. The improvements were almost solely the result of floor amendments.

9

Commodity Politics:
The Passage of the
Farm Bill, 1970-73

While the story of the subsidy limitation controversies showed
that the reign of King Cotton was far from over in the early
1970s, it also indicated that the congressional environment which
now confronts farm bills is increasingly adverse. As the Agriculture committees have become less representative of the larger
groups interested in farm legislation, farm bills written by these
committees have been seriously threatened on the House and
Senate floor by those not represented on the committees whose
interests are ignored in committee bills. By 1973 the drastic decline in the number of members from agricultural districts had
also made the passage of any farm bill more uncertain.

Loss of farm-belt congressional strength seriously imperiled the

215

passage of farm bills in both 1970 and 1973. It forced new strategies upon the Agriculture committee chairmen—strategies that entailed higher risks and required the support of less compatible allies. The new arithmetic of agriculture in Congress points to a truth that the committee leaders no doubt find unpleasant but also ineluctable: to get a farm bill through Congress in the seventies, they are going to have to bargain with their urban colleagues. In 1970 the farm bill passed the House by a slim 191–145 vote. By 1973, forty-one persons who supported the bill had been defeated or retired. There were now two possible ways to pick up the necessary votes, either of which required diplomacy and skill in legislative maneuvering to achieve success. One alternative was to appeal to nonfarm Republicans and administration supporters, who generally view the expensive farm program as much too lavish, by writing a less generous bill. The second was to appeal to nonfarm Democrats by loading the bill with subsidy limitations plus benefits for the poor—increased food stamps for urban constituencies and other provisions related to the problems of poverty and hunger.

Each strategy entailed great risks and potentially high costs for agriculture traditionalists in the House and Senate. The Nixon administration, seeking a major reversal in American agricultural policy, had the stated goal of returning to a free market farm economy and virtual elimination of direct program payments to farmers. Chairman Poage, maneuvering for Republican support, ran the risk of having to concede too much in exchange for it. The potential losses were particularly large for Poage's cotton-growing constituents back in Texas, upon whom a reduction in direct payments would fall hardest.

But the bipartisan approach, for all its hazards, was philosophically more attractive for conservative Democrats like Poage than any alliance with urban and liberal congressmen. In virtually every recent session of Congress conservative committee members have tried to pass amendments specifically denying food stamps to strikers, a calculated slap at organized labor. Labor has a long-standing grievance against southern Democrats for their general failure to support its position on such issues as the minimum wage and the Emergency Employment Act, a program to create state and local public service jobs for the unemployed. City and rural congressmen are increasingly at odds over aid to the cities, mass transit, and environmental protection. These differences seem graver in the 1970s than ever before, creating strong incentives for urban and labor groups to retaliate by withholding support for the farm bill.

The strategy of reaching out to liberals and urban congressmen for support does have its champions on the House committee in the persons of Thomas Foley, John Melcher, and Robert Bergland. It has even stronger support in the Senate committee, with Humphrey and McGovern providing leadership. The difficulty with this strategy is that it in effect pits the wheat and feed-grain farmers of the Midwest, the Great Plains, and the Northwest against the cotton farmers of the South and Southwest. Subsidy limits, for example, may in the future be a *sine qua non* for liberal-urban support in the House. But while wheat and feed-grain farmers can tolerate limiting subsidies to $20,000 a farm, because few receive more than $10,000 in payments, this plan strikes terror to the hearts of big cotton farmers. Chairman Poage has, however, been willing to go along with cuts in subsidies for other commodities if cotton were left alone.

THE REIGN OF KING COTTON

The decline of agrarian power in Congress has strained the traditional relationships between commodity groups and caused subtle but significant shifts in the politics of the farm committees. The most important change has been the gradual withering of the political power of cotton.

The obsolete term "farm bloc" implied a uniformity of interests that now misrepresents the complexity and turmoil of farm politics. In fact, the farm committees preside over a free-for-all among commodity groups for shares of the farm budget. The farm economy is very interrelated, very organic in character.[1] Gains for one commodity in one region are often won at the expense of another commodity in another region. If acres set aside by cotton controls in the Mississippi Valley are planted in corn, feed grain markets in Iowa may suffer; if price supports on feed grains in the Dakotas increase the price for animal feed, chicken farmers in Georgia will complain; when production controls reduce total farm output, the committees' agribusiness constituency—including processors and pesticide, fertilizer, and machinery manufacturers—feels aggrieved.

The relative power of the various commodity groups ebbs and flows over time, but cotton has tenaciously held on to a disproportionate share of federal farm benefits. Despite a great reduction in authorized cotton acreage in 1966 and a gradual shrinking of domestic demand for cotton, cotton farmers continued to receive the great bulk of the larger subsidy payments. In 1970, for example, 90 percent of the $143,700,000 paid out to the cotton, wheat, and feed grain farmers who each received $55,000 or more in federal subsidy payments went to cotton farmers, mostly in Mississippi, Texas, Arizona, and California.[2] In Mississippi, 335 such growers received $29,250,000 in cotton program benefits, an average of $87,300 per farm.[3] During the same period 290 California cotton growers received $44,000,000 for an average payment of $150,000.[4] Total cotton subsidies amounted to $808 million in 1972.

If the federal farm subsidy system is a "taxpayer's hayride," to use Jules Duchas' metaphor, cotton has been the lead horse pulling it along. The basic farm legislation affecting cotton production had its origins in the chronic overproduction crisis of American agriculture, which, in the years before federal controls became conventional, depressed prices to the point where they failed to cover the investment and costs of production.[5] Cotton was directly affected by the technological revolution in agriculture that has helped cause overproduction.

In the 1930s a bale of cotton required 209 man hours to produce. By the 1960s the required time had fallen to 32 man hours.[6] Demand for fiber, however, has remained relatively static as supply has enlarged. Two factors have exacerbated the price crisis in cotton: increased foreign cotton competition[7] and even more significant, competition from man-made fibers such as rayon and polyester.[8] As man-made fibers' share of total mill consumption of fibers increased from 4 to 57.5 percent between 1930 and 1970, cotton's share fell from 86 to 40 percent. More than half of this loss occurred during the 1960–70 period.[9] Between 1968 and 1973 per capita consumption of cotton decreased four pounds while per capita consumption of synthetics increased fifteen pounds.[10] The switch to wrinkle-free permanent-press fabrics further damaged markets, and new federal laws protecting occupational health gave textile firms incentive to switch to synthetics, for cotton dust has afflicted tens of thousands of workers with the lung disease byssinosis. Federally mandated cotton dust controls will cost the textile industry many millions of dollars when the government begins to enforce them by the mid-1970s.

Cotton has always received strong support from southern members of Congress, whose communities are economically dependent on the cotton complex from grower to factory. To meet the problems of overproduction, fluctuating commodity prices, and inadequate farm income, Congress has passed during the past fifty years a series of federal farm programs[11] to help cotton. In the 1920s, legislation was motivated by a drop in prices from about 35 cents a pound in 1919–20 to below 10 cents in 1921.[12] The Agriculture Marketing Act of 1929[13] attempted to stabilize prices but was followed by a further price decline in the early thirties to 5 cents per pound.[14] Under the Agriculture Adjustment Act (AAA) of 1933, cotton farmers became eligible for direct payments as part of an acreage control program.[15] Initially, farmers were paid to plow under ten million acres of cotton, nearly a fourth of the entire crop.[16] These payments derived from a processing tax on cotton manufacturers. Shortly thereafter the Commodity Credit Corporation was created to support cotton prices by means of nonrecourse loans. Both the direct payment and the loan were paid directly to the landlord, who was instructed to dispense a portion of the benefits to his tenants. In 1936 the Supreme Court declared the AAA unconstitutional. Congress immediately passed the Soil Conservation and Domestic Allotment Act, which, although ostensibly enacted for soil conservation purposes, retained the AAA's crop controls and benefit payments.[17]

The price support and supply management programs that were in effect at the end of 1972 emerged in the late fifties[18] and were extended, with certain modifications, by the Agriculture Acts of 1965[19] and 1970.[20] The cotton provisions of the 1970 act (which was drastically modified in 1973) required participating farmers to "set aside" a prescribed proportion of their acreage allotment for cotton (or feed grains or wheat). Having set aside that land, and another small amount for conservation purposes, the farmer could plant any crop he wished on the rest of his land, unless it was restricted by other legislation. He then beame eligible for a government cash payment based on the potential total production of his acreage allotment. The acreage allotment was a specific proportion of his acreage planted between 1966 and 1970. Farmers received from the government 15 cents for every pound of cotton produced on their acreage allotment. They could also sell or lease the allotment, and doing so was often more profitable than growing the crop.

Cotton subsidy policy is set in the Agriculture committees of the House and Senate. Unlike most federal agriculture programs, subsidy matters are not much affected by the Appropriations subcommittees on agriculture.[21] The costs of the subsidy program are determined when Congress sets loan and payment rates, leaving the Appropriations committees little discretion to modify spending.

Southern domination of the Agriculture committees has meant cotton domination. In 1970–71, when the 1970 farm bill was up for consideration, four of the eight Democratic members of the Senate Agriculture and Forestry Committee, including the three top-ranking members, were from major cotton-producing states. Similarly, nine of the twenty-two Democratic members of the House Agriculture Committee, including the three top-ranking members, were from cotton districts. Especially influential on cotton legislation are Representatives Poage and Sisk (D., Calif.) and Senator Eastland (D., Miss.). By 1973, cotton's power had slipped substantially, however. On the Senate committee, only Eastland remained as a strong cotton advocate, although Talmadge and James Allen (D., Ala.) added some support. Talmadge, the new chairman, has weaker cotton interests to contend with in Georgia than his predecessor, Ellender, had in Louisiana. In the House committee members from cotton districts declined from eleven in 1970 to six in 1973.

In addition to Agriculture committee memberships, however, cotton's unique influence in Congress has flowed through key chairmanships of other committees. Congressmen from cotton districts and states are chairmen of the House Appropriations Committee, the House Appropriations Subcommittee on Agriculture, and the Senate Appropriations Committee, and the House Ways and Means Committee. Again there has been a decline from 1970 when cotton Congressman William Colmer of Mississippi also chaired the House Rules Committee, now chaired by Ray Madden, from steel-producing Gary, Indiana.

The hegemony of cotton on the Agriculture committees had perhaps its last hurrah in the formulation and passage of the Agriculture Act of 1970. In the summer of 1969 the House Agriculture Committee began a series of public hearings on a new farm bill. Four months later the Cotton Subcommittee held further public hearings on the cotton program. Testimony was of a general nature, for the administration had presented no bill to the committee. While the pro forma public hearings were being held, basic policy decisions on the new farm bill were being made at a series of unprecedented executive sessions attended by members of the House Agriculture Committee and top officials of the Department of Agriculture. These closed meetings took place virtually every Monday evening for twenty-seven weeks.[22]

An initial purpose of the meetings was to create lines of communication and cooperation between the committee members and the newly appointed USDA officials. Chairman Poage agreed to the meetings on the theory that he would have to have White House support to get a new farm bill through an increasingly skeptical House. By working out strategy with administration officials behind the scenes, he hoped to present a bipartisan bill with more chance of acceptance on the House floor.

Democratic losses in the 1968 election had increased the need for Republican cooperation. Furthermore, as Representative William Randall later revealed on the House floor, the administration had notified the Agriculture Committee that it "would veto any kind of farm bill that was more expensive than a preagreed cost in terms of dollars and even sent word that the President would veto a farm bill which provided for advance payments."[23] Poage doubted that proponents of a farm bill could muster the two-thirds majority required to overturn a presidential veto.[24]

To insure administration and Republican congressional support, Chairman Poage had to work closely with the House Agriculture Committee's ranking Republican, Representative Belcher. The fact that Poage enjoyed a warm personal relationship with Belcher and shared his conservative views on nonagricultural policy helped this strategy work. As Hyde Murray, associate counsel to the House Agriculture Committee, remarked, "There are 125 or so Representatives who automatically vote against all farm bills. If the Agriculture Committee is divided on a bill it doesn't stand a chance on the floor."[25]

Admitting that the bipartisan approach had its advantages

Murray nevertheless noted a serious danger of cooperation in committee:

> The adversary process requires a sharp questioning of all significant sections of a bill. Often this check does not function in committee because of the pressure for cooperation. And the floor of the House is a poorer forum for such challenging than is the Committee.[26]

According to another staff member, "During the course of the many months of meetings, the Administration gradually brainwashed the committee members to accept its position."[27] The extraordinary meetings between the committee and administration officials were closed to the public and to the press and no records were kept. As one former farm lobbyist remarked, "It was like the Star Chamber. We had no opportunity to propose alternatives or criticize the bill they were creating. All we knew was the broad outlines of a bill as discussed in general terms by the Administration in the public hearings."[28]

The bill that emerged from the negotiations between Poage, Belcher, and administration officials struck the following compromise: the White House, wanting a reduction in production restrictions and a shift away from income support to supply management, got the "set-aside" provision; Poage and his allies from the cotton states got increased benefits for cotton; and both, by reducing benefits for wheat and feed grain farmers, got a cheaper farm bill with more assurance of approval in the House. The dominance of cotton at this stage of the negotiation on the bill is illustrated when one compares the benefits of cotton to wheat and feed grain benefits. First, cotton allotments could be leased or sold, a liquidity not conferred on feed grain and wheat allotments. Second, virtually the full cotton crop qualified for price support payments while only one-half the feed grain crop and only that part of the wheat crop to be used for domestic food consumption qualified (approximately 44 percent). Third, the loan to cotton farmers was set at a fixed 90 percent of the estimated average world price.[29] In contrast, the Secretary of Agriculture was granted the discretion to set the nonrecourse loan for wheat at anywhere from 0 to 100 percent of parity.[30] The severing of parity from price supports was a major departure from traditional farm policy.

The price of the consensus bill for Poage was near-revolt within his committee by members representing wheat and feed grain interests. Opposition to the bill was led by the Farm Coalition, an *ad hoc* group of thirty-four farm organizations (the only major group not represented was the American Farm Bureau Federation, which viewed the bill as a warmed-over version of the Orville Freeman program with a few new gimmicks but no substantive change in the direction of a free market agriculture). The coalition wanted additional support for wheat and feed grains, a program that would add $660 million (the Coalition's figure) to $1.5 billion (USDA's figure) to the farm bill. The Coalition, which represented family farmers from the Midwest, the Great Plains, and the Northwest, centered its influence in the Livestock and Feed Grains Subcommittee, chaired by Rep. Graham Purcell of Texas.

Although some cotton is grown in his district, Purcell had been a strong advocate for grain interests. While Poage was working out his compromises with Secretary of Agriculture Hardin, Purcell's subcommittee was working just as hard to torpedo them by approving a program of increased benefits for wheat and feed-grain farmers. When Belcher reported the White House's displeasure to the subcommittee and his fear that no farm bill could be enacted without strong White House support, its members still refused to reverse themselves until April 8, 1970, when Poage and Belcher—who do not sit regularly on the subcommittee but who are ex officio members—provided the winning margin for reversal in a close 9–8 vote. The five representatives from cotton districts on the subcommittee—Rarick, Ed Jones, Sisk, Price, and Montgomery—gave Poage his base of support and Belcher was able to deliver one feed grains Republican, Wiley Mayne of Iowa. The power of cotton congressmen on the Livestock and Grains Subcommittee was significant; wheat and feed grain congressmen by contrast are not strongly represented on the Cotton Subcommittee.

The 1970 farm bill was a critical test of Poage's leadership. Although he eventually kept the bill from being compromised by his subcommittees, he still faced major struggles in the full committee, on the House floor, and with the Senate Committee on Agriculture and Forestry. Here his cotton allies would be outnumbered and it was not at all certain that in the minds of the Republican members, loyalty to the administration would overcome their concern about the bill's unpopularity in the Midwest, the Great Plains, and the Northwest. When Secretary of Agriculture Clifford Hardin announced the compromise bill on February 3, 1970, no member of Congress initially would introduce it and all the farm organizations continued to oppose it.

On June 2, 1970, the full committee met to vote on the wheat, feed grains, and cotton programs, the last major committee action required before the farm bill could be reported to the House. In a surprise move, Representative Foley called for a record vote on Committee Print No. 4, the substitute plan for increased benefits for wheat and feed grains, and the substitute won committee approval.

The vote was an unprecedented repudiation of the chairman's leadership; Poage's fellow cotton congressmen stayed solidly behind him, but Belcher could not keep seven of his Republicans from deserting the administration's bill. The regional split on the vote was dramatic, as all the committee members from the Midwest, the Great Plains, and the Northwest, with the exception of minority leader Belcher, voted for Foley's motion. Had the vote been unrecorded, Poage might well have won. But with a record vote many Republican congressmen feared supporting an administration plan that was not only opposed by all the major farm groups but would also, for the first time, divorce feed grain payments from the cherished concept of parity.*

A committee chairman at bay can be a formidable force. The Purcell-Foley faction that pushed through Committee Print No. 4 was therefore under no illusion that their victory was in any sense final. As long as Poage could keep the farm bill from being reported by the committee, he could work to change its vote. This he proceeded to do, by adjourning the committee's deliberations on the farm bill even before it had voted on the cotton program. Poage scheduled other business and let the committee majority know that he would allow no bill to be reported unless it was the way he wanted it. His position squeezed the committee members and the farm groups which opposed the administration bill, for without new legislation to replace the 1965 agricultural act, the Department of Agriculture would have to fall back on pre-1965 legislation that had led to the depressed farm prices, excess production, and bulging surplus storage bins of the Benson era. By using his power as chairman to declare a moratorium on committee consideration of the farm bill, Poage gained time to work with the administration forces to turn the committee around. Poage generally does not resort to arm twisting or power plays, but in this instance he was equal to the challenge. Republican members were especially vulnerable to pressure. One convert was Representative Catherine May (R., Mo.), whom the administration persuaded to change her vote, a decision for which her wheat farmers punished her in the next election. After a seven-week hiatus during which the Department of Agriculture made ostentatious displays of preparing production plans on the basis of the unpopular basic legislation, Poage reconvened the committee on July 21. That day the committee voted 20–12 to reject Committee Print No. 4. Two days

---

* In fact, the differences between the administration bill and Print No. 4 were not great. The latter would have provided greater payments for wheat, but the former, despite abandoning parity, actually provided greater benefits for feed grains.

later the committee sent the administration-approved bill to the House floor.

On August 5, 1970, the House passed the Agriculture Act of 1970, by a 214–171 roll-call vote, largely as Poage had designed it. In addition to his compromises to win Republican support, Poage demonstrated his flexibility by approving the $55,000 limitation on subsidy payments on any one crop, which was of some help in calming opposition from urban congressmen chafing at big-farmer payments.

With his bill safely through the House, Poage now had to worry about its treatment in the Senate, where the political stakes were very different. Wheat and feed grain advocates were much stronger on the Senate committee than in the House. Moreover, Chairman Ellender, more confident that he could get increased farm payments accepted on the Senate floor (where farm constituencies traditionally have more clout than in the House), was little disposed to bargain with the administration on farm cutbacks. Ellender was certain he could get his bill passed without administration support. In August the Senate Committee on Agriculture and Forestry began formulating its own farm bill, using the House bill as a foundation. Ellender wrote Secretary of Agriculture Hardin that the adminstration's proposals gave the secretary authority "to fix the compensation so low, or the amount of acreage required to be set aside so high, as to defeat any objective of assuring farmers a fair return."[31] Ellender further charged that the administration bill would "tend to destroy the family farm system and result in large corporate-type farming."[32] The bill finally reported by the Senate committee involved substantially higher payments to wheat and feed grain producers and slightly higher payments to cotton producers.[33] In a letter to Ellender, Hardin expressed his opposition to the bill as reported by the Senate committee because of its rigid base acreage allotments and high costs.[34]

One of the difficulties facing Ellender on the floor of the Senate was an effort by midwestern and northern senators to limit payments to $20,000 per crop per farmer. As noted above, the payment limitation would have substantially greater effect on cotton producers than on wheat and feed grain producers. Ellender met this challenge with a classic display in logrolling. After a series of closed-door negotiations, several senators from wheat and feed-grain states, including Mondale of Minnesota and Burdick of North Dakota, agreed to vote against the $20,000 payment limitation if the southern cotton senators would uphold the Senate bill's high wheat and feed grain support levels when the bill reached the House-Senate conference committee. In a lobby off the Senate floor, Ellender of Louisiana, Eastland of Mississippi, Holland of Florida, and Talmadge of Georgia agreed to the deal. In the ensuing vote on the Senate floor, such liberal northern farm senators as Mondale of Minnesota, Burdick of North Dakota, McGovern of South Dakota, Church of Idaho, and Metcalf of Montana voted against the $20,000 payment limitation and the amendment was defeated. On September 15, the Senate passed its version of the Agriculture Act of 1970 by a vote of 65 to 7,[35] and the bill went to House-Senate conference.

At the conference meeting, the House conferees, four Democrats from cotton-producing areas and three Republicans (Poage, Abernethy, Sisk, Purcell, Belcher, May, and Wampler),[36] categorically rejected the Senate bill's support levels which were substantially higher for wheat and feed grains and slightly higher for cotton. Ellender was later to state that Belcher "dominated" the three-week conference,[37] and that when presented with the Senate position, Belcher "got up and hit his chest and said 'I represent the President and I represent the Secretary of Agriculture and we are not going to accept this.'"[38] Faced with such intransigence, Ellender concluded that no compromise bill was possible. At that point four of the seven Senate conferees, including southern Democrats Eastland and Holland and Republican Senators Aiken and Miller, capitulated to the House position despite Eastland's and Holland's previous commitments to the wheat and feed-grain senators.[39]

In addition to Nixon administration support, the dominance of House members in the conference was a product of the different legislative burdens of members of the two Houses.[40] Senators, unlike representatives, simply have too many legislative responsibilities to wait out a conference committee deadlock. Assistant Counsel Murray remarked, "The representatives presented a united front and just wore the Senate conferees out." Furthermore, agricultural matters are often so complex that only members of the House Agriculture Committee can afford to spend the time required to write the legislation. "Most agricultural matters, like most tax matters, are mainly written in the House," Murray says. "The House works out the details and the Senate only modifies the House product."[41] Certainly that was the case in 1970.

After the Senate conferees capitulated to the bulk of the House's demands, the bill went to the two Houses for final ratification. On October 13 Chairman Poage could modestly report on the floor of the House that "Certainly, the basic position of the House was maintained."[42] Ranking Republican Belcher had more difficulty disguising his sense of triumph. "I do not believe," he reported to the House, "that any conference has ever been held between the House and the Senate in which the House has prevailed as much as we did on this particular bill."[43] The House approved the conference report by a 191–145 roll-call vote.

The scene in the Senate chamber was less harmonious. Wheat and feed-grain senators were enraged at what they considered a sellout by the southern members who had voted to accept the basic provisions of the House bill.[44] On November 19, Senator Mondale noted on the Senate floor that the original Senate bill had guaranteed corn farmers the greater of 75 percent parity or $1.35 a bushel through 1973.[45] The conference report, in contrast, allowed only 70 percent parity or $1.35 a bushel in 1972 and gave the Secretary of Agriculture discretion to drop parity to 68 percent in 1973. Mondale charged that the conference report had deleted all the "strong features" of the Senate bill. Senate Agriculture Committee Chairman Ellender opposed the conference reports on the floor of the Senate.[46] According to a former farm lobbyist, Ellender was shaken by the Senate conferees' capitulation, after having given his word to the northern senators to defend in conference the Senate bill's high wheat and feed grain support levels.[47]

Senator Mondale also reported that the Farmers Union Grain Terminal Association Conference, composed of Minnesota, South Dakota, North Dakota, and Montana wheat growers, had overwhelmingly passed a resolution requesting the Senate to reject the conference report.[48] Senator Ralph Yarborough, a liberal Democrat of Texas, argued that the conference report was unacceptable because the 75-percent parity level for corn was lowered, the advance payment program was terminated, and the Secretary of Agriculture was given wide discretion in determining acreage allotments on which support prices were to be made.[49] Several senators wanted the bill returned to conference to be modified in a manner closer to the original Senate bill. Others argued that, although the conference report was unsatisfactory, it was better than no bill at all. On November 19 the Senate passed the conference report by a vote of 48 to 35.[50] The result was a bill which decreased payments for wheat and feed grains but increased payments for cotton.[51]

In 1970, in short, the farm bill narrowly squeaked through, with the support of a coalition of farm interests plus moderates and administration supporters who were persuaded that the bill was lean enough to tolerate. The coalition was familiar, although the margin was uncomfortable.

NEW COALITIONS

The story in 1973, in the House at least, was very different—and was made different by the increasing unrepresentativeness of the committee plus the sudden decline in farm-belt strength following the 1972 reapportionment. The committee leadership, for the first time, lost control of the bill when it came to the floor, and it was significantly amended. The sudden drop in farm-belt strength had forced the committee to construct a new (and more unwieldy) coalition, composed of extremely disparate elements, and in 1973 this coalition proved too precarious for its task. For the first time, an agriculture bill acceptable to cotton supporters was not passed. The ultimate outcome of the farm bill controversy in 1973 did not differ radically from the outcome in 1970: the same kind of bill eventually came out of conference and became law both times. But the process by which this outcome was achieved signaled not only that the new groups interested in agriculture bills are now strong enough in the House to override the committee when they are ignored, but that cotton strength has fallen to a point where cotton interests can get no bill at all through the House without the support of a new-style coalition. In 1973 the Agriculture congressmen, especially the cotton congressmen, found that all possible farm bill coalitions were either too weak to win or required the inclusion of groups whose goals were incompatible with their own. The bill finally passed the House solely because groups that had lost badly in the final House version (i.e., labor and cotton) anticipated (correctly) that logrolling in the conference committee could bail them out of their difficulties.

The Senate, of course, is never reapportioned, hence very much the same Senate considered the farm bill in 1973 as in 1970. And the bill worked its way through the Senate in 1973 with even less conflict and controversy than in 1970. The bill was originally expected to encounter considerable trouble from consumer groups that doubted the wisdom of farm subsidies when agricultural prices were soaring, especially farm subsidies basically designed to lower production. But this land mine of opposition was side-stepped by a fundamental change in the subsidy mechanism, the introduction of what was euphemistically called the "target price" system. Under the old system farmers were paid to leave land fallow, in order to keep production low enough to guarantee adequate prices. But under the "target price" system the effort is not to restrict production but to directly compensate farmers for income lost due to low prices if overproduction occurs. If the market price falls below the "target" (or guaranteed) price, the USDA makes up the difference between the two prices.

This change appeased consumer groups as well as the administration, assuring both that low production would not be encouraged and that no needless subsidies would be paid to farmers to maintain prices already too high.

The bill sailed through the Senate, passing by a large 78–9 margin. The only controversy concerned a set of provisions affecting milk prices; the fundamental structure of the bill was uncontroversial.

In the House, however, the uncertainty began in committee and continued up to the final vote. While the bill was on the House floor two separate coalitions formed in support of it, and both then collapsed. The usual logrolling process of favor trading between interests was replaced by a bizarre *reverse* logrolling process—the somewhat vengeful inclusion of provisions *un*favorable to other interests—which led to the creation of a bill that actually threatened to do more harm than good to all the groups interested in it.

Coalition number one resembled the coalition that had narrowly passed the Farm Bill in 1970—an alliance between cotton and other farm interests, plus administration supporters and fiscal conservatives. To attract administration support, the cotton leadership would have to write a less extravagant bill than they would have liked—they would have to delete an escalator clause providing for increases in payment levels as farm production costs rose. But if this coalition prevailed, it would enable the (conservative) committee leadership to pass a bill that included no major gestures toward labor or the northern liberals.

The decline in the strength of this coalition since 1970 was clearly apparent in the first major floor vote. It was no longer a majority. The administration was supposed to join the cotton leadership in defeating liberal and nonfarm efforts to clamp an effective $20,000 lid on subsidies, aimed especially at cotton subsidies, but administration support was not enough; the subsidy amendment passed easily, 246–163, despite the opposition of Minority Leader Ford (as well as Speaker Carl Albert, Poage, and Sisk). For the first time, an agriculture bill had been significantly rewritten on the floor, by precisely those consumer and nonfarm interests which have no strength whatever on the committee.

The cotton forces also lost in their effort to maintain a $10-million subsidy for Cotton Incorporated, a quasi promotion and research firm. These two major defeats for the committee-administration coalition showed that this alliance had lost so much strength that it was now too weak to win, and the agreements the coalition was premised upon were canceled: cotton would no longer aid in the deletion of the escalator clause. Poage was forced to look elsewhere for allies.

Action on the bill was delayed for five days while Poage struggled to construct a new majority alliance. He finally succeeded: coalition number two was to consist of the farm forces plus the labor-liberals. If the labor-liberals would put the loopholes back into the $20,000 subsidy limit, restore the Cotton Incorporated subsidy, and support the bill with an escalator clause, then the cotton forces would see to it that labor would get a bill otherwise to its liking. Specifically, there would be no ban on food stamps to strikers; certain other restrictions on food stamp eligibility would be eased; and jurisdiction over the Occupational Safety and Health Act would remain with the Department of Labor instead of being transferred to the Department of Agriculture (as many tobacco congressmen desired).

Had this coalition held together, it would certainly have been big enough to carry the day. But it required cooperative action by a group so diverse—and so unaccustomed to mutual cooperation—that it eventually fell apart, amid remarkable chaos on the House floor.

As the July 16 session opened, the new coalition seemed to be holding up well. The liberals rescinded their anticotton amendments, restoring the payment limit loopholes and the Cotton Incorporated subsidy by a vote of 207–190. (Northern Democrats supported the move by a margin of 80–64.) In exchange, the cotton interests helped defeat the Labor Department jurisdiction transfer, which was deleted by a vote of 221–177, with southern Democrats voting in favor by 43–37. The southerners also contributed to the easy passage of liberalized food stamp requirements.

But the labor-cotton coalition collapsed on July 19, when cotton failed to deliver enough southern votes to defeat the ban on food stamps to strikers. The antistriker amendment, offered by William Dickinson (R., Ala.), carried by 212–203, with southern Democrats supporting it by 49–30. In retaliation, the labor-liberal northerners switched back to their original stand against the cotton subsidies, again closing the loopholes in the $20,000 limit and cutting off the Cotton Incorporated subsidy. This coalition, too, had failed, torn apart by its own centrifugal force.

This left the entire bill a shambles; there remained no single group that supported its final form. Administration supporters were bitter over the escalator clause and the administration threatened a veto. The cotton interests were bitter over the subsidy limits and wondered out loud if no bill at all might be better. And, of course, labor was particularly bitter over the food-stamps-to-strikers ban. Had these groups felt that the bill would not be significantly altered in conference it could never have passed the House (which it did, by a narrow 226–182). A rare and remarkable breakdown in the logrolling process had taken place.

Logrolling had not broken down in the Senate, of course. The Senate bill was vastly better for both labor and cotton than the House version—it contained no ban on food stamps for strikers and no $20,000 subsidy limit. Of the 111 differences between the Senate and House bills, 110 were resolved in conference, including retention of the Senate's provision for a $20,000 limit on annual subsidy payments to individual farmers (complete with loopholes). The undecided provision was the bar on food stamps for strikers and their families, a provision that had squeaked into the House bill by a narrow margin, but was not included in the Senate version.

With the prohibition on food stamps for strikers still dangling, the farm bill was stymied. In the Senate, Jesse Helms (R., N.C.) introduced an amendment that would have added the provision to the Senate bill, thereby placing the Senate and House bills in agreement. Acceptance of such an amendment would have jeopardized passage of the farm bill in both the Senate and the House, since many liberal Democrats were opposed to such an amendment. Senator Humphrey moved to kill the Helms amendment and the Senate agreed 58–34. The Senate then approved the farm bill 85–7.

In the House, only a shrewd parliamentary move by Chairman Poage saved the legislation. Representative William Dickinson planned to propose that the House insist on its amendment barring food stamps to strikers. This would have again placed the Senate and House bills at odds with each other. Before Dickinson had a chance to make his move, Poage moved to accept the Senate version along with an essentially meaningless amendment asking that farmers be urged to produce as much as possible. For the sake of saving the farm bill, the House supported by a 349–54 vote a parliamentary maneuver which guaranteed that Poage's motion would not be amended (by the Dickinson amendment, for example), and then proceeded to vote in favor of Poage's motion to accept the Senate version of the bill 252–151.

Nonetheless, this episode carries an ominous lesson for the farm-belt coalition and for the agriculture committees. The chaos in the House was due to the inability of an unrepresentative committee to write a representative bill, plus the need for the cotton interests to forage ever more widely for allies as their own numbers diminished. The same dynamics are also at work in the more pro-farmer Senate; its Agriculture Committee is only somewhat more representative of the whole spectrum of interests covered by agriculture bills than is the House committee, meaning that floor-amended Agriculture bills may become a likelihood in the Senate as well as the House; and urbanization is slowly transforming several formerly reliable farm states into urban-union-consumer profile states, which in time will force the construction of the same precarious coalition in the Senate as in the House if farm bills are to continue to pass.

The success of the farm committees' efforts to protect their jurisdictional turf and defend their bills on the floor will in future depend in part on their ability to convince their colleagues that they will react responsibly to the needs of their heretofore neglected constituencies among the poor and hungry.

10

The Forgotten Constituency: The Agriculture Committees and the Poor*

The Agriculture committees, with among the most ideologically conservative memberships in Congress, control major food relief programs affecting the health and welfare of poor people in the United States and abroad. The food stamp, commodity distribution, and school lunch programs† help relieve malnutrition domestically; the Food for Peace program (Public Law 480) provides hunger relief abroad. Each of these programs was sold to Congress by the farm committees as humanitarian efforts that

---

* This chapter was researched and written in 1972 and does not take into account all the changes in the membership of the farm committees and the structuring of the food programs since that time.

† The school lunch program is under the jurisdiction of the Committee on Education and Labor in the House and the Committee on Agriculture and Forestry in the Senate.

would also benefit domestic farmers. In practice, however, given the committees' hostility to welfare and their concern for producers' interests, humanitarian goals have often been subordinated to economic ones. The committees have thus reflected the interests of their most organized and powerful rural constituents, the wealthier producers who send their representatives to Washington to keep food prices up. Although the poor are numerically large in many of those rural districts, they are in most cases politically impotent. What influence the poor have is found in the Senate committee, where a greater diversity of interests is represented, with Senators Humphrey, McGovern, and Clark acting as spokesmen for the rural poor when the food programs are before the committee.

The farm committees' reluctance to increase aid to the hungry poor, even after malnutrition in rural America had become a national scandal, was a strategic blunder. The resentment it generated among urban, labor, and liberal congressmen and the national media helped turn public opinion against the farm programs. By 1970 it had stimulated efforts among liberals and even some conservative congressmen to reduce the power of the farm committees and retaliate against their bills on the floor. While the committees' handling of the food stamp program attracted the most criticism, the same conflicts in values and mission afflicted the committee's stewardship of the Food for Peace program.

For many years, P.L. 480 was the nation's largest nonmilitary foreign aid program. It grew out of the farm surplus crisis after the Korean war, when public confidence in agricultural policy waned as a deluge of unsalable wheat descended on the market. The government was even forced to convert some of the ships returning from Korea into seagoing silos to provide emergency storage capacity for grain. As the mounting surplus reached the proportions of a national scandal, and farm prices declined, urban congressmen became insistent that the amount of national resources committed to agriculture be reduced.

Fearful of the reforms this pressure might bring, the farm

committees looked for relief to an expanded program of subsidized disposals of agricultural surpluses overseas. The origins of P.L. 480 helped to determine its subsequent character. First, while its nominal goals were mixed—economic development, hunger relief, trade expansion—it was essentially special interest legislation designed to succor the failing farm economy. The policy of maximizing agricultural exports has often conflicted with the needs of developing nations and of United States foreign policy, but the conflicts have been resolved with great consistency. Domestic agricultural interests have invariably prevailed over those of foreign policy and foreign aid.

P.L. 480 was conceived by most observers as a temporary expedient to meet a transitory domestic need. Surpluses were not expected to continue. The American Farm Bureau Federation, a reluctant sponsor of P.L. 480, explicitly warned that it opposed the long-term use of foreign aid programs "as a means of unloading farm surpluses created by unwise domestic policies." But contrary to expectations, surpluses increased hand in hand with P.L. 480 exports ($10 billion worth between 1954 and 1960), until in 1960 grain and dairy surpluses had reached record levels.

In 1954 Food for Peace was begun with $1 billion for three years; six years later it was receiving $2 billion for a single year. By the time of the Kennedy administration, surplus disposal had become the keystone of domestic farm policy. Stopping it then would have required an economic readjustment in agriculture far more severe for millions of farmers than they would have had to make without it in 1954.

P.L. 480 in its first six years was an effective guardian of the status quo in domestic agriculture. With it as a safety valve, price supports in some cases had increased, bringing the program full circle. It had begun as a program to relieve the surplus and had now become a justification for expanding it with greater production incentives. By 1961, P.L. 480 had become the major foreign market outlet for wheat, feed grain, rice, cotton, and tobacco.

The dominance of rural southerners on congressional farm

committees helps to explain this result, for the South, more than other regions, has been dependent on P.L. 480's economic benefits. Its major crops—tobacco, cotton, and (in Louisiana and Mississippi) rice—have suffered from overproduction and increasing competition in foreign markets since the 1950s.

The success of the farm bloc in holding Food for Peace in bondage to domestic economic interests was not built on southern solidarity and seniority alone. As usual, the farm committees protected their interests by making P.L. 480 legislation a grab bag with benefits for a wide range of other interests. For example, 50 percent of all Food for Peace tonnage is required by law to move on American flagships. With freight rates per ton two to three times the rate of foreign competitors, the American merchant marine would not stay afloat without Food for Peace shipments. Although the farm committees are not directly responsible for this cargo preference law, they have used it to win political support from urban states with strong maritime interests, such as Massachusetts. Other sectors of American business also benefit from Food for Peace, including banks with foreign branches in which foreign currency received from P.L. 480 sales is sometimes deposited; and corporations such as Sears, Roebuck and Merck Chemical Company, which have received low-interest loans from these same foreign currency funds to expand their operations abroad. The Food for Peace Act of 1966 contained a stipulation that made "a friendly atmosphere for U.S. capital" a condition for receiving food aid.

The primary beneficiaries of Food for Peace remain domestic agricultural interests, however. In serving these interests the Agriculture committees have often displayed a tunnel vision that gives them an image of selfish parochialism among internationalists concerned with foreign economic development. For example, the committees required nations receiving food aid to agree not to export agricultural products that are in surplus in the United States and not to expand production of crops that compete with American agricultural exports. These product restrictions imposed a heavy burden on efforts to expand farm production in developing nations, for they fell most heavily on cotton, wheat, tobacco, and rice—all crops relied on by developing economies to earn foreign exchange and meet rising food demands. Most of these restrictions were dropped in the late 1960s, when Congress began to phase out P.L. 480 "concessional" sales (sales for foreign currency that was virtually worthless to the United States).

Congressman Poage was particularly adept at using the product restrictions to serve special interests while wrapping them in a mantle of benevolence. For example, in the name of their hungry peasants he attacked India and Egypt for exporting cotton. Complaining that it was inhumane for these nations to divert food crop acreage to cotton production, he sponsored Section 103 (i) of the 1966 Food for Freedom bill—which required the conversion of nonfood crop (i.e., cotton) acreage to food production as a condition of future aid. The fact that cotton is a major earner of foreign exchange for these countries and that any losses would increase their dependence on U. S. dollar aid was overlooked. The local bias of Poage's P.L. 480 policy making was sharply revealed when a witness pointed out that India produced an inferior short staple cotton which did not ordinarily compete with U. S. exports. What the witness did not know was that while relatively little of the inferior cotton is produced in the United States, what there is comes primarily from Texas; predictably, Bob Poage was not persuaded by his argument.

In the past, P.L. 480 came alive only when the Department of Agriculture discovered that it had a surplus and rushed eagerly to unload it. Making food aid dependent on the vagaries of U. S. production has had distressing consequences for malnourished people in recipient countries. For example, in 1959, when an estimated 35 million people receiving assistance from food relief programs were suddenly deprived of milk because the surplus of nonfat dry milk suddenly ended, the Department of Agriculture answered an inquiry from the United Nations Food and Agriculture Office by noting that "the program has always been vulnerable to substantial reductions or temporary interruptions, since it is a residual program, dependent on a condition external to itself. This condition is the supply-demand relationship for non-fat dry milk in the U. S. at support price levels."

The committee's indifference to public opinion beyond the farm sector reached a peak when tobacco was made a Food for Peace staple. P.L. 480 funds have even been used to subsidize tobacco advertising overseas. At the same time the U. S. Surgeon General was warning the American public against the cancer hazard of smoking, the Department of Agriculture was helping to sponsor *World of Pleasure*, a tobacco promotion film, to be shown in Egypt. The film showed tableaux of dreamy young tourists smoking filter kings while they admired the Pyramids, with the following dialogue: "Tobacco is a part of the lives of millions of people throughout the world . . . the pure joy part."

For P.L. 480 to be useful as a development resource, the country receiving aid needs an alert government with a balanced economic plan that coordinates food aid with a development strategy. In some countries—India, for example—P.L. 480 has been helpful, but generally an assessment of P.L. 480 as a development tool reveals a succession of paradoxes. For every positive action that advances a nation's economic welfare, there is the possibility of a negative reaction that might retard it. Food donations by voluntary agencies under P.L. 480 might have the quantity to fill empty stomachs but lack the protein to advance health; food imports might relieve inflationary pressure on the food price in the recipient country but discourage farm production by reducing prices; agricultural progress was a condition of aid but investment in crops that competed with U. S. exports was restricted; family feeding through food donations gave temporary relief to hunger but reduced the incentives for self-help in community development.

Among economists and agronomists who have weighed these paradoxes in light of P.L. 480's twenty-year-history, the dominant view of its utility as a development resource is negative.

Most would agree with Theodore W. Schultz that one of the major obstacles in the way of the United States' doing more to assist poor countries was the belief that U. S. farm surpluses were a powerful resource for economic growth in the underdeveloped countries that receive them. Others have charged that Food for Peace from 1954 to 1966 became a form of food imperialism that depressed foreign markets, discouraged local farmers, and made permanent relief clients of its recipients.

When farm surpluses began to diminish under the production restrictions imposed by Secretary of Agriculture Orville Freeman in the early 1960s, the farm committees began to shift P.L. 480 from a giveaway to a cash-on-delivery basis. Now that P.L. 480 was less important for farm profits, they began to regard it as another foreign aid program and hardened its terms. Relatively little consideration was given to the impact of this change on the economic development plans of dollar-starved recipients.

In their handling of the Food for Peace program, the committees, especially the House Committee on Agriculture, again displayed the traits which suggested that they were becoming increasingly isolated and parochial in their points of view—a dangerous trend in a Congress that was becoming more urban and liberal in the sixties. The lack of sensitivity to the needs of the poor, the somewhat cynical use of economic development rhetoric to mask service to narrow agricultural interests, the indifference to public opinion on such issues as tobacco and malnutrition—these biases the committee could indulge with relative impunity on the issue of surplus disposal overseas. The program was obscure as well as complex, and the recipients—the hungry poor in foreign lands—had no lobby to defend their interests. When the committees displayed these same attitudes toward feeding the hungry poor in the United States, the result was very different. The backlash against the committees not only embarrassed the committees but threatened the farm bill as well.

Millions of Americans, including most of official Washington, were surprised and shocked when the first indications of the extent and seriousness of hunger and malnutrition in the United States began to emerge in the late 1960s. Studies conducted by various private groups, reports by doctors working with the poor, and the national nutrition survey conducted by the Department of Health, Education and Welfare under a December 1967 congressional authorization were in accord: millions of Americans suffered from chronic hunger and malnutrition. The reports further chronicled the results in the form of infant deaths, permanent and irreversible brain damage in infants, retarded growth and learning rates, increased vulnerability to diseases which could prove fatal because of inadequate resistance, and various other conditions stemming from nutritional deficiencies, such as apathy and alienation.

A team of physicians that conducted a field trip to rural Mississippi under the auspices of the Field Foundation graphically depicted the results of nutritional deficiencies in terms of serious skin, ear, and eye diseases; prevalent bacterial and parasitic diseases and severe anemia resulting in loss of energy and ability to live a normal life; and severe malnutrition injuring muscles, bones, and skin, and causing listlessness and exhaustion. The National Nutrition Survey reported that poor children were six months to two and a half years behind their peers in physical development and that more than one-third suffered from enervating anemia and shortages of vitamins A and C. *Their Daily Bread*, a study of the National School Lunch Program, contributed reports from teachers across the nation who spoke of children coming to school without breakfast and often without dinner the night before, too hungry to pay attention and learn, feeling sick and having to return home. Other evidence of the effects of malnutrition began to appear: the infant mortality rate in the United States is higher than in any of the Western European countries; a child born to poor parents in the United States is twice as likely to die before the age of one as a child born to middle-class parents.

The medical testimony that nutritional deficiencies cause permanent brain damage—coupled with evidence that while only 5 percent of children are born mentally retarded, 11 percent are retarded at the age of 12—and reports that inadequate nutrition may stunt physical growth and leave people weak and without energy to learn or work, raised the possibility that billions of dollars were being wasted on education and job training because these programs provided help that arrived too late. Attention began to focus on the congressional Agriculture committees, which have jurisdiction over commodity distribution and food stamps—the general family assistance programs—and the national school lunch program. It soon became apparent that these programs, like Food for Peace, had been designed primarily to aid the farmer and only incidentally to feed the hungry. It became apparent too that the congressional committees and the Agriculture Department still viewed them from much the same perspective.

Food relief was first launched during the depression of the early 1930s, when millions of Americans stood in bread lines while farmers slaughtered their pigs and burned their produce because of low prices. President Roosevelt first authorized the direct distribution of surplus food to the poor on relief in 1934. In 1935 the program was strengthened by Section 32 of the Agriculture Adjustment Act, which gave the Department of Agriculture 30 percent of customs receipts to be used to boost farm prices, including the purchase of surplus food to feed the poor. By 1939 the program was helping to feed 13 million Americans. In that year the Department of Agriculture instituted a complicated food stamp program designed to help the farmer by allowing the poor to buy, in the market place, products that were overproduced (and only those products). At its peak, in 1941, the stamp program had 4 million participants.

These programs were discontinued when World War II created jobs for the unemployed and brought prosperity to the farmer. After the war, the overproduction crisis returned as mechanization, improved seeds and fertilizers, returning manpower, and decreasing demand resulted in food surpluses once again. In 1946,

Congress responded to the farmers' needs with the National School Lunch Act—which provided for the distribution of surplus foods to schools as well as subsidies for all lunches served—and in 1949 it voted additional authorization for USDA to purchase surplus commodities for the poor and for schools. After many unsuccessful congressional attempts to institute a food stamp program, a pilot program was authorized in 1959 and was ordered into operation by President Kennedy during his first month in office. Congress provided for a regular program in 1964.

Thus three major programs to alleviate hunger were in existence when malnutrition began to attract national attention. Clearly, the programs were shockingly inadequate.

Statistics outlined the situation. Current estimates of the number of persons needing some amount of food aid range from 12 to 13 million to 26 million. Yet in 1967 only 5.5 million were participating at all in either of the general assistance programs—2 million in the food stamp program and 3.5 million in the direct distribution program. The child nutrition program was equally inadequate. Of 50 million public school children in the United States, only 18 million participated in the national school lunch program; at least 4 million poor children from families with less than $2,000 annual income were denied the free or reduced-price lunch to which they were entitled.

Investigations by citizens' committees and by Congress revealed that these programs suffered from the congressional farm committees' view that they were to aid the farmers first, as a means of surplus food disposal, and to feed the hungry second. Review of the commodity distribution program indicated that neither these committees nor the Department of Agriculture was interested in insuring the nutritional adequacy of the program. When the Senate Select Committee on Nutrition and Human Need held hearings on hunger in September 1971, it was the first time a congressional committee had ever evaluated the food programs in terms of the needs of the poor. Both the committees and the department conceded that the programs existed primarily to protect the price levels of overproduced products. Robert Choate, a prominent member of the antihunger coalition who at one point worked within the Nixon administration, testified that commodities were selected for distribution as the result of political decisions, "a decision made by people who listen to the screams of orange producers or apricot producers or bean producers." The chance that a combination of products from the loudest screaming producers would provide a well balanced diet was obviously minimal. For years committee members had jealously overseen the use of Section 32 funds, insisting that they be saved in order to be available for a possible overproduction "emergency," instead of being used to improve the commodity distribution program for the hungry. As a result, because of a $300 million maximum carryover provision, over $1.25 billion available for use in the program had been returned to the Treasury by the Department of Agriculture.

The attitude of both the committees and the Agriculture Department was further revealed in Agriculture Secretary Benson's reply to Senator Cooper of Kentucky in 1959, when the senator discovered that large amounts of cooking oil were stored in government tanks and asked why they could not be distributed to the hungry poor in Appalachia. Benson said that government policy gave first priority to overseas sales for dollars, second to Food for Peace sales with payment in foreign currencies, and last priority to distribution to the poor. Similarly, when the White House Conference on Hunger and Malnutrition recommended in 1969 that the food stamp and commodity distribution programs be transferred out of the Department of Agriculture, the administration, while agreeing with respect to the food stamp program, stated that the primary function of the commodity program was to "balance the agricultural economy" and that it served "a different constituency than that concerned with health and nutrition."

The failure of the food aid programs in the sixties reflected the committees' pro-producer, antiwelfare bias. When the food stamp bill was introduced in committee in 1964, it was sold with the promise that it would provide more benefits to the farmers than the commodity programs. Committee oversight of the food programs, such as it was, stressed the need to stop alleged cheating by food recipients, not evaluation of the programs' adequacy in meeting the needs of the poor. The food stamp hearings were characterized as "a snipe hunt for the secretly wealthy poor who pick up their stamps in a Cadillac and eat their purchases before a color TV."

Many of the deficiencies of the national school lunch program and the other child nutrition programs may also be attributed, at least in part, to the influence of the congressional committees. Up to 1967 the program had received congressional examination chiefly from the Appropriations subcommittees, which were determinedly opposed to more aid for poor children on principle and were determined to keep the cash outlays of the program to a minimum. The committee never investigated the program to discover whether funds were adequate to allow schools to meet the act's requirement of providing free or reduced price lunches for the needy. Although the cost of food for a school lunch had doubled since 1946, the average rate of federal reimbursement for each lunch served remained the same, 4.5 cents. In 1962 the National School Lunch Act was amended to authorize $10 million a year in extra funds to assist schools serving predominantly poor children to serve more free or reduced-price lunches. Despite the authorization, however, the committees did not appropriate any funds for this purpose until 1966, when they granted $2 million only because Senator Philip Hart (D., Mich.) threatened a floor fight against the farm appropriations if they refused. As with the commodity distribution program, the school lunch foods available are those in oversupply. Thus schools might one year receive large amounts of beef and the next year receive none but instead be inundated with ripe olives. This situation did not disturb the Agriculture committees or motivate them to try to insure a more dependable supply of commodities, because they were interested in the program mainly as an avenue for the disposal of surplus agricultural products. Representative Whitten said, during consideration of the 1959 budget: "I am now of the opinion that the only way we can get the Department to move fast enough to protect farm prices and the income of the farmer is once again to transfer Section 32 funds to the school lunch program so that they will have to use them." Senator Ellender, discussing the Special Milk Program (which subsidizes the cost of an extra half-pint of milk sold to children at reduced prices) with a lobbyist for the National Milk Producers association, said at a hearing in 1966, "The Special Milk Program was for the producer, rather than a program to assist children."

The committees' view of the food programs has colored their administration by the Department of Agriculture. Many Department officials have background similar to that of members of the farm committees and share their concept of the Department's mission: to further the interests of the large commercial farmers and arbitrate between competing agribusiness interests. The similarity of views also reflects the frequent interchange of personnel between committee staff and the Department. Pressured by the committees and by lobbyists for various commodity interests, agriculture officials had little incentive to respond to the needs of the poor, especially when there were no lobbies on the scene to advocate their views.

More than any other department, Agriculture is honeycombed with congressional patronage, a legacy of the New Deal era when it became the employer of last resort for thousands of displaced farmers with good connections. Congressional patronage control reached its ultimate in the cotton subsidy program, for cotton subsidy administrators could, by law, be hired without regard for civil service regulations. For these reasons, the average Department official is naturally inclined to accept the values of the farm committees. For example, until 1964 the Department opposed the food stamp program. For many years its testimony against food stamps as opposed to commodity distribution was instrumental in preventing the program from being established. Although Secretary Freeman ended direct departmental opposition, funding requests for food stamp programs were usually based on Department estimates of need; the committees, somewhat disingenuously to be sure, have often defended themselves against charges of inadequate funding by asserting that they supplied what the Agriculture Department requested.

Even if the Department had been solidly behind the progressive food programs, the farm committees would not have allowed them to implement them. Usually the committee members need not take any direct action; the knowledge of their presence and oversight is sufficient. When Freeman finally recognized the extent of the hunger problem in the late 1960s, he still felt unable to take the actions to liberalize the programs that were legally within his power. Realizing it would anger his committees, he was reluctant to endanger the Department's future legislative and funding plans. For example, unless Congress specifically legislates another use for them, Section 32 funds are legally available for use at the secretary's discretion. The Department decides what commodities will be purchased and then distributed through the school lunch and direct distribution programs. Freeman refused to use the Section 32 funds to improve the nutritional quality of those programs or to purchase food for emergency relief, although Department officials now admit that virtually all crops can legally be bought with the funds. As Freeman himself was to admit later, he also had the power to issue free food stamps and, by declaring an emergency, to allow surplus commodities to be distributed in counties where thousands could not afford food stamps—actions which hunger fighters had been imploring him to take. Although the committees could not have stopped Freeman from issuing free food stamps, Freeman was fearful that such defiance would lead the committees to kill the program. For example, when Chairman Poage was holding up an extension of the food stamp program in 1968 at a time when Freeman's total budget was under consideration, he pleaded with the food-aid reformers not to press him publicly for reforms until the Department's appropriations bill and the food stamp extension bill had passed Congress.

The views of the Agriculture committees have also influenced the organizational structure and bureaucratic routines of the Department. According to Rodney Leonard, administrator of the food programs under Freeman, because of the committees' emphasis on stopping cheating and waste in the hunger programs, the agency developed procedures that were more suited to providing the Appropriations committees with a mechanical accounting than to informing Congress whether the programs were adequately feeding the poor. Appropriations subcommittee hearings are replete with the figures on how much money is spent for food programs, how it was spent, and the measures taken to guard against fraud, but devoid of information about the adequacy of funds, how great the need is, and whether all who need it are reached by the program. Because the Department is asked to account for its activities in only these limited terms, it is not accustomed to and has not measured programs in terms of human values.

A case in point is the Department's manual of regulations for storage of free food in county warehouses. Sixty pages of regulations instruct local officials in protecting the food from rats, insects, heat, and moisture. *Not one* regulation instructs local officials to locate warehouses near public transportation or in the vicinity of rural ghettos for the convenience of the poor. This disparity exists not because Congress requires it—these regulations are discretionary within the agency—nor because officials delight in inconveniencing the rural poor. It exists because the Department of Agriculture is accustomed to storing food, not to feeding hungry people. In many southern counties food programs are withdrawn, not because the poor have ceased to be hungry, but because the counties lack warehouses that can pass the rigid storage regulations. Other hunger counties (as designated by *Hunger, USA*) are sprinkled with antiseptic warehouses that are waterproof and ratproof but inaccessible to the hungry people eligible to consume their contents.

The tight rein the Agriculture committees kept on the food programs continued into the late 1960s, when the hunger problem was beginning to attract attention. Jamie Whitten, chairman of the House Appropriations Subcommittee on Agriculture, angrily ordered Freeman not to issue free food stamps and not to allow both food stamps and the commodity program in the same county, to provide food for the many who could not afford stamps, when Freeman was considering both moves to appease those who were bombarding him with demands to do something about the situation in 1968. Similarly, when a bill authorizing $10 million of funds for emergency hunger and medical aid to the worst of the cases revealed by early hunger investigators came before the House Agriculture Committee in 1967, it was killed by a vote of 20 to 7.

The bitterness and duration of this opposition to providing those in the lowest income bracket with free stamps (instead of charging the 50 cents per person in the food stamp schedule) attests to the fact that these farm congressmen have opposed social welfare legislation for genuine ideological reasons. The increase in cost that free stamps would represent was too small to justify such opposition; it can be explained only in terms of the social views of the most powerful committee members. For insight into the mind of the House Agriculture Committee, this exchange recorded at a food stamp hearing is revealing. Chairman Poage was presiding. Representative William Green (D., Pa.), the lead-off witness, is urging consideration of free food stamps:

> THE CHAIRMAN: "I know there is considerable effort under way now to say that we will not require anything from these families.
>
> Well, they have been spending something for food. Where it came from is more or less immaterial from the standpoint of their spending something for food. They have been spending something for food or they would not

be here. We see no reason why they can't continue spending something for food, although the Food Stamp Program will greatly increase their variety and desirability and the nutritional value of the food they get.

It seems to me, at the least, that, if we simply give a family spending, let us say, $30 a month for food, a really small amount, but if they have been spending that much and we then turn around and give them all the food with no requirement of expenditure, in too many cases, the $30, to be really frank about it, will go for liquor, or for pot, or for those sorts of things. How are you going to keep it from going that way if you make it 100 percent a giveaway? . . .

. . . It is rather fundamental, as to whether we keep our country on a profit economy, or whether we keep it on a socialistic economy. I think that we can, in a private enterprise economy, care for the needy people, and I think that we should care for the needy people, but I do not think that we have to break down all of the elements of private property and capitalistic economy in order to do it."

MR. GREEN: "I do not think I am suggesting that, Mr. Chairman."

THE CHAIRMAN: "Well, I think when you say you do not care whether anybody pays or whether they get it without doing anything, if I understand the philosophy of socialism, that is all there is to it, that 'regardless of what you contribute, you will be cared for!' "

MR. GREEN: "No, I did not say we were going to take [care of] people regardless of their initiative and regardless of many, many other factors and do everything for them completely. What I said was—what I think I said was this: That I, frankly, when it comes to a matter of food and nutrition, there is a whole generation of young people in our city that has no chance at all; they did not even have good diets and have no way of getting them. Frankly, I think that food and nourishment is so basic that I am certainly willing to go that far, to give any child that needs it all the nutritious food that he needs so that he will have the opportunity to develop himself."

THE CHAIRMAN: "You can't get an argument with any member of this Committee on that point. We will all agree, I am sure, that we want to help every child who needs nutritious food. We want him to have it.

The only question is, as I see it: How will you provide that; whether you will provide it in a manner that will maintain our economic system or whether you simply ignore our economic system for a large part of a substantial portion of our people, let us say, because it is going to grow wider and wider, and obviously, our own figures point out that nearly one-half of the welfare money goes for rent and, obviously, you are going to provide housing for these people as well as food, and, certainly, you are not going to have them going on the streets naked, and you are going to provide clothing as well as food and shelter. You are going to provide all, and we have no disagreement there. They are going to provide all of the essential elements. It is not simply food. They are going to provide all of thise [sic] essential elements.

The question is whether we provide it on the socialistic basis where, as I say, it makes no difference what you contribute, or whether we provide it on the capitalistic basis of contributing at least what you can. . . ."

Chairman Poage went on to say that, to escape the taint of socialism, the poor should pay some money for food stamps, even if they had to steal to get it. In the doublethink of the House Agriculture Committee, as the journalist Nick Kotz has observed, feeding hungry children is socialism, but giving subsidies to wealthy farmers is capitalistic virtue.

This strong conservative antiwelfare attitude characterizes a majority of the members of the Agriculture committees to this day. They feel that their programs should not in any way resemble welfare programs. Behind this attitude lies the familiar belief that those who are suffering from poverty-related malnutrition and hunger are poor because they are too lazy and indifferent to work; that they will never look for work if the government helps them; that many of the malnourished and hungry are so because of ignorance of good nutrition and by personal preference, choosing to spend their money on television sets and luxurious automobiles; that children go hungry because of parental neglect and the federal government should not assume the parent's responsibility; that giving people "something for nothing" will destroy their character.

Exemplifying this attitude was Missouri Congressman Paul Jones' statement at food stamp hearings in 1968: "The thing is, as Mr. Poage said this morning, there are people like that big buck down at the city who said that he went to the so-called Resurrection City to 'get away from that shovel.' Well, I am getting tired of that, myself." Similarly, in 1969, when Nixon's budget for food aid was under consideration, Whitten told George McGovern that "Nigras won't work" if you give them free food, and that McGovern was encouraging a revolution by trying to get free food stamps for the very poor.

Furthermore, in the view of many observers, the southern members of the committees were concerned about the social implications of substantial food aid in the Deep South. By the mid-1960s the blacks in the South had become both an economic superfluity and a political threat; many whites in the area spoke of outmigration as the only solution to the problem. The southern-dominated Agriculture committees rightfully feared that an adequately and impartially administered food program would not only upset the traditional southern social structure, with submissive blacks dependent upon the good will of whites, but would also stem the tide of outmigration.

Despite the resistance of the agricultural committees, the food programs were greatly expanded and improved between 1969 and 1972. A small group of citizens, led by the Citizens' Board of Inquiry into Hunger and Malnutrition (funded by the Field

Foundation); John Kramer, executive director of the National Council on Hunger and Malnutrition; Robert Choate, an independent hunger lobbyist; and Nick Kotz, formed a coalition with liberal and moderate congressmen that made hunger a major national concern and orchestrated sufficient political power to bypass some of the agricultural committees' roadblocks.

The coalition decided that favorable Senate action could best be obtained through a new Senate Select Committee that would constantly focus attention on the problem of hunger and the inadequate attempts to deal with it. Realizing that the Senate Agriculture Committee would regard the move as an attempt to usurp its control over food aid programs and that the Senate, which usually stands together to protect its established institutions, would very possibly defeat the resolution to establish the committee, the reformers decided that members of the Agriculture Committee should lead the fight, so that Ellender could not assert that the purpose of the resolution was to bypass his committee. Senators McGovern, Mondale, Hatfield, and Boggs led the effort, signing up as many co-sponsors as possible for a resolution which had been carefully worded to escape the jurisdiction of the Agriculture and Rules committees. The day after the Citizens' Board of Inquiry released *Hunger, USA*, McGovern, holding a copy of the report, introduced the resolution, which was by then co-sponsored by thirty-eight other senators, and it passed easily.

In the House, the reformers decided that the best way to form a base for legislative action would be to have the liberal Education and Labor Committee consider the hunger issue, but they were fearful that Committee Chairman Carl Perkins would not want to challenge Poage. Choate, however, formulated a plan to pressure Perkins to act. He enlisted the aid of Congressmen Foley and Goodell, who convinced most of the members of Perkins' committee and several from Poage's to request Education and Labor to hold hearings. These congressmen held a press conference to urge that action be taken, and Perkins finally agreed to hold hearings.

By keeping a close watch over hunger legislation, personally urging its adoption at every step of the process, and stimulating the interest and enlisting the aid of congressmen at critical points, the early reformers eventually involved most liberal and moderate congressmen in an attempt to overcome the opposition of the more conservative members of the Agriculture committees to food aid legislation. In this way the coalition did win certain victories in 1968: the commodity distribution program was improved; Congress freed $43 million of Section 32 funds to provide free or reduced price lunches for poor children, and the new Senate committee was formed to explore the hunger issue.

Although there were significant steps forward during the Johnson administration, the major legislation improving the food programs was not passed until after President Nixon took office.

The story of the genesis of the most important legislation in 1970–71 is useful in assessing the performance of the Agriculture committees in dealing with the hunger problem.

Immediately after Nixon took office, the new Senate Select Committee focused attention on the preliminary results of the National Nutrition Survey that had just been released. These provided the scientific proof of hunger and malnutrition that the skeptical had demanded.

The Select Committee planned to increase the pressure for food stamp reform by keeping a constant spotlight on the issue—calling a wide range of expert witnesses, taking further field trips, and enlarging the anti-hunger coalition within Congress. They were aided in the latter effort by Senator Hollings of South Carolina, who broke tradition by testifying before the Select Committee that there was, indeed, hunger in the South. Following his lead, other southern senators such as Talmadge, Cook, and Spong conducted hunger tours in their states and on their return called for immediate food aid reform. McGovern and Javits encouraged further field trips. As well as focusing the attention of the public and the press on the conditions they viewed, the trips convinced those who took them of the need for food aid reform. Even Senator Ellender advocated better programs after his trip to Florida.

Clifford Hardin, the new Secretary of Agriculture, was also an eager advocate of reform. He realized that if he were not more successful in dealing with the hunger problem than Freeman, it could be his political ruin. In addition, many representatives of commercial agriculture's interests were urging him to support efforts to improve the food programs and to keep them within the Department of Agriculture. Realizing that support for expensive farm subsidy programs was at an all-time low, and that farm programs were receiving more scrutiny because of the food aid reformers' disconcerting trick of juxtaposing the amounts spent to protect the farmer from the results of overproduction and the amounts spent to feed those who were unable to obtain enough food, agribusiness wanted to keep food programs where support for them could be bartered for support for farm programs. Consequently, under his leadership, the food and nutrition committee created by the Urban Affairs Council to review the hunger issue developed a $1 billion reform of the food stamp program.

Despite Nixon's apparent early enthusiasm for reforming the food programs, the issue was soon lost among domestic needs competing for limited dollars. His first budget message recommended spending only $15 million more for food aid programs than Johnson's last budget had. After this message the pressure on Nixon increased, reflecting the success of the two-year effort of the anti-hunger coalition and especially the effect of the Select Committee and the National Nutrition Survey. As the results of the survey were made public, state and local officials began calling for food aid programs in their areas or asking that they be included in the study. Groups such as the National Council on Hunger and Malnutrition, formed to continue the work done earlier by the Citizens' Board of Inquiry, generated further pressure by lobbying, developing local support for food programs, bringing lawsuits and publishing reports focusing on administration inaction.

In addition, McGovern focused attention on and attacked any plan that the administration was considering. Many other Democrats in Congress who had restrained their criticisms of Johnson now felt free to attack the new administration's actions. These attacks increased Agriculture Department sensitivity and led Hardin to press Nixon harder.

In May 1969 McGovern increased the pressure by asking Secretaries Finch and Hardin to testify before the Select Committee. Knowing they would be in the impossible position of being asked why their reform proposal had not been implemented and unable to come up with satisfactory testimony, they approached Nixon again immediately before the hearings and the President finally agreed to introduce the program.

The day after the President's hunger message, the Senate Agriculture Committee met and decided that with the President now committed to action the committee must formulate and introduce legislation in order to retain jurisdiction of the food programs. This was essential not only so they could keep the programs in hand, but also so they could continue to provide the large farm subsidies so important to commercial agriculture by bartering support for the food programs.

The administration's Food Stamp Reform Bill established the food stamp allotment at the level of the Agriculture Department's Economy Diet plan and authorized expenditures for the program of $315 million for fiscal 1970, $610 for fiscal 1971, and open-ended authorizations for fiscal 1972–73. McGovern introduced another bill setting the allotment of stamps at the level of USDA's Low Cost Diet, which is about 25 percent higher than the Economy Diet level, and containing a provision for open-ended authorization. These bills were referred to the Agriculture Committee, which reported out its own bill in July 1969. The bill set the allotment level at the Economy Diet and authorized expenditures of $750 million in fiscal 1970 and $1.5 billion in fiscal 1971 and 1972.

When the bill came to the Senate floor in September, Senators McGovern and Javits offered a substitute bill, one of the principal methods congressional members of the anti-hunger coalition use

to obtain more liberal food programs than the Agriculture committees are likely to approve. The bill set the level of benefits at
the Low Cost Diet and contained authorizations of $1.25 billion
for fiscal 1970, $2 billion for fiscal 1971 and $2.5 billion for
fiscal 1972. In addition, it contained national eligibility standards
which had the potential for increasing participation greatly. The
Senate adopted this substitute bill in place of that of the Agriculture Committee.

On December 16, 1970, fourteen months after Senate approval
of the food stamp bill, the House finally approved its bill. The
House Agriculture Committee had not reported the bill out until
August 10 because of delays imposed by Chairman Poage. As
reported out, the bill was much more restrictive than the Senate
version. It authorized funding at the level requested by the administration; provided for the allotment of food stamps at the level of
the Economy Diet; and required that adults register for work or
accept available employment as a condition for eligibility. Representative Thomas Foley fought within the committee for higher
spending levels but was supported only by Representative Allard
Lowenstein.

Having lost in committee, Foley set about building a coalition
that would support his position and might produce a victory when
the committee's bill was considered. Following the procedure
used before, he enlisted the aid of Republican Congressman Albert Quie to develop a bipartisan food stamp proposal that could
be supported by a majority of the House with varying philosophies. John Kramer of the National Council on Hunger and Nutrition functioned as chief draftsman of the proposal, and in this
role worked closely with representatives of organized labor and
civil rights and other groups that advocate increased federal food
aid for the poor. Trying to come up with a proposal that would
appeal to a broad range of congressmen, the draftsmen, against
much opposition, included a work requirement, but also increased
the allotment for a family of four to $128 worth of stamps a
month, authorized spending levels of $2 billion in fiscal 1971,

$2.5 billion in fiscal 1972 and $3 billion in fiscal 1973, and ordered that a food stamp program be established in every county and independent city. The group also organized a lobbying campaign that was conducted by labor leaders and religious groups as well as by the congressmen and their staffs.

Despite these efforts, the proposal was defeated 116–119 and the Agriculture Committee's bill was adopted. The defeat was due to active administration opposition to the proposal: a letter opposing the measure from Hardin to Belcher, the ranking Republican on the House Agriculture Committee, was widely distributed and Minority Leader Ford and Republican Whip Leslie Arends exerted pressure for Republican votes against it. Behind the administration's low budget request and opposition to the Foley-Quie substitute bill was a growing concern over the costs of the program. Officials argued that the proposal would not be acceptable from a budgetary viewpoint.

As this review of the evolution of the food stamp program indicated, the role of the Agriculture committees in the program's development has not been an enthusiastic one. Rather than taking the lead in developing and financing programs when the need was uncovered, the committees resisted improving the program as long as possible. They were galvanized into action—developing a program and holding hearings—only when President Nixon's apparent strong support indicated to them that they could no longer stop the establishment of an adequate food stamp program because the support of a Republican president would provide the swing votes and the coordinating effort necessary for a successful legislative campaign.

The powerful committee chairmen began to formulate their own programs and to act favorably on and provide the requested funding for the administration's proposals not only because they wished to protect their own jurisdiction over the issue so they could use it for vote-trading, but also because they sought to protect their own power by maintaining the appearance of invincibility. In addition, the chairmen often supported administration requests in an effort to keep the program as controlled as possible, knowing that there was pressure for more liberal programs and higher appropriations.

That the apparent support for the food stamp program is to be explained largely by such views and interests, rather than by a true change in attitude, is attested to by the comments of many committee members as the legislation worked its way through Congress. When the conferees seemed in deadlock over the 1970 Food Stamp Act, Poage took the floor in the House to urge a conservative compromise: "In the final analysis, the whole matter boils down to this: Do we want to exchange our social, economic and religious philosophy that 'in the sweat of his brow shall man eat bread' for the philosophy of the socialistic countries which proclaims that man shall share the good things of the world not in proportion to his contribution but in proportion to his need?" Similarly, during House consideration of the conference report, Belcher expressed the view that the program was beginning to look like another welfare program, when it was only intended to be a supplement to the regular diet. Poage's delay in reporting out the bill further substantiated the claim that with regard to food stamps the Agriculture committees had been reacting largely to the politics of the issue instead of its substance, the needs of the hungry.

The obvious pattern of development underlying final legislation further reveals the role of the Agriculture committees as well as one of the important reasons why some liberal anti-hunger legislation has been adopted. Almost without exception, both the Senate and the House Agriculture committees and Appropriations subcommittees have approved legislation embodying administration recommendations and requested funding levels, and the whole House has then adopted the bills as reported out by the committee. In the Senate, however, McGovern or someone else acting for the Select Committee usually offers a substitute bill or an amendment that liberalizes the program or increases the level of appropriations. The Senate then almost always adopts the substitute or amendment and the conference committee reaches a compromise that is somewhat more liberal than the position of the Agriculture committees.

The Select Committee has been largely responsible for the more liberal provisions passed by the Senate. It is not just a matter of offering amendments to bills developed by the Agriculture Committee (as the Foley-Quie effort indicates). Rather, in addition to keeping a constant spotlight within the Senate on the hunger issue, the Select Committee has built a strong coalition of moderates and liberals who acknowledge the committee's expertise in the area of nutrition and hunger, and who follow its lead on most issues. Committee members and staff feel that this is its most important accomplishment, that in so doing it has become the real center of action for food stamp legislation. Thus it has become much easier to successfully challenge on the floor the work of a committee that has jurisdiction of an issue. In addition, the repeatedly proven ability of the Select Committee to secure passage of the programs it endorses serves to keep the Agriculture committees moving forward on food programs.

If it is true that the Agriculture committees are responding politically to the pressure generated by the anti-hunger coalition, and if the general food aid programs remain in their jurisdiction (which is by no means certain), continued improvements in the program—or even maintaining the status quo—depend on continued pressure. Many members of the hunger coalition feel that if the pressure were to subside, the Agriculture committees would attempt to cut back the programs.

The reaction of the committees to efforts to improve the school lunch program has been critically different from their role in changing the food stamp program. Although action had to await exposure of the deficiencies of the programs, and some of the protest and pressure for reform that followed these revelations, once these occurred, the Senate Agriculture Committee, with Talmadge taking the lead, stepped in to develop a program that would serve the poor. This was not just a token move to keep the program within the jurisdiction of the Agriculture committees. Although members of the Select Committee and of the hunger coalition in the Senate did suggest amendments to the School Lunch Act, they did not try to develop their own substitute program. Rather, they worked with the Agriculture Committee as much as possible, joining as co-sponsors of the bill, offering their amendments to the committee for consideration first, and taking care to explain on the floor that they were offering only minor changes and were very pleased with Talmadge's bill. Members of the Select Committee staff say that although the attitude of the Agriculture Committee toward the Select Committee was at first hostile, as time went on, at least with regard to the school lunch program, the Agriculture Committee began to consult the Select Committee on problems concerning the program.

The alacrity with which the committee and especially Talmadge responded to USDA's attempt to limit reimbursement rates in 1971 further revealed that they were genuinely interested in establishing an adequate program. Many explain the committee's different attitude by the fact that, unlike the food stamp program, the school lunch program is supported by a large middle-class constituency, and especially by the fact that Talmadge feels it is very popular in Georgia.

That this may be the case is indicated by the apparent attitude of the Senate Agriculture Committee toward improvements in other child nutrition programs, such as the breakfast and the non-school feeding programs. These were developed mainly to serve the poor by congressmen outside the Agriculture committees and were initially established on a very small scale. The attitude of the Agriculture committees and the Appropriations subcommittees toward these programs has been less friendly, with the committees letting others take the lead in pushing for reforms.

The fact that the school lunch program is under the jurisdiction of the House Education and Labor Committee, chaired by Perkins, a powerful congressman who is in a position to grant or withhold important support, may have served as an additional incentive for the Senate Agriculture Committee to establish an adequate program. In addition, the program had been initiated by members of the committee and they had long pointed with pride to its accomplishments and benefits.

POSTSCRIPT 1973

Because of the hunger coalition's success in maneuvering around the farm committees in the House and the Senate, as well as the growing sensitivity of the committees' members (at least in the Senate) to the problems of the poor, public participation in food programs increased dramatically between 1968 and 1973. Funding for the programs rose from $687 million in fiscal 1967 to $4.32 billion in fiscal 1973. Although this is great progress, the Citizens' Board of Inquiry reported in 1972, in *Hunger USA Revisited*, that there are still more than 24 million people living at or below federally defined poverty levels. The expanded food programs still reach only half of those in poverty. As the Senate's Select Committee on Nutrition noted in 1973, the plate of the nation's poor is still half empty. With the soaring inflation of the 1970s, there is little doubt that the condition of the hungry poor has worsened.

If the United States is to complete its unfinished business of providing an adequate diet for all its citizens, and to meet its obligations to the hungry overseas, strong and imaginative congressional leadership is required. This leadership can come from the farm committees only if substantial changes are made in their structure and membership.

11

Recommendations

For the most part, changes in the farm committees' structure and procedures must come from within the committees, and we have seen that their most powerful members are those largely satisfied with the status quo. In 1973, after the debacle of the farm bill in the House—which was spurred by continuing national debate over the consumer implications of farm policy—the committees began to sense that they could lose part of their control of future farm policy if they did not become more representative and responsive to national interests. The narrow producer orientation of the committees appears to be no longer acceptable to the House or the Senate. The following recommendations, if adopted, would help open up the committees and bring about a more equitable balance between consumer and producer interests.

1. The committees' membership must be made more representative of Congress as a whole. With food prices soaring, and the world becoming more and more dependent on U. S. agricultural

266

exports, farm policy has become too important to be left to the farmers (and the agribusiness corporations). Congressmen who identify with the poor, the consumer, the environmentalists, and the urban public should serve on the committees to balance those who serve specific commodity interests.

2. Hearings and markup sessions should be open. The farmer committees remain among the most secretive in Congress. Such secrecy denies the public information about farm policy at a time when public education in agricultural economics and policy is more important than ever before. The committees should begin holding field hearings to get a wider exposure to the public interest in agricultural policy.

3. Staffs on the committees should be substantially increased, to give the committees more expertise in scrutinizing administration proposals and administration performance. The present lack of professional economists is intolerable if the committees are to exercise any independence in setting agricultural trade policy, which is bound to remain a major issue during the rest of the 1970s.

4. Each subcommittee should have its own staff. Such staffing will greatly increase the investigative potential of the subcommittees and encourage oversight of the Agriculture Department bureaucracy.

5. The committees should seek out representatives of the poor and of consumer and environmental groups to testify at hearings. If the committees do not listen to their views, these neglected constituencies will continue to attack committee priorities on the House and Senate floors.

6. Jurisdiction over the food stamp and commodity distribution programs should be taken away from the farm committees. The hunger programs are and should be essentially welfare programs. They ought not to be controlled by committees congenitally hostile to welfare as a concept and indifferent to the problems recipients have with the agriculture bureaucracy that administers the program. In a period of rising food prices and

strong world-wide demand for U. S. farm products, whatever reason there may have been for making relief part of the farm program has evaporated.

7. Members of the Agricultural committees should refuse to accept contributions from any lobby group that has legislation pending before the committees. This rule should apply to the milk lobby as well as to the pesticide makers. The fact that a commodity lobby group has a large membership of producers does not remove the conflict of interest inherent in acceptance of such contributions, particularly when the committees should now be balancing consumer and producer interests to insure an adequate food supply at reasonable prices.

Members of the Agriculture Committees

Majority:

Herman E. Talmadge, Chm.
(Ga.)
Allen J. Ellender (La.)
James O. Eastland (Miss.)
B. Everett Jordan (N.C.)
George S. McGovern (S. Dak.)
James B. Allen (Ala.)
Hubert H. Humphrey (Minn.)
Lawton Chiles (Fla.)

Minority:

Jack Miller (Iowa)
George D. Aiken (Vt.)
Milton R. Young (N. Dak.)
Carl T. Curtis (Neb.)
Bob Dole (Kans.)
Henry Bellmon (Okla.)

Subcommittee on Agricultural Credit and Rural Electrification

Majority:	*Minority*:
McGovern, Chm.	Aiken
Allen	Miller
Ellender	Dole
Humphrey	

Subcommittee on Agricultural Exports

Majority:	*Minority*:
Chiles, Chm.	Miller
Jordan	Bellmon
McGovern	

Subcommittee on Agricultural Production, Marketing and Stabilization of Prices

Majority:	*Minority*:
Jordan, Chm.	Young
McGovern	Miller
Eastland	Curtis
Ellender	Bellmon
Humphrey	

Subcommittee on Agricultural Research and General Legislation

Majority:	*Minority*:
Allen, Chm.	Dole
Jordan	Young
Eastland	Curtis
Chiles	

Subcommittee on Environment, Soil Conservation and Forestry

Majority:	*Minority:*
Eastland, Chm.	Bellmon
Jordan	Aiken
Chiles	

Subcommittee on Rural Development

Majority:	*Minority:*
Humphrey, Chm.	Curtis
Ellender	Dole
Eastland	Bellmon
Allen	

SENATE COMMITTEE ON AGRICULTURE AND FORESTRY, NINETY-THIRD CONGRESS

Majority:	*Minority:*
Herman E. Talmadge, Chm. (Ga.)	Carl T. Curtis (Neb.)
James O. Eastland (Miss.)	George D. Aiken (Vt.)
George McGovern (S. Dak.)	Milton R. Young (N. Dak.)
James B. Allen (Ala.)	Robert Dole (Kans.)
Hubert H. Humphrey (Minn.)	Henry Bellmon (Okla.)
Walter D. Huddleston (Ky.)	Jesse A. Helms (N.C.)
Dick Clark (Iowa)	

Subcommittee on Agricultural Credit and Rural Electrification

Majority:	*Minority:*
McGovern, Chm.	Aiken
Allen	Dole
Humphrey	Helms
Huddleston	

Subcommittee on Foreign Agricultural Policy

Majority:	*Minority*:
Humphrey, Chm.	Bellmon
McGovern	Helms
Huddleston	

Subcommittee on Agricultural Production, Marketing, and Stabilization of Prices

Majority:	*Minority*:
Huddleston, Chm.	Young
McGovern	Bellmon
Eastland	Dole
Humphrey	Helms
Clark	

Subcommittee on Agricultural Research and General Legislation

Majority:	*Minority*:
Allen, Chm.	Dole
Eastland	Young
Clark	Bellmon
McGovern	

Subcommittee on Environment, Soil Conservation and Forestry

Majority:	*Minority*:
Eastland, Chm.	Helms
Allen	Aiken
Huddleston	

Subcommittee on Rural Development

Majority:	Minority:
Clark, Chm.	Curtis
Humphrey	Dole
Eastland	Bellmon
Allen	

HOUSE COMMITTEE ON AGRICULTURE, NINETY-SECOND CONGRESS

Majority:	Minority:
W. R. Poage, Chm. (Tex.)	Page Belcher (Okla.)
John L. McMillan (S.C.)	Charles M. Teague (Calif.)
Thomas G. Abernethy (Miss.)	William C. Wampler (Va.)
Watkins M. Abbitt (Va.)	George A. Goodling (Pa.)
Frank A. Stubblefield (Ky.)	Clarence E. Miller (Ohio)
Graham Purcell (Tex.)	Robert B. Mathias (Calif.)
Thomas S. Foley (Wash.)	Wiley Mayne (Iowa)
Eligio de la Garza (Tex.)	John Zwach (Minn.)
Joseph P. Vigorito (Pa.)	Robert D. Price (Tex.)
Walter B. Jones (N.C.)	Keith G. Sebelius (Kans.)
B. F. Sisk (Calif.)	Wilmer D. Mizell (N.C.)
Bill Alexander (Ark.)	Paul Findley (Ill.)
Bill D. Burlison (Mo.)	John Kyl (Iowa)
John R. Rarick (La.)	La Mar Baker (Tenn.)
Ed Jones (Tenn.)	
John Melcher (Mont.)	
John G. Dow (N.Y.)	
Dawson Mathis (Ga.)	
Bob Bergland (Minn.)	
Arthur A. Link (N.D.)	
Frank E. Denholm (S. Dak.)	
Spark M. Matsunaga (Hawaii)	

Subcommittee on Cotton

Majority:	*Minority*:
Abernethy, Chm.	Mathias
de la Garza	Price
Sisk	Mizell
Burlison	
Jones (Tenn.)	

Subcommittee on Dairy and Poultry

Majority:	*Minority*:
Stubblefield, Chm.	Wampler
Vigorito	Miller
Jones (Tenn.)	Zwach
Dow	
Abbitt	

Subcommittee on Forests

Majority:	*Minority*:
McMillan, Chm.	Teague
Foley	Kyl
Burlison	Baker
Vigorito	
Dow	

Subcommittee on Livestock and Grains

Majority:	*Minority*:
Purcell, Chm.	Mayne
Foley	Zwach
Rarick	Price

Majority:

Abbitt
Jones (N.C.)
Sisk
Melcher
Bergland
Link
Denholm

Minority:

Sebelius
Findley
Kyl

Subcommittee on Oilseeds and Rice

Majority:

Jones, Chm. (N.C.)
Rarick
Alexander
Burlison
Mathis

Minority:

Wampler
Mizell
Baker

Subcommittee on Tobacco

Majority:

Abbitt, Chm.
McMillan
Stubblefield
Jones (N.C.)
Mathis

Minority:

Wampler
Miller
Mizell

Subcommittee on Conservation and Credit

Majority:

Poage, Chm.
Stubblefield
de la Garza
Alexander
Bergland

Minority:

Teague
Goodling
Mayne

Subcommittee on Domestic Marketing and Consumer Relations

Majority:	Minority:
Foley, Chm.	Goodling
Sisk	Zwach
Denholm	Findley
Link	
Matsunaga	

Subcommittee on Department Operations

Majority:	Minority:
de la Garza, Chm.	Mathias
Abernethy	Sebelius
Purcell	Mayne
Jones (Tenn.)	
Matsunaga	

Subcommittee on Family Farms and Rural Development

Majority:	Minority:
Vigorito, Chm.	Goodling
Purcell	Miller
Melcher	Kyl
Mathis	
Dow	

HOUSE COMMITTEE ON AGRICULTURE, NINETY-THIRD CONGRESS

Majority:	Minority:
W. R. Poage, Chm. (Tex.)	William C. Wampler (Va.)
Frank A. Stubblefield (Ky.)	George A. Goodling (Pa.)
Thomas S. Foley (Wash.)	Robert B. Mathias (Calif.)

Majority:

E. de la Garza (Tex.)
Joseph P. Vigorito (Pa.)
Walter B. Jones (N.C.)
B. F. Sisk (Calif.)
Bill Alexander (Ark.)
John R. Rarick (La.)
Ed Jones (Tenn.)
John Melcher (Mont.)
Dawson Mathis (Ga.)
Bob Bergland (Minn.)
Frank E. Denholm (S. Dak.)
Spark M. Matsunaga (Hawaii)
George E. Brown, Jr. (Calif.)
David R. Bowen (Miss.)
Charles Rose (N.C.)
Jerry Litton (Mo.)
Bill Gunter (Fla.)

Minority:

Wiley Mayne (Iowa)
John M. Zwach (Minn.)
Robert Price (Tex.)
Kenneth G. Sebelius (Kans.)
Wilmer Mizell (N.C.)
Paul Findley (Ill.)
Le Mar Baker (Tenn.)
Charles Thone (Neb.)
Steven D. Symms (Idaho)
Edward Young (S.C.)
James P. Johnson (Colo.)
Edward R. Madigan (Ill.)
Peter Peyser (N.Y.)

Subcommittee on Cotton

Majority:

Sisk, Chm.
de la Garza
Jones (Tenn.)
Bowen
Rose
Mathis

Minority:

Price
Mizell
Young

Subcommittee on Dairy and Poultry

Majority:

Jones, Chm. (Tenn.)
Stubblefield

Minority:

Wampler
Zwach

Majority:
Bergland
Brown
Bowen

Majority:
Findley
Thone

Subcommittee on Forests

Majority:
Rarick, Chm.
Foley
Vigorito
Melcher
Gunter

Minority:
Goodling
Baker
Thone
Symms

Subcommittee on Livestock and Grains

Majority:
Foley, Chm.
Rarick
Jones (N.C.)
Sisk
Melcher
Bergland
Denholm
Matsunaga
Litton
Gunter

Minority:
Mayne
Zwach
Price
Sebelius
Findley
Thone
Johnson
Symms

Subcommittee on Oilseeds and Rice

Majority:
Jones, Chm. (N.C.)
Rarick

Minority:
Wampler
Baker

Majority:
Alexander
Mathis
Rose

Minority:
Johnson
Madigan

Subcommittee on Tobacco

Majority:
Stubblefield, Chm.
Jones (N.C.)
Mathis
Rose
Litton

Minority:
Mizell
Wampler
Madigan
Young

Subcommittee on Conservation and Credit

Majority:
Poage, Chm.
Stubblefield
de la Garza
Alexander
Bergland

Minority:
Zwach
Goodling
Mayne
Madigan

Subcommittee on Domestic Marketing and Consumer Relations

Majority:
Vigorito, Chm.
Foley
Sisk
Denholm
Matsunaga

Minority:
Goodling
Findley
Johnson
Symms

Subcommittee on Department Operations

Majority:	*Minority*:
de la Garza, Chm.	Price
Jones (Tenn.)	Mathias
Matsunaga	Sebelius
Denholm	Mayne
Litton	

Subcommittee on Family Farms and Rural Development

Majority:	*Minority*:
Alexander, Chm.	Sebelius
Vigorito	Mizell
Melcher	Baker
Mathis	Young
Brown	

III

THE HOUSE SCIENCE AND ASTRONAUTICS COMMITTEE AND THE SENATE AERONAUTICAL AND SPACE SCIENCES COMMITTEE

All unattributed quotations in this text are based on interviews conducted in 1972 and 1973 with present and former committee members and staffs and held confidential at their request.

12

Science and Space

The French and Italians were awed, the Germans asked for details, the Russians were chagrined, and the Tahitians, who disbelieved the whole story, called it lunacy. In 1969, astonished Americans joined people all over the planet to watch Ohio's Neil Armstrong make the first giant footprint for mankind on the colorless sand of the barren moon.

The primers and pushers on Capitol Hill said it was the most significant moment in twentieth-century history. The press proclaimed it a triumph of talent, teamwork, and technique, and the American public was jetted into the mainstream of media excitement. Only a few, less dazzled, asked why we had to go at all.

Talent and hardware, though dramatic, were not the most significant factors in the "triumph." Backstage, in the political committee wings where the gigantic show was seeded and steered, all-too-human foibles were instrumental in the lift-off. "Mission

NOTE: This chapter was researched and drafted by Douglas Harbit.

control" may also have included the vaulting political ambition of a ubiquitous Texas senator, the corrupt machinations of an Oklahoma tycoon, the rumored need to find a haven for an incompetent Louisiana legislator with seniority, and the necessity for a young president with a bad press on a foreign policy decision to demonstrate dynamism. But the triumph unquestionably demonstrated the use of science and technology for targeted policy goals.

UP, UP AND AWAY:
THE WAY IT BEGAN

The sputter in America that followed Russia's soaring Sputnik achievement in 1957 sobered the executive branch but galvanized the legislative branch.

President Dwight D. Eisenhower augmented what had been a desultory[1] post–World War II program of exploration on rockets and missiles by the appointment of a Scientific Policy Advisory Committee (SPAC), headed by MIT's distinguished Dr. James R. Killian. When Killian left in 1960 he offered this assessment of appropriate space objectives:

> I believe that, in space exploration, as in all other fields we choose to go into, we must never be content to be second best, but I do not believe that this requires us to engage in a prestige race with the Soviets . . . We should insist on a space program that is in balance with our other vital objectives and that does not rob them because they are currently less spectacular. In the long run we lower our international prestige by frantically indulging in unnecessary competition and prestige-motivated projects . . .[2]

In the halls of Congress in 1957, however, Sputnik's ascent generated a scramble for prestige and power. Analyst Thomas Jahnigne notes that "the military missile men, civilian government scientists with the NSF [National Science Foundation] and

NACA [National Advisory Committee on Aeronautics][3] and nongovernmental scientists of the National Academy of Sciences and the American Rocket Society" took their views to Congress. "Prior to the launching of Sputnik they had carried on their fight for a more aggressive satellite program solely within the executive branch . . . [where] they had been held in check by the Administration and the upper echelons of the Department of Defense."[4]

The administration's failures were thoroughly aired by four congressional subcommittees. The most extensive hearings were held by Senate Majority Leader Lyndon Johnson in the Preparedness Investigating Subcommittee of the Senate Armed Services Committee. It was Johnson who spearheaded the Senate drive to establish a blue-ribbon "Select Committee on Space and Astronautics" and to make him chairman of the special group.

The rationale for breaking with precedent by making the majority leader chairman of the committee was that the investigations and recommendations were bound to cross jurisdictional lines. The practical result of the action put the ambitious Texan into a position of power over established Senate committee chairmen. The composition of the new space group included chairmen and ranking minority members of other "interested committees" (those with possible jurisdictional claims over space and science affairs).[5]

The establishment of such an illustrious committee on the Senate side forced the House to set up one of its own.* John McCormack (D., Mass.), the House majority leader, followed Johnson's lead and became chairman. Unlike the Senate committee, however, the House special space committee did not seek members who already chaired other "interested committees." And only one was a ranking minority member of another committee—Leslie Arends (R., Ill.) of the Armed Services Committee. Representatives Metcalf (D., Mont.), Sisk (D., Calif.), Keating (R., N.Y.), and McDonough (R., Calif.), were members of committees

* The House Committee on Science and Astronautics was renamed the Committee on Science and Technology, effective 1975.

which had no jurisdictional claims on subsequent legislation.[6] (Table 12 shows the composition of the first committees in both the Senate and the House.)

In 1958, when the initial Senate committee moved from "se-

TABLE 12.

Senate Special Committee on Space and Astronautics, 1957
Chairman: Lyndon Johnson, *Majority Leader of the Senate*

Democrats	Republicans
Russell (Ga.), chairman, Armed Services Committee	Bridges (N.H.), ranking minority member, Appropriations Committee
Green (R.I.), chairman, Foreign Relations Committee	Wiley (Wis.), ranking minority member, Foreign Relations Committee
McClellan (Ark.), chairman, Government Operations Committee	Hickenlooper (Ia.), ranking minority member, Atomic Energy Committee
Magnuson (Wash.), chairman, Commerce Committee	Saltonstall (Mass.), ranking minority member, Armed Services Committee
Anderson (N.M.), vice chairman, Atomic Energy Committee	Bricker (Ohio), ranking minority member, Commerce Committee
Symington (Mo.), member, Armed Services and Government Operations Committees	Mundt (S.D.), ranking minority member, Government Operations Committee

House Select Committee on Astronautics and Space Exploration, 1957
Chairman: John McCormack, *Majority Leader of the House*

Democrats	Republicans
Brooks (La.), member, Armed Services Committee	Martin (Mass.), ranking minority leader of the House
Natcher (Ky.), member, Appropriations Committee	Arends (Ill.), ranking minority member, Armed Services Committee
Hays (Ark.), member, Foreign Affairs Committee	Ford (Mich.), member, Appropriations Committee
O'Brien (N.Y.), member, Interstate and Foreign Commerce Committee	Fulton (Pa.), member, Foreign Affairs Committee
Metcalf (Mont.)	Keating (N.Y.)
Sisk (Calif.)	McDonough (Calif.)

lect" to "standing" status, becoming the Aeronautical and Space Sciences Committee, Johnson again became chairman. This was a major step in the Texan's career. Although he was majority leader in 1958, Johnson had been in the Senate only ten years. Under seniority rules he could not have become chairman of a standing committee for many years. But as they say on the Pedernales River, "If there's one stallion in a herd of geldings, he'll find a way out of the corral."

The congressional decision to create separate Senate and House committees instead of one joint committee with membership from both houses of Congress, similar to the Joint Committee on Atomic Energy, was no accident. It is clear that on the Senate side Johnson wanted a committee chairmanship.* Educator Vernon Van Dyke[7] suggests that the provision on the House side was the result of Speaker Sam Rayburn's opposition to joint congressional committees in general. An even more interesting explanation for the House decision to establish a standing committee comes from Thomas Jahnige,[8] who suggests that the House leaders wanted to dump an incompetent but senior legislator, Overton Brooks (D., La.):

> Brooks, who was generally considered to be one of the least competent legislators in the House, had, through seniority, risen to the number two position on the House Armed Services Committee. The only factor which separated him from control of this committee was the aging body of Carl Vinson (D., Ga.), chairman of the committee.
>
> In the event of Vinson's death or retirement, Brooks would become chairman of this most important committee. This was a prospect which the leadership viewed with alarm. Creation of a new space committee gave the leadership the opportunity to offer Brooks an immediate chairmanship of a committee whose jurisdiction dealt with a program which,

---

* Johnson, conscious of the power and prestige of a committee chairmanship, feared that if a joint committee were formed, the position would go to a House member.

although glamorous, was not yet very significant. The leadership did, in fact, manage such a feat. Brooks became chairman of Science and Astronautics and gave up his seat on Armed Services.*

One of the first Senate committee acts was to set up the National Aeronautics and Space Administration (NASA). The NASA Act, written primarily by Senator Lyndon Johnson and his staff, was signed into law July 29, 1958. On October 1, 1958, three days short of the first anniversary of Sputnik I, NASA was open for business—the exploration of the peaceful uses of space "for the benefit of mankind." The nucleus of the new agency, the old National Advisory Committee on Aeronautics, had its entire staff of eight thousand scientists and supporting personnel transferred to NASA as soon as it became operational. Dr. T. Keith Glennan, highly respected in the scientific community, was chosen as its head by President Eisenhower. The space committees now had a defined oversight function.

THE MOONSTRUCK EXECUTIVE

In April 1961, when cosmonaut Yuri Gagarin became the first man to fly in space, his single orbit seemed to confirm America's second place in the space race. On April 14, just forty-eight hours after the Soviet launch, President John F. Kennedy summoned adviser Ted Sorenson and other consultants to the White House. The President was grasping for straws. "What this meeting disclosed more than anything was the sight of a man obsessed with failure. . . . the image of dynamism . . . had to be avenged. . . ."[9]

Three days later, the CIA-funded Bay of Pigs debacle further depressed American prestige and self-confidence. An American success on the moon was no longer a technological bauble but rather a hard political necessity. President Kennedy decided that

---

* One of Brooks's staff appointments was Charles Ducander, formerly counselor for the Armed Services Committee. In 1973 Ducander was replaced by astronaut John Swigert.

space exploration on a grand scale should become a national priority program, no matter what the cost. The next day Kennedy sent a memo to Lyndon Johnson, who was now his Vice-President:

> Do we have a chance of beating the Soviets by putting a laboratory in space, or by a trip around the moon, or by a rocket to land on the moon, or by a rocket to go to the moon and back with a man? Is there any other space program which promises *dramatic results in which we could win?* [Emphasis added.]
>
> . . . How much additional would it cost?
>
> . . . Are we working twenty-four hours a day on existing programs? If not, why not? If not, will you make recommendations to me as to how work can be speeded up?
>
> . . . Are we making maximum effort? Are we achieving necessary results?
>
> I have asked Jim Webb [NASA administrator], Dr. Wiesner [science adviser to the White House], Secretary McNamara, and other responsible officials to cooperate with you fully. I would appreciate a report on this at the earliest possible moment.[10]

Under the watchful eye of the Vice-President, Jim Webb and Robert McNamara (then head of the Department of Defense) wrote the report to the President. Johnson placed his findings in Kennedy's hands the same day Kennedy pinned the Distinguished Service Medal on America's first astronaut, Alan Shepard. The report made clear that international prestige was the most important aspect of the American adventure:

> It is man, not merely machines, in space that captures the imagination of the world. All large-scale projects require the mobilization of resources on a national scale.
>
> They require the development and successful application of the most advanced technologies. Dramatic achievements in space therefore symbolize the technological power and organizing capacity of a nation. It is for reasons such as

these that major achievements in space contribute to national prestige.

. . . Major successes, such as orbiting a man as the Soviets
have just done, lend national prestige even though scientific,
commercial, or military value of the undertaking may, by
ordinary standards, be marginal or economically unjustifiable.

. . . Our attainments are a major element in the international competition between the Soviet system and our own.
The non-military, non-commercial, non-scientific but "civilian" projects such as lunar and planetary exploration are,
in this sense, part of the battle along the fluid front of the
cold war.[11]

Kennedy's address to Congress on May 25, 1961, naming a
much more aggressive program in space as one of his "urgent
national goals," was widely accepted. The congressional committees were in general agreement on the need to beat the Soviet
Union to the moon. In the early days of NASA funding there was
little question of objectives, or of the massive nature of America's
space effort. House committee member James Fulton (R., Pa.)
typified the congressional attitude when he asked: "How much
money would you need to get us on a program that would make
us even with Russia . . . and probably leapfrog them . . . ? I want
to be the firstest with the mostest in space, and I just don't want
to wait for years. How much money do we need to do it?"[12]

The Kennedy push in 1961 made NASA the fastest-growing
agency in recent history. NASA authorizations ballooned from
$961 million in fiscal 1961 to their highest mark of just over $5
billion in fiscal 1965. By the time Johnson ended his career in
public service, the space agency he designed in 1958 had spent
well over $32 billion. (See Table 13.)

Evidence of the heady context in which members of Congress
viewed space exploration can be found in the NASA memorabilia
that still decorate their walls and desks. Plastic satellites serve as
paperweights; pencils and pens have rocket heads; astronauts

TABLE 13.
History of NASA Funding
(Millions of Dollars)

Fiscal Year	Administration Request	Authorized Amount	Percent of Change
1959	$ 280.5	$ 222.8[a]	− 20.6
60	508.3	485.1[a]	− 4.6
61	964.6	961.0	− 0.1
62	1,940.3	1,825.3	− 5.9
63	3,787.3	3,674.1	− 3.0
64	5,712.0	5,100.0	− 10.7
65	5,445.0	5,250.0	− 3.6
66	5,260.0	5,175.0	− 1.6
67	5,012.0	4,968.0	− 0.9
68	5,100.0	4,588.9	− 10.0
69	4,370.4	3,995.3	− 8.6
70	3,715.5	3,715.5	
71	3,333.0	3,410.9	+ 2.3
72	3,271.5	3,355.0	+ 2.6
73	3,407.6[b]	3,444.2	+ 1.1
74	3,016.0	3,064.5	+ 1.6

[a] Funds actually available in first two years somewhat increased by transfers from other agencies.
[b] Budget request as amended.
SOURCE: *Congressional Quarterly Almanac, 1973* (Washington: Congressional Quarterly, Inc., 1974), p. 877.

beam owlishly behind their helmets on autographed photographs; maps of the Sea of Tranquillity and other lunar landmarks bear little red pins for each Apollo landing; and computer-created film stills show the minute ridges and craters of Mars. One framed congressional memento is a *New Yorker* cartoon showing an irate American astronaut and an irate Russian cosmonaut on a landscape barren except for two lunar vehicles, each with a dented fender. That the drug culture of the sixties coined the expression "spaced out" as an indicator of high fantasy is not surprising. Space exploration became more than a responsibility for these members of Congress; it was also a mystique.

A new frontier also meant new money for congressional districts. As an illustration, multimillionaire Senator Robert Kerr

(D., Okla.), who became chairman of the Senate science committee when Johnson became Vice-President, never made any bones
about mixing politics and business. "I represent myself first, the
state of Oklahoma second, and the people of the United States
third, and don't you forget it."[13] It was Kerr who proposed that
James Webb, a Kerr protégé, be appointed director of NASA.
Before winning appointment in February 1961, Webb had been
"assistant to the president" of Kerr's uranium empire, Kerr-
McGee Oil Industries, Inc. Taking over as NASA chief, Webb left
his McDonnell Aircraft Company directorship and divested himself of his aerospace holdings. As late as May 1962, however, he
still held nearly $800,000 of stock in the Fidelity Bank and Trust
Company in Oklahoma City, a Kerr-run enterprise.

A generous patron himself, Kerr understood the finer arts of
patronage. The Oklahoma senator owned a large tract of land just
outside Tulsa; he hoped it would be used to construct a canal
linking Tulsa to the Mississippi. When the canal idea died, the
land was sold to a manufacturer of space hardware, a subsidiary
of North American Aviation. And North American was awarded
one of NASA's largest contracts—by James Webb.

As former House space committee member Joe Karth (D.,
Minn.) remarked, Webb knew how to pass around the pork.*
Texas and Oklahoma were not alone. In 1961 there was an item
in the proposed NASA budget for a new research installation in
Cambridge, Massachusetts. Karth was puzzled by the request. He
argued that existing electronics firms and NASA labs could do the
work. But House Speaker John McCormack (D., Mass.) called
Karth in and said, "You don't understand. We *need* that new
plant in Cambridge." Karth sensed the request had little to do

---

* It must be added, however, that Webb was a dynamic administrator and
deserves credit for NASA's well-honed bureaucratic machinery. Staff people
at the National Science Foundation, now confronting some of the same
problems that beset the early space effort, sometime yearn wistfully for
Webb's skills.[14]

with NASA requirements, and he continued to refuse to approve the new authorization, which was under the jurisdiction of the subcommittee he chaired. President Kennedy then invited Karth to the White House for a chat. Kennedy told Karth that he hadn't originally known that the Cambridge project was going to be in the budget, but now that it was, it would look bad if it wasn't reported out of committee. When Karth still refused to compromise, the item was simply taken out of his subcommittee and put on the docket of another subcommittee—where it passed. Karth told an interviewer that he doubted that McCormack had actually requested the new installation; the request was more likely a result of the fact that "Jim Webb was a smart politician" and knew where his rockets were oiled. (The Cambridge NASA installation was phased out a few years ago.)

Political considerations also overruled logic in locating the control center for manned space flights. There was sufficient space at Cape Canaveral (now Cape Kennedy), Florida, for both the launch site and the control centers. Hugo Young[15] states that "the congressman in charge of the Appropriations subcommittee with responsibility for space funding was Albert Thomas (D., Tex.), and Albert Thomas was a power in the city of Houston." No one was really surprised, then, when Rice University donated land for the manned spacecraft center in Houston, making this site relatively less expensive than other alternatives. Rice's generosity had its own Catch-22. Humble Oil Company had given the land to Rice University with the restriction that the tract be donated to NASA. The industrial giant, too, like the congressman and the university, was seeking no honors for altruism: the company owned an even larger parcel of land in the immediate area. When the Houston space facility was built, Humble Oil was there to cash in on all the supporting business required by a newly developed community.

Locating the control center a thousand miles away from the launch facility caused serious communication problems. The chairman of the board of inquiry investigating a disastrous fire that took the lives of three astronauts in 1967 attributed some of the errors to the "interface between the Manned Spacecraft Center [Houston, Texas] and the Kennedy Spaceflight Center [Florida]."[16]

THE MOONSHINE EXPERTS

The scientific community was far from united on the executive proposal to send men to the moon. Dr. Polycarp Kusch, a Nobel Prize winner and chairman of the Physics Department at Columbia University, testified at a congressional hearing in 1961 that lunar landing should not be a priority for the 1960s: domestic problems like pollution and the eroding water table in western America deserved higher status.[17] Dr. Simon Ramo, vice-president of a corporation under industrial contract to NASA, saw danger in space as a new military arena for the world's superpowers. On the other side was Dr. Lloyd Berkner, chairman of the Space Science Board of the National Academy of Sciences. In testimony before the Senate in the same hearings, he stated that the enterprise was a contest, "a genuine test of technological capacity, in the sense that the peoples of emerging nations size up the developing potentialities and inevitably back the winner."[18]

Projected costs of a moon landing were suitably astronomical. Dr. Warren Weaver, a mathematician and vice-president of the Alfred P. Sloan Foundation of New York, did a few elementary computations on what earthly goods and services could be purchased with the estimated $30 billion that would have to be spent on space:

> With that sum ($30 billion) one could give a 10 percent raise in salary, over a 10-year period, to every teacher in the United States from kindergarten through universities (about $9.8 billion required); could give $10 million each to 200 of the better small colleges ($2 billion); could finance 7-year fellowships (freshman through Ph.D.) at $4,000 per person per year for 50,000 new scientists and engineers ($1.4 bil-

lion); could build and largely endow faculties for all 53 nations which have been added to the United Nations since its original founding ($13.2 billion); could create three more permanent Rockefeller Foundations ($1.5 billion); and one would still have left $100 million for a program of informing the public about science.[19]

But the battle was unequal, reason vs. romance, prudence vs. adventure. The public imagination had been captured and private industry foresaw a bonanza. The voyage of man to the moon was on and the costs of manned spaceflight missions increased accordingly (see Table 14).

TABLE 14.
Manned Space Flight Costs
(*Millions of Dollars*)

Fiscal Year	Total NASA R & D Funds	Manned Flight Costs	Percent of Total
1959	$ 195.3	$ 49.7	25.4
60	305.3	119.4	39.1
61	617.7	296.3	48.0
62	1,145.2	538.0	46.9
63	2,509.7	1,502.0	59.8
64	3,977.4	2,717.9	68.3
65	4,285.3	2,961.0	69.9
66	4,486.3	3,199.5	71.3
67	4,175.0	3,024.0	72.4
68	3,967.6	2,789.0	70.4
69	3,201.4	2,177.5	68.1
70	3,066.0	2,031.0	66.2
71	2,606.1	1,474.2	61.2
72	2,603.3	1,320.5	50.7
73	2,637.4	1,224.4	46.4
Totals	$39,779.7	$25,424.4	63.9

SOURCE: *Congressional Quarterly Almanac, 1972* (Washington: Congressional Quarterly, Inc., 1972, p. 169).

13

The Space Committees in Orbit

What powers do the space committees have? Which agencies are under their purview? What rules determine the scope of their work? Who are the committee members in charge and how effective are they?

JURISDICTION

The Senate and House space committees do not have exactly the same jurisdictions. The Senate Aeronautical and Space Sciences Committee is concerned only with issues of space and deals almost exclusively with NASA: there are no subcommittees. Its formal rules specify concern with activities in aeronautical and space sciences only (although scientific aspects of these are included).[1] In the Ninety-third Congress, thirteen men sat on this committee.

The House Science and Astronautics Committee handles much broader issues, in basic science as well as space.[2] Six subcommittees—Manned Spaceflight; Aeronautics and Space Technology; Science, Research and Development; Space Science and Applications, International Science; and NASA Oversight (replaced in 1973 by a subcommittee on energy)—apportion these wide-ranging responsibilities among the House members. According to the formal rules, the House committee handles all legislation and other matters relating to three agencies: NASA, the National Science Foundation,* and the National Bureau of Standards.† The House space committee is also caretaker of "astronautical research and development (including resources, personnel, equipment, and facilities); exploration and control of outer space; and science scholarships and scientific research and development." Thirty-one representatives sat on this committee in the Ninety-third Congress.

Neither of the space committees is supposed to deal with the military aspects of space. This division of labor reflects the early decision to keep the civilian and military space programs separate, to forestall diluting any of the power of the Armed Services Committees in both chambers.

---

* NSF is a twenty-three-year-old administrative agency identified with basic research in the "hard sciences" and the encouragement of excellence in scientific education. Its mission is to enhance the nation's scientific capability, and it functions largely as a funding conduit for university experimenters and investigators who advance the state of scientific knowledge.

† NBS is a government laboratory, largely focused on applied research and technology, that maintains and develops standards for all kinds of instrumentation in all fields of science, both for researchers and industry. The four institutes at NBS conduct research and development on a diverse range of social and economic problems—from consumer product-safety controls and the precise delineation of air pollutants to standardization in measurements via atomic clocks and computer components. At the upper levels, NBS and NSF jurisdictions allow for some overlap, especially where both techniques and data in a certain scientific area are still to be charted.

Fragmentation

The science (nonspace) activities covered by the House committee are scattered through different Senate committees, resulting in little coordination and less liaison between the two chambers. Thus the Bureau of Standards is handled by the Senate Commerce Committee and the National Science Foundation is handled by the Senate Committee on Labor and Public Welfare.

In fact, at various times from 1962 to 1972, there were more than twenty-five separate subcommittees in the Senate with some jurisdiction over scientific and technological activities; there were thirteen in the House.

Such fragmentation sometimes makes it difficult to enact even watered-down legislation. Conversion to the metric system, for example, was the subject of hearings by the Science, Research and Development Subcommittee of the House space committee in 1969.[3] In 1971 the Metric System Subcommittee of the House Select Committee on Small Business held other hearings. Yet when the Senate Commerce Committee and the Senate finally passed a bill, in February and August 1972, respectively, providing that the metric system shall be the predominant system of weights and measures in the United States, no one in the House was ready to pick up the ball at the end of the Ninety-second Congress. Action was also stalled in the Ninety-third. At the end of 1974 the United States was the only high-technology country in the world that had not converted to the metric system.

Committee Composition

Between 1959 and 1974, thirty-nine different senators—eighteen Democrats, twenty-one Republicans—have held seats on the Senate space committee. Turnover can be attributed to death, retirement, lost elections by incumbents, and the desire of members to serve on committees with jurisdiction over affairs of greater concern to their constituents (plus the 1973 increase by 2 seats in the size of the committee). Although there has been considerable turnover at the junior levels in the Senate committee, a few senior members are long-time space buffs: Barry Goldwater (R., Ariz.), Stuart Symington (D., Mo.), and Howard Cannon (D., Nev.). Goldwater's sophistication in aeronautics (he is a major general in the Air Force Reserve) is a technical plus for the committee. Symington is a former secretary of the Air Force.

The committee is not the major assignment for any of its members. Half the Democrats and 40 percent of the Republicans double up on space and defense committees, an infrequent occurrence for their House counterparts. The Senate space committee's prestige dipped to a new low when recruiting difficulties in the Ninety-second Congress forced a reduction in membership from fifteen to eleven because seven vacancies could not be filled, though in 1973 the size of the committee was increased to thirteen seats. *Aviation Week*, a magazine widely read in the aerospace industry, said in February 1971 that the committee is now only a "temporary assignment for freshmen senators."[4] The committee seems almost moribund today: its "inquiries and investigations" budget was the lowest of all standing committees in the Senate in the Ninety-second Congress: $10,000.* This compares with $7,589,000 for the Senate Judiciary Committee on the high end, and $35,000, the next lowest budget, for the Senate Finance Committee.[5]

Part of the Senate committee's problem stems from the fact that its jurisdiction is restricted to NASA only. But its House counterpart, the Science and Astronautics Committee, has been having similar problems, even though its jurisdiction is considerably broader. Turnover rate for the House is between four and five members a year, nearly three times higher than that of the Senate (one or two annually). Eighty-eight representatives have served over the past thirteen years, including fifty-six Democrats and thirty-two Republicans. At the end of the Ninety-first Con-

---

* Actual expenditures were $6,194.96.

gress the Democratic side of the committee lost nine of its eighteen members. In the Ninety-second Congress the total committee membership was reduced from thirty-two to twenty-nine, but it increased to thirty-one in 1973. In 1971 the committee had lost two members with the death of its ranking Republican, Representative James Fulton of Pennsylvania, and the resignation of one of its most active and capable leaders, Representative Joe Karth. The House space committee's budget figures reflect their much heavier work load, the detailed inquiries and investigations they have undertaken, and the use of outside consultants. Authorized expenditures for the Ninety-second Congress were $380,000; a supplementary resolution later in the same Congress added $410,000 for a total of $790,000. The House employs thirty-two staff members.

Increasingly the House committee has come to be of interest to representatives with large aerospace constituencies. For instance, in the Ninety-second Congress its membership included three representatives from the Los Angeles area, and others whose districts included the Kennedy Space Center, Seattle, St. Louis, and Long Island, all areas with large NASA or aerospace employment. It is not surprising that there is a predisposition among these members of Congress to advocacy rather than criticism of the space program.

The political allegiance of individual committee members indicates that they generally tend toward the more conservative spectrum, judging from the ratings that special interest groups give members of both the Senate and House space committees for their floor votes.[6] (See ratings for members in Table 15.)

THE PERSONALITY PARADE

Personalities are as much a part of the space program as propellants and nose cones. In addition to one minor mutiny, there are two examples of despotism: one created by the arrogance of the chairman of the House subcommittee on manned space flight (who now chairs the full committee); the other by the pique of an elderly California congressman at references to his age.

Mutiny in Committee Room 2321

So far, the one real intracommittee rebellion was, at that, a transistor-sized tempest. This was an attempt in 1970 by a few House committee members to chop off funds that the committee as a whole had added to an administration request for the space shuttle, the largest projected project at NASA. (See Table 16.)

TABLE 15.

House Science and Astronautics Committee Ideology:
Floor Vote Ratings of Members (1971)

Rating of:	Median	Mean	Standard Deviation	Committee Chairman
Americans for Democratic Action (Liberal)	24	39.4	30.6	41
Average	30	39.6	32.2	xxxx
Americans for Constitutional Action (Conservative)	57.5	50.8	26.5	30
Average	54	51.0	31.8	xxxx
Committee on Political Education (Labor)	46	53.5	28	91
Average	50	53.2	33.1	xxxx

Senate Aeronautical and Space Sciences Committee Ideology:
Floor Vote Ratings of Members (1971)

Rating of:	Median	Mean	Standard Deviation	Committee Chairman
Americans for Democratic Action (Liberal)	30	31.8	27.4	48
Average	41	46.6	33.3	xxxx
Americans for Constitutional Action (Conservative)	57	57.8	28.5	26
Average	39	43.8	30.2	xxxx
Committee on Political Education (Labor)	42	45.5	30.2	75
Average	56	53.1	27.7	xxxx

TABLE 16.

Projected Breakdown of Allocations for NASA Objectives, 1973–78

Budget Authority:	1973	1974	1975	1976	1977	1978
			(in millions)			
Aeronautics	$151	$171	$159	$142	$128	$117
Space science	679	584	483	413	335	256
Space applications	189	153	146	124	87	74
Manned space flight, advanced mission studies	957	582	345	226	218	218
Space shuttle	200	475	850	1,100	1,190	1,090
Space research and technology	65	65	65	65	65	65
Nuclear power and propulsion	17	4	4	4	4	4
Technology utilization	4	4	4	4	4	4
Tracking and data acquisition	248	250	254	254	254	247
Construction of facilities	77	112	150	100	80	70
Research and program management	715	707	707	707	707	707
Total budget authority	$3,302	$3,107	$3,167	$3,139	$3,072	$2,852
Total outlays	$3,062	$3,136	$3,231	$3,219	$3,145	$3,043

SOURCE: *National Journal*, May 12, 1973, p. 642.

Representative Joe Karth, then chairman of the Space Sciences and Applications Subcommittee, began the mutiny. Playing Captain Bligh opposite Karth was Texan Olin Teague, then chairman of the Manned Space Flight Subcommittee. Karth's efforts to push the space applications area in NASA had been rewarded; a separate office had been established, and one of its several significant achievements, the Earth Resources Technology Satellite (ERTS), was funded in 1970 and again in 1973.* Karth and his bipartisan mutineers—four Democrats and three Republicans, including Charles Mosher, the subcommittee's ranking Republican—took

* ERTS contracts have stimulated business for at least one private firm. The two-year-old Earth Satellite Corporation of Washington, a natural resources consulting firm specializing in extracting data from satellites and aircraft (such as mapping river basins and making land-use inventories), in 1973 recorded nearly $2 million in sales and assets of $1 million.[7]

the unprecedented step of categorically opposing a committee-approved bill—the space shuttle fund increase.

Karth claimed he was not against the shuttle but simply wanted to slow development to "a more rational pace."[8]* Mosher said he opposed the funding increase because of the tight budget situation. But in a speech on the floor, Mosher gave outsiders a glimpse of the bickering behind closed doors that had preceded the full committee's action: "Our subcommittee deferred a number of projects in the space applications program, only to find the manned flight subcommittee was coming in with a $300 million increase in their segment. We just couldn't support it."[9]

"Tiger" Teague prevailed. Karth's open break with the committee, Teague said, was "just plain stupid." He dismissed the incident with, "Karth could have had much more influence had he worked within the committee, but instead he went out and made a bunch of speeches and got nowhere." Representative Karth left the Science and Astronautics Committee in 1971 for a seat on the powerful Ways and Means Committee, and Teague became chairman of the full committee in 1973.

The Genial Tyrant

There is considerable difference of opinion as to how good Teague's predecessor was. Representative George Miller (D., Calif.), committee chairman until 1973, was a proselytizer for space exploration and considered himself an amateur scientist. He had even less patience than most space advocates with those who were skeptical of some NASA programs. During our discussion he accused the interviewer of "scoffing" at space exploration.

Miller's style of leadership was very personal, which is not unusual for senior committee chairmen. This occasioned some run-ins with Representative Ken Hechler, chairman of the Sub-

---

* Karth had previously fought excessive costs on the Ranger and Surveyor projects (unmanned geolunar projects of the Jet Propulsion Laboratory in Pasadena, California).

committee on Aeronautics and Space Technology. For example, at that time the rules of the Democratic Caucus, which determines positions favored by the majority of House Democrats, provided that a subcommittee chairman "shall be entitled to select and designate at least one staff member for his subcommittee." Miller "cheerfully and consistently" opposed the implementation of this rule, a move that Hechler opposed, since he wanted to appoint staff to his subcommittee. When asked about this, Miller simply replied that he hired and fired all staff members.[10] Reminded of Hechler's feeling about this issue, Miller angrily acknowledged that Hechler "is unhappy about a lot of things."

Hechler thinks his relationship with the chairman soured when he had the temerity to suggest mandatory retirement at the age of seventy for members of Congress. Miller, well past seventy, took this as a personal affront, and his response was to harass Hechler. For example, several times when Hechler had important constituents as guests at committee hearings, Miller would try to belittle him with comments like "That is not a very smart question."

On the other hand, Miller gave great latitude to former Congressman Emilio Q. Daddario (D., Conn.), who from 1963 to 1970 chaired the important Science, Research and Development Subcommittee. That subcommittee was amazingly prolific and served as the primary congressional link to the outside scientific community. But then Miller reportedly liked Daddario personally.

Under the jurisdiction of the science committee Miller created a study group on energy resources, under Representative Mike McCormack (D., Wash.), two years before the public recognized the energy crisis. Since McCormack was too junior to warrant a subcommittee chair, the policy area of energy was subsumed under a task force structure that functioned somewhat like a subcommittee. When Miller was defeated, in 1972, McCormack became a full-fledged chairman of a subcommittee on energy.*

---

* Intense political battles are now being waged in both houses of Congress to determine what committees have major jurisdiction over energy matters. In addition to McCormack's subcommittee, there are a national fuels and en-

Space activities in the House during the Ninety-second Congress included over 200 pages of testimony on the new U.S.-USSR cooperative agreements and the joint space mission scheduled for 1975; studies on fire research and safety; a two-year study on materials research and development (published in the spring of 1973); a study of international environmental science problems via a joint colloquium with the Senate Commerce Committee; and a nationwide survey of water research conducted by the federal government, local and state agencies, and private industry. Hearings of all subcommittees and the full committee took fifty-seven days in the first session of the Ninety-second Congress, and sixty-six days in the second session, for a total of 125—an index that exhibits a very superior effort compared to that of other House committees. Between 1962 and 1972, seventy-two reports, studies, or surveys were published under the House committee's aegis. (See House space committee votes, Table 17.)

The Senate Atmosphere

Calmer—and less colorful—space committee members in the Senate generally worked at a slow pace. The former chairman, Senator Clinton Anderson (D., N.M.), was widely considered a fair-minded executive who did not exploit patronage possibilities. When NASA decided to close down the White Sands engine-testing facility in Anderson's home state, the senator did not try to use his influence to keep it open. He merely asked NASA to mothball, rather than destroy, the facility so that it could be used again if the need should arise. In failing health for several years, Anderson took a progressively less vigorous role in running his committee. (He retired in 1972.)

---

ergy study within the Senate Interior and Insular Affairs Committee (set up by Senate resolution), a new science and technology subcommittee in the Senate Commerce Committee, and an energy subcommittee in the Joint Committee on Atomic Energy. Ironically, the minimal attention getter in all these committees is solar energy—the only nondepleting, nondestructive, nonpolluting, lasting energy source available to this planet.

TABLE 17.

Science and Astronautics Key Committee Votes, 92nd Congress

1. To report NASA authorization, increasing the administration request by $49.95 million (primarily for aeronautical research and technology programs for aircraft noise reduction, aeronautical safety, and automatic approach and landing R & D) (H.R. 12824). Yes: 23; No: 0.
2. To strike the authorization limitation on funds for National and Special Research Programs under the "Research Applied for National Needs" program. Had the amendment succeeded, it would have permitted funding for the program at a higher level than the $50.4 million specified in the bill. Opponents of the amendment feared that new money given over to applied research would divert even more money away from basic research considered by some to be vastly undersubsidized. (McCormack amendment to H.R. 4743, National Science Foundation Authorization for FY 1972.) Yes: 8; No: 17.
3. To provide that subcommittee chairman handle legislation on the floor, and hire their own subcommittee staff. Also, to provide that no member could chair more than one legislative subcommittee. (Hechler amendment to the committee rules to conform rules to the Hausen Reform Committee recommendations.) This would lessen the power of the committee chairman. Yes: 3; No: 22; Present 4.

		Voting					
Democrats	1	2	3	Republicans	1	2	3
Miller	Y	N	N	Fulton	—	N	N
Teague	Y	N	N	Mosher	Y	N	N
Karth	—	N	N	Bell	Y	Y	N
Hechler	Y	Y	Y	Pelly	Y	N	N
Davis, J.	Y	N*	N	Wydler	Y	—	—
Downing	Y	—	N	Winn	Y	N	N
Fuqua	Y	N	N	Price	Y	N	N
Cabell	Y	N	N	Frey	Y	—	N
Symington	Y	Y*	N	Goldwater	Y	N	N
Hanna	—	Y	N	Esch	Y	N	N
Flowers	—	N	N	Coughlin	Y	N	N
Roe	—	N	N	Camp	Y	N	N
Seiberling	Y	Y	Y				
Cotter	—	—	Y				
Rangel	—	Y	—				
Murphy	—	Y	—				
McCormack	Y	Y	—				
Davis, M.	Y	—	—				
Bergland	Y	—	—				

* The House space committee had no key recorded votes during 1973.

A distinctively new complexion for the Senate space committee emerged in the Ninety-third Congress. The new chairman, Frank Moss (D., Utah), a strong space supporter, faces challenges from two new members, Senators Abourezk (D., S.D.) and Haskell (D., Colo.). For the first time the committee's unanimous acquiescence to space programs is being questioned. In April of 1973 Senator Abourezk set up a special "dialogue" between opponents and proponents in hearings on the space shuttle. In alliance with a noncommittee member, Senator William Proxmire (D., Wisc.), Abourezk is seeking projected plans and costs for the space agency for the next decade—and particularly the impact of ever rising costs for the space shuttle. Robert Allnutt, formerly a general counsel for NASA, became the new staff director in the Ninety-third Congress. (See Senate space committee vote, Table 18.)

TABLE 18.

Aeronautical and Space Sciences Key Committee Vote, 1973*

To allocate $131 million from the space shuttle program to other (unmanned) space programs (Abourezk amendment to H.R. 7528). Yes: 2; No: 10.

	Voting		
Democrats		Republicans	
Moss	N	Goldwater	N
Magnuson	N	Curtis	N
Symington	N	Weicker	N
Stennis	N	Bartlett	N
Cannon	N	Domenici	N
Abourezk	Y		
Haskell	Y		

* The Senate space committee had no recorded votes during the 92nd Congress.

INFORMATION RESOURCES

Beyond all the jurisdictional and personality problems that affect space science policy making is an even more critical problem—

where to get reliable data. So far, committee policy has been based on the information most readily at hand. The most knowledgeable source of scientific information for congressional committees has been the National Academy of Sciences, an elite group in diverse scientific fields elected by their peers, who are experts not only in these fields but in the peripheral regions as well. Two major organizations, the American Association for the Advancement of Science (biological sciences) and the American Chemical Society (chemical sciences), have offices in Washington. (The American Physical Society's national office is in New York.) A special-interest activist group, the Federation of American Scientists, has been operating and offering information since 1946; and in the last decade organizations such as the Center for Science in the Public Interest have provided some information to the committee.

On the whole, however, NASA is the primary source and the aerospace industry the secondary source for nearly all the information the committees gather on space. One has to look long and hard to find a witness at a committee hearing who is not affiliated with NASA or the industry. For example, in the Senate authorization hearings for the 1973 budget, out of twenty-eight witnesses who testified, only three were independent—and two of those had a NASA contract. Outsiders frequently submit written material, but theirs is only a small fraction of the supplementary material supplied by NASA and the industry.

Members make this situation more limited by their own attitudes and procedures. They perceive NASA not only as the major source of information but as practically the *only* relevant source. In general, nonspace technical men are inexperienced and ineffective in the political arena, and face a communication problem of some dimension even with interested members of Congress.* The

---

* Some of the professional scientific organizations began a special program in 1972, fielding scientists and engineers at Capitol Hill as "Congressional Fellows" under association grants. Only three or four have been involved, at this writing. Representative Mike McCormack of the House space commit-

views of dissenting scientists are often discounted by members and staff if the scientists stray in the slightest from their special areas of expertise, but even a space scientist's view may be ignored if he contradicts NASA. In our interview with the former chairman of the House committee, George Miller, this was clear:

> Q. How do you respond to the claims of some scientists that the scientific payoff of space is not as great as it should be?
>
> A. Well, you can believe them if you want. You can find scientists to criticize the thing, and then you can condemn the program and say it spends too much money. Scientists are funny people. You can find scientists to say anything to support you when you condemn the space program.
>
> Q. But how do you, as a decision maker, go about evaluating the conflicting claims?
>
> A. If a man is in biology, and he is talking about earth sciences, then he has no business making a judgment.
>
> Q. How about some of the scientists in the space sciences field who criticize manned space programs?
>
> A. Like who? I'm not aware of any.
>
> Q. For example, James Van Allen. He's opposed to the shuttle.
>
> A. Jim Van Allen is a good friend of mine and a neighbor of my brother. I don't know that he's opposed. Where did you see that?

In fact, Dr. Van Allen, the space scientist for whom the radiation belt around the earth is named, had submitted a statement of his opposition to the space shuttle to the Senate committee.

Digging for information encompasses more than formal hearings. Among the committee's sources of information a few are generally dominant, although different members place varying emphases on each of them. First is the committee staff. In spite of the esoteric nature of the space committee's work, there is no

---

tee welcomed the program of scientific congressional interns eagerly. "There is a tremendous gulf of ignorance," he said, "on both sides."

indication that the members rely very much on the staff for scientific expertise. Only one staff member holds a doctorate in a scientific field. In addition to relying on NASA, committee members listen to representatives of other government agencies, notably the Department of Defense. A third frequently mentioned source is the Library of Congress, which is occasionally commissioned to do special projects for the committees. Finally, committee members rely on the senior members' own experience and "feel" for situations. None of the committee members pretend to understand the fine technical details, but they may understand some of the less complex technical issues and options.

1. *The Broader Questions.* The context in which space issues are discussed, however, is quite narrow. In fact, underlying questions about the space program are rarely asked. Like most other congressional committees and government agencies, the space committees proceed by an incremental style of decision making.

NASA and committee members frequently point out all the earthly benefits of the space program. For example, Senator Goldwater entered a summary of highlights of NASA's 1972 achievements in the *Congressional Record*: the space agency won plaudits in avionics, aerodynamics, and astronomy (by way of the Mariner explorations of Mars); in foreign relations (through the Nixon-Brezhnev agreement for a joint venture in 1975); and in agriculture, forestry, geology, geography (land use), hydrology, and ecology, among others (through applications of space discoveries to earthly problems). Some of the technological innovations included an ultraclean laminar air-flow technique for cleaner hospital surgeries; a rapid-scan infrared tire tester; a computer design program to test structural stress; a heat pin for cooking; and a paper-thin flat electrical conductor for household use.[11]

What is never assessed by the committees, however, is whether these advances could have been obtained more cheaply and in greater number by a less lavishly funded program of pure and applied research directed specifically toward problems on earth.

That might or might not have been possible, but the point is that the question seems never to have been asked.

How are the men of government—many of them intelligent, educated, and enlightened, but laymen nonetheless—to deal with the advice of the men of science? Like President Franklin Roosevelt, who had nothing more than his faith in Einstein when he committed the United States to study the potential of the atom, members of the science committees depend on their own faith in the scientists who serve as their information sources. Representative John Davis (D., Ga.), current chairman of the House Science, Research and Development Subcommittee, remarks:

> There is just not any way to know when you are not a scientist yourself. You are in the same shape when you have a watchmaker work on your watch. I find, after 9½ years on this committee, I don't believe there is any group of men in the country that is more reliable, or who cherishes the integrity or validity of their views more jealously than the scientific community. I think the examples have been the scientific advisors of the president and the great parade of witnesses who come before this committee. I have no misgivings whatsoever.

But this expression of faith misses the point that is most frustrating to laymen: sincere scientists may reach conclusions that are 180 degrees apart. With competent people aligned on various sides of an issue, the dilemma of the decision maker is a search for criteria.

The problem of dealing with experts on complex subjects is not limited to science policy making. Taxation, revenue sharing, welfare reform—all these issues involve their own complexities, have their own experts, and employ their own languages. But in complex nonscience areas some members of Congress can acquire substantial expertise. It is not an invidious comparison to point out that Clinton Anderson and George P. Miller, chairmen of the congressional space committees in the Ninety-second Congress, could not through mere diligence develop expertise comparable to that of the scientists; they would need substantive formal training in physics and engineering.

Second, there is the matter of the location of expertise. If one wants to know about toy safety, for example, available experts are not only those in the toy industry or a government agency. Any number of independent pediatricians, toxologists, and others would be competent to testify. On space issues, committee members claim that the aerospace industry and NASA are the only sources of relevant expertise.

Many members of Congress seem to be dissatisfied with the adequacy of their technical information. A recent Stanford University workshop questionnaire asked them about their need for technical advice. The response was small (seventy-three returns), but perhaps the results show a trend. To the question "Is Congress adequately informed on the technical issues involved in legislation?" seventeen members answered yes, while thirty-six answered no. The Stanford questionnaire also asked whether resources of technical advice, and those of Congress in general, were adequate to the tasks of initiating legislation. Thirty-one said yes; twenty-nine said no. Especially startling was Congress' perception of its position compared with that of the executive branch. Only seven members considered congressional resources of technical advice adequate to oversee the operation of government agencies; fifty-two members said they were not.

The need for such advice, however, is endemic in Congress. Representative John Davis, chairing the most active of the six House subcommittees on space, ran a spot check on bills introduced in the House subcommittees and found that, excluding private bills, *half of all legislation* contained some major scientific or technological component or was allied to or dependent upon science and technology.

And the problem won't go away. The scientific and technical information explosion, rather than slowing, is expected to roar ahead, "with greater escalation," according to a study by French economist J. G. Anderia, a Sorbonne professor who headed a study on the question for the Organization for Economic Cooperation and Development. Anderia indicated that by 1987 output of scientific information would increase six to seven times the 1970 level, creating even greater problems for national governments that wish to insure each citizen "a legal right" to access to scientific information.

2. *On the Horizon: Expertise.* In March 1967, when House Science and Astronautics committee member Emilio Daddario introduced a technology assessment bill, Congress tried to develop a new, dependable expert information structure of its own, as a supplement to space industry and executive branch experts for the science committees and as a source of technological advice for all members. In Daddario's bill (H.R. 6698), technology assessment was defined as

> identifying the potentials of applied research and technology and promoting ways and means to accomplish their transfer into practical use; and identifying the undesirable by-products and side-effects of such applied research and technology, in advance of their crystallization, and informing the public of their potential in order that appropriate steps may be taken to eliminate or minimize them.

Later in 1967, as part of the discussion about Daddario's bill, a blue-ribbon seminar of scientists and other scholars was convened, a move that was to become a pattern for the House science subcommittee. Separate studies of technology assessment were made by the National Academy of Sciences (National Academy of Engineering) and the Science Policy Division of the Library of Congress. Reports were unanimous in urging such a program. After hearings in 1969 a bill was drafted and circulated to "a selected group of government officials and private individuals." A second draft, H.R. 17046, was then introduced by Daddario and Representative Mosher; and a third bill (H.R. 18469) in 1970.

This last was introduced by Committee Chairman George P. Miller and ranking minority member James G. Fulton; all the Science Research and Development subcommittee members co-sponsored it. An attempt to attach it to the Legislative Reorganization Act of 1970 failed, however, for it was ruled not germane. No further House action was taken on it until 1971.

By this time the subcommittee composition had changed: Daddario had left Congress and John Davis had assumed his post as subcommittee chairman. On September 8, 1971, a new technology assessment bill (H.R. 10243) was reported out. It provided for an Office of Technology Assessment within Congress, responsible only to Congress, consisting of a Technology Assessment Board and an administrative staff. Before floor amendments, it provided for an eleven-member board, including four public members, to be appointed by the president *pro tempore* of the Senate. Technological assessment studies could be initiated by any committee chairman or ranking minority member, or by the majority of any committee.

The bill went to the floor in February 1972, where H. R. Gross (R., Iowa) argued:

> To hear this bill explained, one would think that the millennium had been achieved or we were on the threshold of the millennium; that the creation of a new board in government is going to save I do not know how many millions of dollars. Yes, we are told, there will be wondrous savings accruing from the creation of another board that will cost us $5 million to get started and $7 million to $8 million a year after that.[12]

Jack Brooks (D., Tex.) moved to change the staffing provision, suggesting a ten-member technology assessment board consisting of five members of the House and five senators, with no provision for public members. This was passed 29–19—a vote demonstrating the near-invisibility of the legislation, if nothing else. A slightly different technology assessment bill cleared the Senate

Committee on Rules and Administration and was passed on the floor. A conference committee successfully resolved the differences and the Technology Assessment Act became law on October 13, 1972. As enacted, the bill established a thirteen-member board, consisting of an equal number from the House and the Senate, plus the director of the Office of Technology Assessment as an *ex officio* member. Five million dollars was authorized for the first two years.

Slated for the first two years of operation (1972–74) were these members from the Senate side: Edward Kennedy (D., Mass.), Hubert Humphrey (D., Minn.), Ernest F. Hollings (D., S.C.), Peter H. Dominick (R., Colo.), Clifford P. Case (R., N.J.), and Richard Schweiker (R., Pa.). From the House, the following were selected by Speaker Carl Albert (D., Okla.): Olin Teague (D., Tex.), Morris Udall (D., Ariz.), Charles Mosher (R., Calif.), James Harvey (R., Mich.), and Charles Gubser (R., Calif.). Former congressman Emilio Daddario was named director of OTA.

Panels and seminars are expected to include not only scientists from specific disciplines but "associated" personnel—from labor unions, industry, and public interest and consumer groups—who have special expertise in a study area.

It remains to be seen whether the Office of Technology Assessment can override the objections facing it. Scientist Hugh Folk wonders whether members of Congress would accept so-called objective advice on important questions in which they have an interest: "Most politicians know what kind of advice they want, and will make sure that they get it."[13] Folk also warns that expertise is rarely neutral. To an extent, the Technology Assessment Act contains safeguards against the bias of experts who are assessors for Congress; for example, assessments are to be contracted out rather than done by a permanent agency. Of course meaningless assessments could result if the contracts went only to organizations with predictable interests of their own (such as affiliates of corporations with financial stakes in science programs). Another safeguard should at least expose such assessments, because all panels, seminars, meetings, reports, and other data gathering in the OTA's jurisdiction are to operate under the "sunshine law"—that is, with public access at all times.

In the end, members of Congress do not have to follow OTA's advice. OTA information gathering is not a decision-making process in itself. There is even disagreement about whether technology assessments should identify only "bad" consequences or should identify positive consequences as well. And should OTA provide information on "intangibles"? In *Technical Information for Congress*,[14] the Congressional Research Service* argues that "measurement [should] involve noneconomic, subjective values as well as [provide] direct, tangible quantifications."

At any rate, H.R. 10243, as passed by the House, probably represents the House space committee's finest hour. As passed by the whole of Congress, it is potentially the most constructive and creative congressional endeavor of the past few years.

---

* The Congressional Research Service was established by Congress to provide information and conduct research at the request of members of Congress, committees, and staff.

14

The Star Issue

The shades of Buck Rogers and Jules Verne romanticize what is likely to be the major space controversy of the seventies. According to the *National Journal*, a Washington weekly that reports on federal policy making, the tug of war is between those who favor a "space shuttle"—involving manned flight and a new system of "transportation" (new rockets, engines, and plane designs)—and those who favor the high maintenance of space science applications and research, unmanned flight, and the use of existing "hardware."

No one is against the latter option. According to the *National Journal*:

> [opposing] sides do not disagree on the prospective uses of space. The most fruitful opportunities, both would agree, are found in the sciences, including physics, astronomy, the life sciences, and planetary (unmanned) probes; in space applications, including already substantial benefits from commu-

nications, navigation, weather observation and earth resources satellites . . .[1]

The space agency, too, wants both: but unless the agency budget
goes up again, from its peeled-down, stable $3.1 billion (to some-
where near $3.4 billion, according to deputy NASA director
George Low), something will have to give. Proponents of man in
space and new hardware say it will occur in the valuable research
and applications areas.

THE SPACE SHUTTLE

One of NASA's dreams—a station in space—was already old
when the first man walked on the moon. Public discussion began
when President Johnson said, "The year 1965—the year of Gem-
ini, Ranger, and Mariner*—is a brilliant preface to the coming
years of Apollo, stations in space, and voyages to the planets."
The dreams included the space station (a man-made, life-support-
ive "mini-moon" in the middle of the wild blue yonder); a space
shuttle (an earth-to-station ferry to supply the station); two lunar
stations, one on the satellite and one in its orbit; and, for the
decade of the eighties, missions to carry out manned exploration
of the planets in our solar system.[2]

The dreams were as ethereal as the probabilities. After the
summer of NASA's remarkable moon walk triumph (1969),
budget plans for fiscal 1971 were dismissed by the Office of Management and Budget (OMB, the "executive bookkeeper") as a
collection of moonbeams. NASA hastily dropped several of its
incandescent notions and concentrated solely on the space shuttle.
The original reason for the inclusion of the shuttle in the planning
stage was that NASA had discovered that two-thirds of the cost
for the space station was for ordnance—that is, supplies.[3] Whatever the reason, the space shuttle has now become the central

NOTE: This section was researched and drafted by Judith Lichten.
* Respectively two-manned orbital flight; unmanned lunar mapping; and unmanned Mars mapping.

issue around which the entire space program of the seventies revolves.

Models and Money

At one point, everybody in Washington was designing his own shuttle. "Reusability" was a key factor: NASA's current hardware is all "disposable." The first shuttle design was schizoid, a fully reusable two-stage vehicle that "darts up like a rocket and lands like an airplane," the *New York Times* reported in a story headlined "Billions Were Up for Grabs."[4] NASA claimed that this 1969 design would cost $6 billion to build, an estimate so low it caused the space agency a sharp loss of credibility.[5] A long design battle ensued to make the high-flying shuttle a low-cost bonanza. The idea of scrapping the shuttle rather than the design was not genuinely considered.

In January 1970 the OMB asked NASA for a cost-benefit analysis of the shuttle. The result was a study by a firm of economic consultants, Mathematica, Inc., which was completed in May 1971. The consultants estimated that the nonrecurring costs (research, development, testing, and evaluation) for the fully reusable shuttle would be $12.8 billion between 1979 and 1990. They did not endorse the design.[6] NASA awarded contracts to Lockheed, Grumman Aerospace, and the Chrysler Corporation to study less complicated and less expensive shuttle designs. More than nine different designs were studied between June 1971 and January 1972.[7]

A second Mathematica study was completed for the simpler design that was selected on January 31, 1972. The conclusion this time was that the shuttle would be economically feasible as long as there was space activity at least equal to the U.S. unmanned space program of the past eight years.[8]

Early in 1972 President Nixon announced that he supported the new, simplified shuttle model, whose development costs would be approximately $5.15 billion over the next six years. Caspar Weinberger, at that time a deputy director of the Office of Man-

agement and Budget, affirmed his support of space but added,
". . . as to what exactly it is the shuttle will be taking up and back
to orbit, I must say I don't know."[9]

Delta-winged, the shuttle will be launched into orbit vertically
by a two-part booster, and then change its plane of orbit to return
to earth, landing horizontally with the assistance of jet engines. It
is designed to deliver unmanned satellites into orbit. A pressur-
ized cabin, called a "sortie module," fits inside the shuttle and can
be used as a space laboratory for experimental scientists without
space suits. The major design difference in the new model is that
the booster will be expendable; only the orbiter will be reusable.

To support the shuttle, NASA severely cut three programs: the
Grand Tour mission (an eleven-year flight past Jupiter, Saturn,
and Pluto); the NERVA program (a nuclear rocket engine for
galactic use); and three of the seven planned experiments for the
Mariner 9 satellite circling Mars.[10]

The shuttle, boosted by the space committees—Senator Cannon (D., Nev.) called it "a lean and fully defensible system"—
met strong head winds on the floor of Congress. Three times in
May 1972 Senator Walter Mondale (D., Minn.) attempted to
scuttle the shuttle funding and failed. In the House, both Bella
Abzug (D., N.Y.) and Les Aspin (D., Wisc.) tried and failed—
and vowed to try again. Aspin managed to secure only eleven votes
on a floor amendment to delay development pending release of a
study by the National Academy of Sciences.

Opponents of the shuttle have challenged the conclusions of the
Mathematica report on which NASA bases its claim that, during
the next decade, the shuttle will result in a saving of $7 billion
over use of the current system of throwaway rockets. They assert
that NASA's intention to develop the shuttle is only a device to
continue the manned space program. Shuttle proponents counter
that it will be useful to unmanned practical applications of satellites and to scientific space experiments as well. Its military uses
are obvious as well as enormous. Proponents point out obliquely

that economy is only one of several reasons for developing the space shuttle.

With the passage of the NASA budget authorization for 1973 (which included $227.9 million for shuttle development), both sides have shelved their arguments temporarily. These deserve a close examination, however. They are likely to arise again as NASA's annual budget requests for the shuttle steadily become larger.

The Payload Debate

Spokesmen for NASA have stated that the shuttle will reduce per-pound payload launch costs from their current levels to $160,[11] $100,[12] or $75.[13] NASA does not give solid figures to back up the lesser amounts, but if the cost per launch (which NASA estimates to be $10.5 million[14]) is divided by the total payload capacity of 65,000 pounds, the figure of $160 is obtained.

It is difficult to assess the meaning of this figure without determining first what is meant by "payload." Criticism has centered on the large amount of payload to be sent up with the shuttle. Bella Abzug saw the possibility of secret military missions:

> In 1969 there were 37 space launchings carrying a total payload of 381,400 pounds. Yet, according to NASA predictions, the payload level for future shuttle flights would increase to the astronomical figure of over 2.6 million pounds of payload/year between 1978–90. With this increase of over two million pounds per year, it is obvious that the shuttle is being designed to facilitate far more than mere satellites for space travel. Could this space shuttle system possibly serve as a primary transport carrier of heavy military equipment for use in outer space?[15]

James Van Allen says he could envision sending up to one ton of satellites into orbit per week and no more.[16] Senator Mondale points out that over a year's time this would amount to less than one shuttle flight.[17]

What "payload" means is still not clear. "Destination payload," in NASA terminology, refers to the satellite that is to be put into orbit, but payload can refer to everything that would be sent up in the shuttle: fuel, an additional propulsion stage, and the sortie module as well as the satellite.

According to former Secretary of the Air Force Robert C. Seamans, Jr., the heaviest satellite weighs 5,000 pounds. If it were to be carried into a geosynchronous orbit, the remaining 60,000 pounds of capacity would be utilized for propellant and for the propulsion stage to send the satellite from a lower to a higher orbit.[18] Dr. Ralph Lapp, a physicist, says the cost per pound would be much higher if this 60,000 pounds were subtracted from the payload weight. It would then cost $2,000 a pound rather than $160 a pound to send up a 5,000-pound satellite.[19] House Science and Astronautics Committee Chairman Olin Teague's claim that the shuttle's launch cost is "far less than any other space vehicle with an equivalent payload capacity" is, on this analysis, misleading.

The "Space Screwdriver"

A stronger economic argument is NASA's assertion that payloads will be cheaper for two reasons: first, the shuttle will be a "space screwdriver," bringing satellites back to earth from orbit or repairing them in orbit; fewer payloads will have to be built. Second, the shuttle's payload costs would be cheaper because its large cargo bay would make expensive miniaturization of satellite components no longer necessary. According to NASA administrator James C. Fletcher:

> We can substantially reduce the cost of designing, building, and operating all kinds of satellites. Satellites will not have to be so restricted in size, shape, and weight. We can use more standard, off-the-shelf components. The process of putting space-craft together and testing them will be simplified. The time it takes to design a new payload for a specific mission may well be reduced from five or six years to five or six months.[20]

There is strong scientific disagreement with Fletcher. One scientist, Dr. Thomas Gold, director of Cornell University's Center for Radiophysics and Space Research, stated at Senate hearings that "for the Shuttle there could still be major technical problems and neither time schedules nor completion costs can yet be regarded as reliable."[21]

Dr. Brian O'Leary, an astronomer and ex-astronaut, suggests that satellites in a near-earth orbit become obsolete in one or two years. Before satellites can be refurbished there will be the need to standardize them, which would, presumably, involve more time and money. Dr. O'Leary also pointedly notes that the major cost of building a satellite is in electronics and that a large cargo bay would not affect this cost.[22]

NASA uses the Mathematica study to bolster its claim that repair and retrieval of satellites will save money, but this report does not say conclusively that there will be savings: "The interactions between considerations of payload lifetime, reliability, retrieval, refurbishment/updating and reuse with other space transportation system aspects are so complex that the ultimate cost savings remain to be shown."[23]

NASA hopes to build a space "tug," an unmanned vehicle to fire payloads into orbits 22,300 miles from earth (deep space), retrieve them, and repair them in the space shuttle's lower orbital shop. Development, however, is not expected until 1985. Without the space tug nothing can be retrieved from deep orbit—which is the destination of 50 percent of all satellites.[24] Mathematica based its study on the assumption that there *will* be a tug to retrieve and repair these. The tug's nonexistence certainly affects the projected payload savings to be achieved through repair and refurbishment.

The "Input" Argument

Chalkboard or computer, what comes out when you add and subtract depends largely on what you put in. Mathematica has been charged with bias because data for the study were obtained from Aerospace Corporation, a space project contractor (which obtained its projected models from NASA and the Department of Defense), and from the space division of Lockheed Corporation, which worked on payload effects. Mathematica, however, claims to be absolutely independent. When asked how Mathematica's independence was achieved, Dr. Oskar Morgenstern, codirector of the study, replied:

> It is written into the contract, and I think the whole record of our personal lives as well as our company is such that we have never allowed any contractor to interfere with our work. And I must say that NASA has never attempted to direct us or to ask us for a particular answer or the like. On the contrary, at the beginning, it was extremely difficult to come to any common language even, because we were at opposite ends, as I have indicated. We were very skeptical that the whole thing would work and I must say that independence was secured as far as possible.[25]

Personal integrity and noninterference are obviously inadequate responses to a query on how independence is achieved with only biased data sources. The consultant's answer is not to the point.

Nor were the congressional space committees very helpful. In a hearing before the Senate committee, a question about possible bias in the Mathematica study was phrased this way:

> SENATOR CURTIS: Dr. Fletcher, my next question concerns the economic merit and justification of the space shuttle. I have in mind the economic analysis of the space shuttle as prepared by the advanced technology economics group at Mathematica, Inc. I am informed that Mathematica, as your contractor, was given an unusual degree of independence from NASA's more usual practice of close control and direction. Is this the case?[26]

Justification is, of course, based on analysis, and analysis is based on input, not just independence. The senator's question is not to the point.

THE QUESTION OF PRIORITIES

According to NASA's deputy secretary, George Low, the United States cannot keep a "presence" in space unless there are manned flights.

Many disagree. The problem of manned versus unmanned flight is closely related to the space shuttle's position in the context of today's social priorities. Von R. Eshleman, professor of radar astronomy at Stanford University, contends that "NASA needs a focus. I believe the focal point should be in space applications, where there's human and national payoffs. . . ."[27]

Some nonscientists hold the same view. According to *Counterbudget: A Blueprint for Changing National Priorities*, "The excitement of space adventure needs to be replaced by a more rational approach. The overemphasis on manned exploration must give way to the less exciting but more scientifically productive automated missions."[28]

At the request of Senator Mondale, the General Accounting Office (the fiscal investigatory arm of Congress) undertook an analysis and concluded that the shuttle would "not be justified economically if it experienced cost overruns of over 20 percent."[29] The average, in the past, has been 40 percent.

In August 1972 Senator Proxmire took over the chairmanship of the HUD, Space, Science and Veterans Subcommittee of the Appropriations Committee, which approves the Senate space committee's authorizations. Under Proxmire's direction the GAO again studied (and released in June 1973) an analysis of cost-benefit ratios in the space shuttle program. NASA and GAO, in negotiations over the content of the report, battled over esoteric and complicated systems analysis and cost discounting techniques. The report is highly critical of the conclusions of the earlier Mathematica study.

There is little doubt, however, that the shuttle will cut deeply and sharply into space applications and research—unless NASA's authorizations are upped, which is an unlikely probability in the opinion of the OMB and in view of the fact that Congress had yet to do so through fiscal 1975. The expenditure will hit the billion-dollar peak in 1976, as can be seen from Table 16. The table also indicates the deep incisions to be expected in appropriations for both pure science and earth-technology applications.

The Cloud Cover: DOD

Over half of the missions now cited to justify the shuttle involve military uses. Because these are classified, it becomes necessary to discuss the purposes of the shuttle without knowing just what they are.

Before NASA's budget crunch in 1969, the Department of Defense and the space agency were each developing pilot space stations and shuttles (the manned orbiting lab, the SV-5D, Dyna-Soar, etc.). After the cuts, NASA sought the cloudy shelter of the militaristic rationale for NASA programs. It is true that the co-operative effort is cheaper, but why should "civilian" NASA foot DOD's bills? The space agency had to meet Air Force specifications for such things as the ability to maneuver crosswise 1,100 miles (which requires a delta-winged vehicle, a more expensive one than the straight-winged design a "civilian" NASA would need).[30] One committee senator asked this question of Dr. John Foster, head of defense research for DOD:

> SENATOR GAMBRELL: The view is sometimes expressed that, since DOD will use the space shuttle, DOD ought to fund at least a part of it. What are your thoughts with respect to that view?
>
> DR. FOSTER: . . . I think it is quite reasonable . . . either way. My personal view is . . . one agency has to be in charge, and . . . should be the one that . . . prepares and defends the case put before Congress.[31]

The "reasonable" view, of course, makes DOD's budget (now over $80 billion) look a little better than it is. Senator Proxmire commented, "The Pentagon refuses to contribute to the system . . .

[they know] the shuttle could not survive if it were stacked up against other military priorities in the DOD budget," and Professor Courtland Perkins of Princeton confirmed Proxmire's view.[32] Hearings in April of 1973, undertaken at Senator Abourezk's behest, proved "conclusively," according to Proxmire, that "the shuttle is really a Defense Department program that is being piggybacked onto the space agency." If NASA willingly bears the onus of a military cloud, it is because its political administrators know its civilian function—"peaceful uses of space for the benefit of mankind"—will not gain much political support.

As one agency official dryly put it, "The benefit of mankind is diseconomic."

Listening with the Third Ear

Most members of both the Senate and House committees have been less than receptive to critics of the shuttle. In the House committee, just before Representative Bella Abzug (D., N.Y.) was to testify, Representative Louis Frey (R., Fla.) asked the following question of Thomas G. Downall and Caleb B. Hurtt, president and vice-president, respectively, of Martin-Marietta Aerospace: "If you had a minute or two, and no more, to answer someone from, say, New York City, who says the shuttle is a playtoy, the shuttle is just a waste of $121 million or so, what would your answer be?"[33]

Before Dr. Ralph Lapp began his statement against the shuttle at a Senate committee hearing, the following exchange took place:

> DR. LAPP: Thank you very much, Senator Anderson. I appreciate very much the opportunity to appear here today as an independent scientist. I might remark that the definition of independent for me consists of having no contract with NASA. . . .
>
> SENATOR CURTIS: I do not think that that is a very good definition because—I do not say that you are, but somebody might be motivated by the very fact that they did

not receive money from NASA. If money can reward some people, it can disappoint others. I do not believe, for example, that a defeated candidate for president is independent in evaluating the acts of the successful candidate because he does not possess the office.

DR. LAPP: I think the point is valid with respect, Senator Curtis, to the question of the degree of objectivity that a NASA contractor can bring to evaluation of a technical issue wherein he has a possible future for more contracts. I am speaking of the two contractors here to Mathematica; namely, Aerospace and Lockheed. I would, in a completely independent and objective evaluation, prefer not to have companies that will benefit from the Space Shuttle be the ones to make the inputs as to its worth. . . .

SENATOR CURTIS: But the monetary consideration and the status of honor that comes with it is a two-way street. If somebody can be influenced into having a favorable impression because they [sic] are employed and because they have been selected and, therefore, honored, it follows that somebody else could lack independence because they were not employed and selected. I think your definition is pretty narrow. That is all.[34]

A communication process, according to telecommunications expert Colin Cherry, requires a transmitter, a message, and a receiver. There is not much communication when the receiver isn't turned on.

The Sun Shelter

Probably the only significant civilian rationale for the shuttle's existence offered by any member of either space committee at any time came from Representative Mike McCormack (D., Wash.), then the only scientist in Congress (he is a chemist).* McCormack

* James Martin of North Carolina, a former professor of chemistry, won a House seat in the Ninety-third Congress and was appointed to the Science and Astronautics Committee.

chairs the Energy Subcommittee of the House Science and Astronautics committee. In a speech on the floor of the House about the energy crisis, one option he mentioned was "satellite solar energy," which would be dependent on the shuttle. As he explained it:

> . . . satellites will be stationed in synchronous orbit, converting solar heat to electricity with solar panels, which are conceived to be many square miles in area. The energy would be transmitted to earth as a focused beam of microwaves, and converted to usable electricity at receptor stations adjacent to load centers.[35]

The satellite system of procurement is only one of several ideas about how to harness the sun's endless source of abundant power. In 1973 an international conference on solar energy, held in Paris, concluded that nearly "one out of every ten new homes built" in America will be "partially heated and cooled by solar energy" within ten years. Representative McCormack and Representative Symington,* both especially argumentative in this area, have warned that—although they are "enthusiastic" about solar energy's promise—there are formidable economic factors to be overcome.[36] In the short term, the current energy crisis must be met by dependence on "fossil fuels."

The philosophical question—whether the shuttle is the best, the most appropriate, or indeed the necessary, national space objective—is not really considered, any more than the moon shot was.

The changing climate of the Ninety-third Congress does not obscure the fact that in the Ninety-second, committee members saw themselves as advocates of the shuttle, not assessors. Sometimes their earnest partnership with NASA caused a real gaffe. Representative Don Fuqua (D., Fla.) said it was disturbing for members of the House space committee to hear of NASA's deci-

---

* Chairing the energy and the space appropriations subcommittees, respectively, in the House.

sion to drop the fully reusable two-stage shuttle configuration because he "had just finished defending one configuration on the floor [of Congress] and then suddenly they [NASA] announced they were going to change it."[37] Fuqua's problem was a typical committee problem of the past decade.

15

Science, the New Battleground

The real arena for the seventies for the House Committee on Science and Astronautics will not be the outer atmosphere.* Committee priorities were sharply changing even before the Ninety-second Congress drew to a close. Charles Mosher of Ohio, its ranking minority member, in testimony before the Committee on Committees (a select committee that was studying the restructuring of congressional work), noted that "space committee" is an erroneous designation. "I would like to enter a vigorous protest against [that] careless habit . . . an ever-increasing amount of our committee time and effort is necessarily devoted to a variety of science and technology problems not involved in the space program." Mosher, in fact, asked that the committee be renamed the

NOTE: This section was researched and drafted by Thomas Lichten.
* The Senate space committee, however, has jurisdiction only over NASA.

Committee on Science and Technology (which was done) and added that "there seems to be very little real understanding in Washington of the meaning and significance of a coherent national science policy."[1]* Recent events and the unease of the general scientific community bear him out.

The changing fortunes of the National Science Foundation illustrate what Representative Mosher called the "erratic, go and stop, hurry up and wait" policy. Gray, faceless, the National Science Foundation—created by President Truman in 1950 to fund basic research in the "hard" sciences and to encourage scientific education—has often been the butt of congressional jokes. The late Senator Harry F. Byrd (D., Va.) referred to a sample of NSF output as "An Analysis of the Sitting Pressures of Man."

Oversight of the new independent agency was minimal until the House Science and Astronautics Committee set up the Subcommittee on Science, Research and Development in August of 1963. Subcommittee chairman Emilio Q. Daddario, an enterprising and energetic congressman from Connecticut, enlisted the aid of the National Academy of Sciences† for a study of federal options in science and technology. The academy recommended that Daddario's subcommittee forge strong links with the outside scientific community, which it did—with great zeal.

When the subcommittee first turned to look at NSF, it found, in effect, a gaping hole. Perhaps spurred by the success of NASA, which was then flying high, NSF had decided to dig down as deeply as possible. "Project Mohole" was an effort to drill a hole six miles deep through the ocean and the earth's crust into the earth's very mantle. In 1963, when the project was begun, the

---

* The energy situation is the prime example.

† NAS is nominally a private, nonprofit organization. Actually it is a quasi-governmental institution, founded over a hundred years ago with a proviso that no government funds were to be used for its support, except for commissioned studies. However, the last NAS annual report available showed some $2 million in income from private sources and some $25 million in taxpayer funds from studies conducted for nearly every regulatory agency in Washington.[2]

cost was estimated at $68 million. By 1965 the cost had jumped to $110 million.[3] The subcommittee—then hoping to stimulate the scientific education area at NSF—was distressed at the diversion of funds and they wanted something done about it.

There was also some question as to what was being shoveled. The drilling contract was awarded to Brown & Root, Inc., of Houston, Texas, headed by George R. Brown, whose family had presented Lyndon Johnson's President's Club with a gift of $25,000. In the preliminary evaluation of bids for the Mohole contract, a consortium headed by Socony Mobil (including Texas Instruments and Standard Oil) had come in first with 936 out of a possible 1,000 points; Brown & Root was fifth. In the second round of evaluations a bid from Global Marine Exploration (a joint venture with Aerojet-General and Shell Oil) came in first; Socony Mobil was second, and Brown & Root now third. Nevertheless, NSF awarded the contract to Brown & Root, even though that firm was charging a management fee of $1.8 million and overhead charges of 3 to 5 percent on all costs.[4] The same man who had divided NASA facilities with a thousand miles between Houston and Cape Kennedy, Representative Albert Thomas, was then chairman of the House Appropriations subcommittee through which the NSF appropriation passed.

In 1966, after the death of Representative Thomas, the House Appropriations Committee refused to provide any more money for Project Mohole. The Senate Appropriations Committee tried to restore the funding, but, after the House rejected this in a floor vote, the project was finally terminated.

The end of Mohole was less important than other far-reaching recommendations to amend the NSF charter: that the NSF fund applied research as well as basic research; that NSF fund research in the social sciences as well as physical sciences; and that it fund research at profit-making institutions. The proposals were not considered radical: the rationale was to transform hard-won research results into positive applications that would prove of benefit to the society that paid for them. It was, according to Representative John Davis, both "a complete overhaul" and "an extension of scope" for NSF.[5]

A bill embodying these changes passed the House in 1966 and 1967, and finally passed the Senate in 1968. The Senate added a requirement of annual authorization, giving the House committee and its Senate counterpart (the Labor and Public Welfare Committee, not the Senate space committee) more power over the agency.[6] By 1971 the Science, Research and Development Subcommittee was urging that appropriations be on a line-item basis.

RANN: THE PACE IS A WALK

Under the changes adopted in 1968, the National Science Foundation hesitantly began to explore the "translation" of "hard" science from laboratory to community.

By 1971 NSF had consolidated its social, environmental, and technological areas into RANN (Research Applied to National Needs).[7] The first year's funding was only $34 million; in 1972 this rose to $55.9 million—still less than 10 percent of the total appropriation for NSF that year. (Some $448 million went to support the physical sciences and other projects.)

Space committee staff people began to notice that the Office of Management and Budget had turned committee attempts to fund RANN into a robbing-Peter-to-pay-Paul routine. When the funds for RANN went up, the science education budget suffered a sharp decrease and there was a deluge of mail from irate teachers and students. The drain in funds for science education was real: from $208 million in fiscal 1968, appropriations fell to $86 million in fiscal 1972 and $68 million in fiscal 1973.[8] The *Washington Post* reported that the drop in graduate science education support was from 7,800 students in 1968 to 1,450 in 1972. Behind the eroding figures was the shadow of William A. Niskanen, an OMB evaluator.

A Niskanen memorandum, meant for OMB internal use only

and not publicly released to Congress, reportedly argued that an oversupply of scientists and engineers resulted from artificial stimulation by NSF traineeships and similar programs in support of graduate science education. Niskanen argued that such programs should be unnecessary, because normal market forces would work to produce a sufficient supply of scientists and engineers. If there were a demand for them, Niskanen said, the potential professional would find a way to finance his own education.

Both the Science, Research and Development Subcommittee and the full House space committee strongly supported NSF's science education program. It is certain that they would not have agreed with the reasoning behind Niskanen's paper. (Time has since proved Niskanen wrong.)

Miffed, the full committee cut RANN's 1972 appropriation by $8.9 million and were thus able to increase the funding for scientific education by $12 million; in the bill that was passed, they stipulated that certain minimum amounts must be spent in this area. The administration, however, simply impounded the increased funds for scientific education—and at the same time maintained the decrease for RANN. When the 1973 authorization came up, the committee again added more money for scientific education—this time without sacrificing the RANN budget—even though they had little hope that the increased education funds would be utilized.

Initially the subcommittee members had envisioned the RANN program only as an auxiliary to NSF's basic-research role; they did not intend to support its expansion beyond the 15 percent level. This modest objective, however, began to change in 1972.

The ambivalence toward social sciences in the House space committee, occasioned by the RANN-education brouhaha, is now lessening, and committee members are showing increasingly favorable attitudes. (The strongest opponent of social science research on the committee, former Representative James Fulton of Pennsylvania, died in 1971.) In 1971 an attempt by Mike Mc-

Cormack (R., Wash.) to add $10 million to the RANN authorization lost in the subcommittee by a vote of 2–8. Representatives Alphonzo Bell (R., Calif.) and Richard Hanna (D., Calif.), who opposed McCormack's move then, both serve districts in southern California that are plagued by aerospace unemployment. Bell remarked several years ago, however, that he was now "inclined to think that maybe we should have a larger budget for RANN." The slow pace of that program and the static funding for all NSF programs are changing. But the prospect may not be as bright as it seems: funding stability is a prime requisite in scientific effort, and NSF's newly acquired RANN glamour may not be provocative if the agency becomes—as is likely—a battleground between national political factions jockeying for power in the science-technology area.

EXECUTIVE MOVE, CONGRESSIONAL COUNTERMOVE

In March 1972 the President announced a special joint program for NSF and the National Bureau of Standards—the Experimental Research and Development Incentives Program—designed to "improve the climate for technological innovation" and, presumably aid the deteriorating trade balance. Congress followed the President, appropriating some $18 million for NSF and some $22 million extra for NBS. The House space committee was a strong sponsor. But a year later NSF had seen only $2 million of this, and NBS $1 million. OMB had impounded the rest,[9] ostensibly because the "NSF's planning and management [was] flawed."[10] But by Christmas of 1972 another reason for the odd presidential impoundment of funds—authorized, after all, at presidential initiative—was becoming clear. The Office of Science and Technology at the White House was disbanded, and its people and functions were moving into NSF. The OST White House office— once called a "coat rack for Nobel Prize winners"—had served for nearly fifteen years as a prime policy maker: its sudden death was difficult to explain. Later, however, it became fairly clear that funds were being held back until the executive had fully established its operative control of NSF.

The *National Journal* reported that the scientific world had "profound misgivings" at this arbitrary Nixon move.[11] Harvard Professor Harvey Brooks called it a "downgrading of science . . . a misperception of the role of science in public policy." Phillip Handler, the president of NAS, bleakly confirmed Brooks's view.[12] *Science* noted that the NSF was "not sufficiently dynamic, or politically attuned to do the job" needed.[13] John Davis in the House and Edward Kennedy in the Senate joined the critics. The former director of the NSF, William McElroy, noted, "There are many fine people at NSF, but they have no tradition or taste for the kind of political and bureaucratic infighting they will face if the Administration is serious in its plans for them." Harvard chemistry professor Paul M. Doty, an adviser to NSF described the "quality of the staff" as "pretty mediocre . . . not equipped to deal with the alleged new responsibilities." Not everyone, however, expressed negative views. Outgoing OST director Ed Davis was certain the NSF staff was "up to the jobs they've inherited" and Roger W. Heyns, president of the American Council on Education and vice-chairman of the National Science Board, expressed the view that he had always thought NSF "should press for larger responsibilities."

In any event, NSF is in charge of policies for the entire executive branch on a federal research and development budget totaling more than $17 billion. The new NSF funding control (nearly six times as large as that of NASA, the space agency) has given the congressional committees with jurisdiction over NSF a new growth potential. In the House, the space committee's expertise and activity in science is undeniable. Heretofore both had been centered in Representative Davis's Subcommittee on Science, Research and Development, but in the Ninety-third Congress the chairman of the full committee, Olin Teague, moved to assert full commit-tee interest by holding a set of hearings in July 1973—a "com-prehensive inquiry into Federal science policy" and goals.[14]

In the Senate, however, the jurisdictional problem is trickier. NSF oversight now rests with a NSF subcommittee (chaired by Senator Kennedy) of the Labor and Public Welfare Committee, which already oversees a huge proportion of the federal budget, including federal education funds. A tug of war may be expected here, but the only real contender, the Senate space committee—unlike its House counterpart—has a lackluster record and very lit-tle real input from the scientific community.

PATENTS

The Nixon joint program for research and development also in-volved the complex area of patents. There is no uniform gov-ernment-wide pattern of disposal of patents to develop inventions created in government labs. Each agency with a scientific program —whether in agriculture, mining, health, space or transportation —sets its own policy. Until recently NSF's policy, since basic research is at the heart of all development, was very cautious. Developmental rights were generally "deferred" on initial award, until the contractor had completed the assigned work and an evaluation had been made to determine the feasibility and/or de-sirability of government control of the invention, according to NSF's general counsel. Since the usual ratio of research to devel-opment costs is 1:15, it is necessary to "farm out" research re-sults for applications, if the public is to benefit from the discov-ery. Rights protecting the people's interests, such as the development time allowed, royalties, or public access, were con-sidered for each case.*

---

* NASA's initial policy was in accord with the 1958 Space Act, which re-quired all patents to remain in the public domain. Under "pressures" in the early sixties, according to committee counsel Philip Yeager, the House space committee spent nearly three years studying the equitability of this patent

In 1971, however, President Nixon suggested a new policy of granting private firms "exclusive" rights on award—that is, before the private commercial interest has spent a penny on development. The rationale was the very real need to stimulate technological diversity without undue strain on risk capital, and the heavy cost burden borne by the developer, who might end up spending on a pig in the poke. The fact that development could also yield a different animal—an exclusive golden goose—was, obviously, another factor in the determination to give away rights for inventions underwritten by taxpayer support.

In hearings on the technology incentives program in 1972, the House Science and Astronautics Committee asked Dr. Raymond Bisplinghoff, deputy director of NSF, to provide a concise statement of NSF policy with regard to patents on government-owned inventions.[15] Via the incentives program there is a new relationship between NSF and industry, a relationship in which charges of political nepotism are almost a certainty. But nobody has yet come up with a workable general formula for the reconciliation of need and greed.

---

arrangement and recommended some "relief" for contractors. Under Kennedy the first ties were loosened, and commercial interests developing new space hardware won new patent rights.

16

Conclusions

Most committee members and staff believe sincerely in the value of space exploration for the nation and the world. They are not simply rationalizing in a cynical effort to line their own pockets, but are inspired by patriotic aims for America's destiny in space. Their sins are sins of perspective, and of missionary zeal, so that the assumption that space is the next frontier is never closely examined. Questions of cost are never raised strongly enough to cause fear for NASA's vitality. Programs have been cut back— for example, the space station—but new ways to spend smaller amounts of money are always found, as was the case with the space shuttle.

A recent Harris poll shows that only 5 percent of the people felt that space exploration was among the "two or three biggest benefits you feel you have obtained from scientific progress." There is no one except the committees to represent the general public interest in minimizing waste and setting balanced priorities, and, unfortunately, the committees tend to become a part of the forces only they can check.

The space committees should represent the general public interest in minimizing waste. In the main, however, members tend to conceive of waste as a terminated NASA project rather than mismanagement of funds in a current program. For example, when the NERVA program for the development of a nuclear rocket engine for galactic exploration was ended in 1972, Senator Howard Cannon (D., Nev.) then called the program "a tragic example of waste and mismanagement" of a $1.5 billion investment.

Theoretically the committees can add or delete projects requested by NASA and increase or reduce the budget request for particular projects. In practice there has been very little congressional alteration of the NASA budget. In one of the few attempts to pressure NASA, committee members in both chambers moved to increase research in aeronautics, after Representatives Ken Hechler and James Symington had worked diligently to swing committee interest in that direction. Thus in the NASA authorization bill for fiscal 1973 the House Science and Astronautics Committee added $48.45 million to the administration's $9 million research request, specifically for research on reducing noise in commercial jets and improving aviation safety (through radio and radar guidance). In the Senate, however, the Aeronautical and Space Sciences Committee majority failed to go along with the increase, although Senator Goldwater entered a strong dissent at the end of the committee's report. A floor amendment by Senator Cannon then added $24 million to the original $9 million administration request, meeting the $48 million House increase halfway.

In general, the committees have not significantly exercised their legislative oversight responsibility in either policy guidance or checkup for the regulatory agencies. The major test of the committee's role as NASA watchdog came after the January 27, 1967, fire that killed astronauts Grissom, White, and Chafee in an Apollo cabin during a test on the launching pad at Cape Kennedy.

After this tragedy, both committees, as well as NASA, held hearings to investigate the cause of the fire. At the close of the House committee's official probe, Chairman Teague pontificated, "We are all to blame."[1] A year later the Senate Aeronautical and Space Sciences Committee issued a report on its hearings.[2]

According to other sources, safety recommendations had been made to North American, the prime contractor involved, and to NASA itself, in a confidential report by General Samuel Phillips in 1966, well before the tragedy. These concerned exposed wiring and "unnecessary flammable material in the cabin that, if removed, might have prevented the fire and the astronauts' deaths."[3] If the committees had had the courage to probe more deeply, they might have found management weaknesses at North American, but these would have raised embarrassing questions about the political origins of the Apollo contract award to North American. The courts were not as loath to cite failure as the politicians. On March 9, 1972, Grissom's widow accepted $350,000 in an out-of-court settlement of her suit against North American Rockwell Corporation for negligence in causing her husband's death.[4]

The introduction of policy-making powers into the National Science Foundation may give the committees a chance to formulate a genuinely coherent science and technology program to be voted on; perhaps the NASA experience (too much, too soon, too unplanned) will guide the congressmen, too many of whom are prone to either leap or falter. But one observer, Harvard's Paul Doty, has expressed skepticism about the new executive arrangements: "It's all a sham. Stever's phone will never ring."[5]* If the shift in the locus of power over the federal research and development funding is real, however, genuine congressional contributions can be made in the seventies.

Representative Davis, in a statement to the congressional group that is restructuring committees, has posted some future goals for the House committee, including a regional system of national

---

* The reference is to Dr. Guyford Stever, director of the National Science Foundation, who is now also the White House adviser on science policy.

environmental laboratories; investigation of technology's impact on the economy; promotion of materials research; genetic engineering; and a voluntary world-wide standards system. Brighter developments could come through these plans for assessments of future technology. The public has become increasingly concerned about the effects of new scientific developments, and such assessment may offer some means of exercising social control over the frontiers of new technology. There are no guarantees, but at least here the House space committee has begun to function in a way that represents the interests and concerns of a majority of citizens.

1. The Rules of the House of Representatives, insofar as they are applicable, shall govern the committee and its subcommittees. The rules of the committee, insofar as they are applicable, shall be the rules of any subcommittee of the committee.

2. (A) The meetings of the committee shall be held every Tuesday at 10 a.m. and at such other times and in such place as the chairman may designate.

(B) Three members may file in the offices of the committee a written request for a special meeting, specifying the measure or matter to be considered. The committee clerk shall notify the chairman of the request. If within 3 days after the filing of the request the chairman does not call the requested meeting, to be held within 7 days after the filing of the request, a majority of the members of the committee may file their written notice of a special meeting, specifying the date and hour and the measure or matter to be considered. The committee clerk shall immediately notify the members of such meeting, giving the date and hour, and the measure or matter to be considered.

(C) All mark-up and business sessions of the committee shall be closed, except where the committee by majority vote decides otherwise.

(D) Subcommittee meetings shall not be held while the full committee is meeting, unless prior approval has been granted by the chairman.

3. A regular Tuesday meeting of the committee may be dispensed with by the chairman.

4. A majority of members of the committee shall constitute a quorum. A majority of a subcommittee shall constitute a quorum of such subcommittee.

* Adopted February 23, 1971.

5. No general proxies may be used for any purpose. A member may vote by special proxy, which must be in writing and signed, or by telegraph, dated, and delivered to the clerk of the committee. It must identify the member to whom the proxy is given. It must identify the particular bill or resolution and amendments thereto, motion, or other specific matter under consideration. Such a proxy may be used in the full committee or by a subcommittee.

6. A proxy may not be used for the purpose of establishing a quorum, nor may a proxy be used at the organization meeting at the beginning of each Congress.

7. A rollcall of the members may be had at the request of three or more members. The result of each rollcall in any meeting of the committee shall be made available for inspection by the public at reasonable times in the commitee offices. The information shall include a description of the motion or other proposition voted on, and the name of each member voting for and each member voting against such motion or proposition, and whether by proxy or in person, and including the names of those present but not voting. With respect to each record vote on motion to report any bill of public character, the total number of votes cast for and the total number of votes cast against the reporting of such bill shall be included in the committee report.

8. No measure or recommendation shall be reported or tabled by the committee unless a majority of the committee is actually present.

9. The chairman may name standing or special subcommittees.

10. All other members of the committee may have the privilege of sitting with any subcommittee during its hearings or deliberations and may participate in such hearings or deliberations, but no such member who is not a member of the subcommittee shall vote on any matter before such subcommittee.

11. A majority vote of any subcommittee will be required to report any bill, resolution, or other matter to the full committee, or to table any bill, resolution, or other matter before it.

12. The chairman shall have the authority to refer all bills, resolutions, or other matters to any subcommittee(s) of the full committee. A subcommittee to which a bill, resolution, or other matter has been referred shall proceed with all possible diligence, if a majority of a quorum so directs, with appropriate inquiry, and report its findings and recommendations to the full committee, but the chairman of the full committee shall have authority to discharge a subcommittee from

consideration of any bill, resolution, or other matter referred thereto and have such measure or matter considered by the full committee.

13. The order of business and procedure of the committee and the subjects of inquiries or investigations will be decided by the chairman, subject always to an appeal to the committee.

14. Bills will be taken up for hearing only when called by the chairman of the committee or subcommittee or by a majority vote of a quorum of the committee or subcommittee, except those matters which are the subject of special-call meeting outlined in rule 2.

15. The time any one member may address the committee on any bill, motion, or other matter under consideration by the committee or the time allowed for the questioning of a witness at hearings before the committee will be limited to 5 minutes, and then only when he has been recognized by the chairman, except that this time limit may be waived by the chairman or acting chairman. The rule of germaneness will be enforced by the chairman.

16. No private bill will be reported by the committee if there are two or more dissenting votes. Private bills so rejected by the committee will not be reconsidered during the same Congress unless new evidence sufficient to justify a new hearing has been presented to the committee.

17. The chairman and ranking minority member shall serve as ex officio members of all subcommittees and shall have the right to vote on all matters before the subcommittees.

18. All hearings conducted by the committee or its subcommittees shall be open to the public except where the committee or subcommittee by majority vote decides otherwise.

19. Reports and recommendations of a subcommittee shall not be considered by the full committee until after the intervention of 3 calendar days, excluding Saturday, Sunday and holidays, from the time the report is submitted and printed hearings thereon shall be made available, if reasonably possible, to the members, except that this rule may be waived in the discretion of the chairman.

20. No committee or subcommittee hearing may be held unless one member of the majority and one member of the minority are present.

21. Whenever any hearing is conducted by the committee on any measure or matter, the minority members of the committee shall be entitled, upon request to the chairman by a majority of the minority members, to call witnesses selected by the minority to testify with re-

spect to the measure or matter at least 1 day during the hearing.

22. Any member requesting to file minority or additional views for any legislative report shall be granted 3 days for the preparation of same, provided the request is made to the chairman at the time the bill is approved by the committee.

23. The committee report on a measure approved by the committee, if not sooner filed, shall be filed within 7 days (exclusive of days on which the House is not in session) after the day on which there has been filed with the committee clerk a written request signed by a majority of the committee requesting the reporting of that measure.

24. Each witness appearing before the committee shall file 48 hours in advance a written statement of his proposed testimony and shall limit his oral presentation to a brief summary.

25. The committee may not sit without special leave while the House is reading a measure for amendment under the 5-minute rule.

26. Public notice shall be given of committee hearings at least 1 week in advance unless the committee determines otherwise.

APPENDIX 2.
Rules of the Senate Committee on Aeronautical and Space Sciences

---

SOURCE: Committee Calendar 1973.

Rules governing the Procedure of the Senate Committee on Aeronautical and Space Sciences, adopted pursuant to Sec. 133(b) of the Legislative Reorganization Act of 1946, as amended by Sec. 130(a) of the Legislative Reorganization Act of 1970.

1. GENERAL

All applicable requirements of the Standing Rules of the Senate and of the Legislative Reorganization Act of 1946, as amended, shall govern the committee and its subcommittees.

2. MEETINGS

The meetings of the committee shall be on Tuesday of each week at 10:30 a.m. or upon call of the chairman.

3. NOMINATIONS

Unless otherwise ordered by the committee, nominations referred to the committee shall be held for at least seven (7) days before presentation in a meeting for action. Upon reference of nominations to the committee, copies of the nomination references shall be furnished each member of the committee.

4. HEARINGS

(a) No hearing on an investigation shall be initiated unless the committee or subcommittee has specifically authorized such hearings.

(b) No hearing of the committee or any subcommittee thereof shall be scheduled outside of the District of Columbia except by the majority vote of the committee or subcommittee.

(c) No confidential testimony taken or confidential material presented in an executive hearing of the committee or subcommittee thereof or any report of the proceedings of such an executive hearing shall be made public, either in whole or in part or by way of summary, unless authorized by a majority of the members of the committee or subcommittee.

(d) Any witness summoned to a public or executive hearing may be accompanied by counsel of his own choosing who shall be permitted, while the witness is testifying, to advise him of his legal rights.

5. QUORUM

Three Senators, one of whom shall be a member of the minority party, shall constitute a quorum of the Senate Committee on Aeronautical and Space Sciences for the purpose of taking sworn testimony, unless otherwise ordered by the full committee. Each duly appointed subcommittee of the Committee on Aeronautical and Space Sciences is instructed (1) to fix, in appropriate cases, the number of its entire membership who shall constitute a quorum of such subcommittee for the purpose of taking sworn testimony, and (2) to determine the circumstances under which subpoenas may be issued and the member or members over whose signatures subpoenas shall be issued.

Members of the
Science Committees

SENATE COMMITTEE ON AERONAUTICAL AND SPACE SCIENCES, NINETY-SECOND CONGRESS*

Majority:

Clinton P. Anderson, Chm.
  (N. Mex.)
Warren G. Magnuson (Wash.)
Stuart Symington (Mo.)
John C. Stennis (Miss.)
Howard W. Cannon (Nev.)
David H. Gambrell (Ga.)

Minority:

Carl T. Curtis (Nebr.)
Margaret Chase Smith (Maine)
Barry Goldwater (Ariz.)
Lowell P. Weicker, Jr. (Conn.)
James L. Buckley (N.Y.)

SENATE COMMITTEE ON AERONAUTICAL AND SPACE SCIENCES, NINETY-THIRD CONGRESS*

Majority:

Frank E. Moss, Chm. (Utah)
Warren G. Magnuson (Wash.)
Stuart Symington (Mo.)

Minority:

Barry Goldwater (Ariz.)
Carl T. Curtis (Nebr.)
Lowell Weicker, Jr. (Conn.)

* The Senate committee has no subcommittees.

Majority:

John C. Stennis (Miss.)
Howard W. Cannon (Nev.)
James Abourezk (S. Dak.)
Floyd K. Haskell (Colo.)
Howard M. Metzenbaum
   (Ohio)

Minority:

Dewey F. Bartlett (Okla.)
Jesse A. Helms (N.C.)
Pete V. Domenici (N. Mex.)

HOUSE COMMITTEE ON SCIENCE AND ASTRONAUTICS, NINETY-SECOND CONGRESS

Majority:

George P. Miller, Chm. (Calif.)
Olin E. Teague (Tex.)
Ken Hechler (W. Va.)
John W. Davis (Ga.)
Thomas N. Downing (Va.)
Don Fuqua (Fla.)
Earle Cabell (Tex.)
James W. Symington (Mo.)
Richard T. Hanna (Calif.)
Walter Flowers (Ala.)
Robert A. Roe (N.J.)
John F. Seiberling, Jr. (Ohio)
William R. Cotter (Conn.)
Charles B. Rangel (N.Y.)
Morgan F. Murphy (Ill.)
Mike McCormack (Wash.)
Mendel J. Davis (S.C.)

Minority:

Charles A. Mosher (Ohio)
Alphonzo Bell (Calif.)
Thomas M. Pelly (Wash.)
John W. Wydler (N.Y.)
Larry Winn, Jr. (Kans.)
Robert D. Price (Tex.)
Louis Frey, Jr. (Fla.)
Barry M. Goldwater, Jr. (Calif.)
Marvin L. Esch (Mich.)
Lawrence Coughlin (Pa.)
John N. Happy Camp (Okla.)

Subcommittee on Aeronautics and Space Technology

Majority:

Hechler, Chm.
Davis (Ga.)

Minority:

Pelly
Wydler

Majority:

Cotter
Rangel
McCormack

Minority:

Goldwater
Esch

Subcommittee on International Cooperation in Science and Space

Majority:

Symington, Chm.
Davis (Ga.)
Roe
Cotter
Murphy
Davis (S.C.)

Minority:

Frey
Bell
Winn
Goldwater

Subcommittee on Manned Space Flight

Majority:

Teague, Chm.
Fuqua
Cabell
Hanna
Flowers
Roe

Minority:

Winn
Bell
Wydler
Price
Frey

Subcommittee on NASA Oversight

Majority:

Fuqua, Chm.
Teague
Downing
Hechler
Flowers
Rangel

Minority:

Wydler
Frey
Camp

Subcommittee on Science, Research and Development

Majority:	*Minority*:
Davis, Chm. (Ga.)	Bell
Cabell	Frey
Symington	Esch
Hanna	Coughlin
Seiberling	
McCormack	

Subcommittee on Space Sciences and Applications

Majority:	*Minority*:
Downing, Chm.	Mosher
Symington	Winn
Seiberling	Price
Murphy	Goldwater

HOUSE COMMITTEE ON SCIENCE AND ASTRONAUTICS, NINETY-THIRD CONGRESS

Majority:	*Minority*:
Olin E. Teague, Chm. (Tex.)	Charles A. Mosher (Ohio)
Ken Hechler (W. Va.)	Alphonzo Bell (Calif.)
John W. Davis (Ga.)	John W. Wydler (N.Y.)
Thomas N. Downing (Va.)	Larry Winn, Jr. (Kans.)
Don Fuqua (Fla.)	Louis Frey, Jr. (Fla.)
James W. Symington (Mo.)	Barry M. Goldwater, Jr. (Calif.)
Richard T. Hanna (Calif.)	Melvin L. Esch (Mich.)
Walter Flowers (Ala.)	John N. Happy Camp (Okla.)
Robert A. Roe (N.J.)	John B. Conlan (Ariz.)

Majority:

William R. Cotter (Conn.)
Mike McCormack (Wash.)
Bob Bergland (Minn.)
J. J. Pickle (Tex.)
George E. Brown, Jr. (Calif.)
Dale Milford (Tex.)
Ray Thornton (Ark.)
Bill Gunter (Fla.)

Minority:

Stanford E. Parris (Va.)
Paul W. Cronin (Mass.)
James G. Martin (N.C.)
William M. Ketchum (Calif.)

Subcommittee on Aeronautics and Space Technology

Majority:

Hechler, Chm.
Davis
Cotter
Pickle
Thornton

Minority:

Wydler
Goldwater
Conlan
Parris

Subcommittee on Energy

Majority:

McCormack, Chm.
Fuqua
Symington
Hanna
Roe
Bergland
Pickle
Brown
Milford
Thornton
Gunter

Minority:

Goldwater
Wydler
Esch
Conlan
Parris
Cronin
Martin
Ketchum

Subcommittee on International Cooperation in Science and Space

Majority:	*Minority*:
Hanna, Chm.	Frey
Symington	Bell
Davis	Winn
Roe	Camp
McCormack	Ketchum
Milford	

Subcommittee on Manned Space Flight

Majority:	*Minority*:
Fuqua, Chm.	Winn
Flowers	Bell
Roe	Wydler
Cotter	Frey
Bergland	Camp
Gunter	Ketchum

Subcommittee on Science, Research and Development

Majority:	*Minority*:
Davis, Chm.	Bell
Symington	Esch
Hanna	Conlan
McCormack	Parris
Fuqua	Cronin
Flowers	Martin
Cotter	
Pickle	
Brown	
Thornton	

Subcommittee on Space Science and Applications

Majority:	*Minority*:
Symington, Chm.	Esch
Downing	Winn
Bergland	Goldwater
Brown	Camp
Milford	

Notes

Part I. The House and Senate
Interior and Insular Affairs Committees

CHAPTER 1. LAND, LAW, AND LOOPHOLES: UNCLE SAM AND GRANDMOTHER EARTH

1. *One Third of the Nation's Land* (Washington: Government Printing Office, June 1970), p. 327.
2. Ibid., p. 327.
3. Ibid., p. 27.
4. Ward Sinclair, "Strip Mining: Scourge of the Land," *Progressive,* August, 1973, p. 20.
5. *One Third of the Nation's Land,* p. 327.

CHAPTER 2. THE LAND LORDS: RICH MAN, POOR MAN, BEGGAR MAN, THIEF, BANKER, REALTOR, INDIAN CHIEF

1. David W. Rohde, Michigan State University, and Kenneth A. Shepsle, Washington University, St. Louis, "Committee Assignments in the House of Representatives: Strategic Aspects of a Social Choice Process," unpublished paper, p. 10.

2. Ibid., p. 10.
3. *Citizens Look at Congress*, Ralph Nader Congress Project (Washington: Grossman Publishers, 1972).
4. Rohde and Shepsle, "Committee Assignments . . . ," p. 12.
5. "The Dirty Dozen," *Environmental Action*, June 24, 1972, p. 13.
6. Aspinall interview, July 31, 1972.
7. Paul L. Leventhal, "Turnover in Key Committee Chairmanships Foreshadows Policy Changes in 93rd Congress," *National Journal*, October 11, 1972, p. 1755.
8. Ibid., p. 1756.
9. "The Dirty Dozen."
10. Sierra Club files.
11. Ibid.
12. Michael Barone, Grant Ujifusa, Douglas Matthews, *1972 Almanac of American Politics* (Boston: Gambit, 1972), p. 121.
13. Leventhal, "Turnover in Key Committee Chairmanships . . . ," p. 1756.
14. Ibid.
15. Frank Warner, Congress Project Profile on John D. Saylor, *Citizens Look at Congress*, p. 11.
16. Sierra Club files.
17. Ibid.
18. Warner, Congress Project Profile, *Citizens Look at Congress*, p. 15.
19. Sven Holmes and Charles J. Brown, Congress Project Profile on James A. Haley, *Citizens Look at Congress*, p. 1.
20. Ibid., p. 13.
21. Ibid., p. 9.
22. U.S., Congress, House, Committee on Interior and Insular Affairs, Subcommittee on Mines and Mining, *Regulation of Strip Mining: Hearings on H.R. 60 and related bills*, 92nd Cong., 2nd sess. (1972), pp. 174–177.
23. Hosmer press statement, January 22, 1974, "Hosmer Will Not Seek Re-election."
24. Claudia Townsend, Congress Project Profile on Roy A. Taylor, *Citizens Look at Congress*, p. 1.
25. U.S., Congress, House, Committee on Interior and Insular Affairs, Subcommittee on Parks and Recreation, *Voyageurs National Park: Hearings on H.R. 10482*, 91st Cong., 2nd sess. (1970), p. 262.
26. Ibid., p. 263.
27. Ibid., p. 278.
28. Ibid., p. 297.
29. Campaign Finance Monitoring Project, *1972 Congressional Campaign Finances, West Coast States* (Washington: Common Cause, 1974), p. 15.
30. Daniel Epstein, Congress Project Profile on Morris K. Udall, *Citizens Look at Congress*, p. 15.
31. Marjorie Silverberg and Joan Claybrook, Congress Project Profile on Philip Burton, *Citizens Look at Congress*, p .12.

32. Brad Michaelson, Congress Project Profile on John Melcher, *Citizens Look at Congress*, p. 15.
33. George C. Wilson, "Bill to Pay Ranchers to Stop Using Public Lands Stirs Fight," *Washington Post*, October 1, 1973, p. 4.
34. Ibid.
35. Ibid.
36. Ibid.
37. *Congressional Record*, September 18, 1973, p. H.8008.
38. Ibid., p. H.8009.
39. Ibid.
40. Meeds's Newsletter, March 1972, p. 4.
41. *Seattle Times*, April 26, 1972.
42. Meeds's Newsletter, p. 2.
43. Ibid., p. 3.
44. Ibid.
45. Ibid.
46. *Seattle Times*.
47. Robert Vining, Congress Project Profile on Sam Steiger, *Citizens Look at Congress*, p. 1.
48. U.S., Congress, House, Committee on Interior and Insular Affairs, Subcommittee on Public Lands, *Oil and Natural Gas Pipeline Rights-of-Way, Part II: Hearings on H.R. 9130*, 93rd Cong., 1st sess. (1973), pp. 861–863.
49. Campaign Finance Monitoring Project, *1972 Congressional Campaign Finances, Southwestern States*, p. 10.
50. Ibid., p. 6.
51. Robert Sussman, Congress Project Profile on Henry Jackson, *Citizens Look at Congress*, p. 1.
52. Ibid., p. 18.
53. Ibid., p. 19.
54. *Congressional Record*, March 24, 1971, p. S.3867.
55. Ibid., p. S3868.
56. Ibid., p. S3867.
57. Ibid.
58. U.S., Congress, Senate, Committee on Interior and Insular Affairs, *National Environmental Policy: Hearings on S.1075, S.237, and S.1752*, 91st Cong., 1st sess. (April 16, 1969), p. 205.
59. Taylor Branch, "The Sunny Side of the Energy Crisis," *Harper's*, March, 1974, p. 16.
60. *Congressional Record*, February 19, 1974, pp. S.1890–1891.
61. Peter Petkas, Congress Project Profile on Lee Metcalf, *Citizens Look at Congress*, p. 8.
62. Ibid.
63. George Douth, *Leaders in Profile: The United States Senate* (New York: Sperr and Douth, 1972), p. 245.
64. *Congressional Record*, February 28, 1974, p. S.2414.

65. Ibid.
66. Carol Payne and Margaret Carpenter, Congress Project Profile on Frank Church, *Citizens Look at Congress*, p. 4.
67. Ibid., p. 15.
68. Ibid.
69. Ibid., p. 16.
70. U.S., Congress, Senate, Committee on Interior and Insular Affairs, Subcommittee on Water and Power Resources, *Geothermal Resources: Hearings*, 93rd Cong., 1st sess. (August 10–11, 1973), Part II, p. 296.
71. Ibid., p. 299.
72. Ibid.
73. U.S., Congress, Senate, Committee on Interior and Insular Affairs, Subcommittee on Public Lands, *Grazing Fees on Public Lands: Hearings*, 91st Cong., 1st sess. (February 27–28, 1969), p. 35.
74. *Congressional Record*, June 14, 1973, p. S.11137.
75. March 1974 form letter from Haskell to constituents who had written him about S. 425.
76. Mark Gruenberg and Susan Perry, Congress Project Profile on James Abourezk, *Citizens Look at Congress*, p. 1.
77. *Congressional Record*, February 19, 1974, p. S.1909.
78. *1974 Almanac of American Politics*, p. 385.
79. *Congressional Record*, February 25, 1974, p. S.2161.
80. Ann Kelly, Congress Project Profile on Clifford P. Hansen, *Citizens Look at Congress*, p. 5.
81. *Congressional Record*, February 19, 1974, p. S.1916.
82. Campaign Finance Monitoring Project, *1972 Congressional Campaign Finances, Mountain States*, p. 77.
83. *Congressional Record*, May 14, 1971, p. S.6959.
84. Ibid.
85. *The Living Wilderness*, Spring 1973, p. 44.
86. Ibid.
87. Ibid., p. 48.
88. Ibid., p. 47.
89. Memo to the Sierra Club Board of Directors from Citizens Opposing Teton National Park, in the Sierra Club files and in the *Congressional Record*, December 3, 1971, p. S20462.
90. Ibid.
91. *The Living Wilderness*, p. 49.

CHAPTER 3. THE LAND RAPERS: THEY GOT THE BREAD, WE GOT THE CRUST

1. U.S., Congress, House, Committee on Interior and Insular Affairs, Subcommittee on the Environment and Subcommittee on Mines and Min-

ing, *Regulation of Surface Mining: Hearings on H.R. 3 and related bills,* testimony by Rep. Hechler (D., W.V.), 93rd Cong., 1st sess. (April 1, 9, 10, 16, 17; May 14, 15, 1973).

2. James A. Noone, "Environment Report/Congress Digging Into Debate on Stronger Strip Mining Regulations," *National Journal,* June 30, 1973, p. 944.
3. "The Strip Mining of America," Sierra Club, p. 3.
4. Ibid., p. 2.
5. Ibid., p. 3.
6. "Report from Appalachia," *Southern Exposure,* Summer/Fall 1973, p. 52.
7. *Regulation of Surface Mining: Hearings.* Hechler testimony, p. 783.
8. Ibid.
9. U.S., Congress, House, Committee on Interior and Insular Affairs, Subcommittee on Mines and Mining, *Regulation of Strip Mining: Hearings on H.R. 60 and related bills,* 92nd Cong., 1st sess. (September 20, 21; October 21, 26; November 29, 30, 1971), p. 60.
10. *Regulation of Surface Mining: Hearings,* p. 290.
11. "The Strip Mining of America," p. 3.
12. *Regulation of Surface Mining: Hearings,* p. 790.
13. Anthony Ripley, "Strip-Mining Bill Dies in Congress," *New York Times,* October 15, 1972.
14. James A. Noone, "Congress Digging Into Debate on Stronger Strip Mining Regulations," *National Journal,* June 30, 1973, p. 945.
15. *Regulation of Surface Mining: Hearings,* Part II, p. 1439.
16. Ibid., p. 1435.
17. "Congress Digging Into Debate," p. 947.
18. U.S., Congress, Senate, Committee on Interior and Insular Affairs, *Regulation of Surface Mining Operations: Hearings on S.425 and S.923,* 93rd Cong., 1st sess. (March 13, 14, 15, 16, 1973).
19. U.S., Congress, Senate, Committee on Interior and Insular Affairs, Markup of S. 425, Minutes of the Committee, June 25, 27, 1973.
20. Ibid., June 27.
21. Ibid., September 10.
22. *Congressional Record,* October 9, 1973, p. S.18875.
23. *Congressional Record,* October 8, 1973, p. S.18870.
24. Ibid., p. 18762.
25. *Congressional Record,* October 9, 1973, p. S.18897.
26. James A. Noone, "Coal Lobby Seeks House Action to Offset Senate's Tough Strip Mine Bill," *National Journal,* October 20, 1973, p. 1573.
27. *Congressional Record,* March 21, 1974, p. S.4166.
28. *Congressional Record,* October 8, 1973, p. S.18771.
29. Ibid.
30. "Coal Lobby Seeks House Action," p. 1573.
31. Ibid.
32. Ibid.
33. Bagge-Overton letter, p. 2.

34. *Congressional Record*, October 10, 1973, p. S.18950.
35. James A. Noone, "Strip Mining Lobby Groups Focus on House Interior Committee," *National Journal*, January 26, 1974, p. 139.
36. Ibid., p. 140.
37. Morton's letter to Haley, November 9, 1973, pp. 1–3.
38. "Strip Mining Lobby Groups," January 26, 1974, p. 142.
39. Ibid.
40. Seiberling's letter to William E. Simon, November 20, 1973, p. 1.
41. Ibid., p. 2.
42. Whitaker's letter to Haley, February 6, 1974.
43. Hosmer's statement on the introduction of the Surface Coal Reclamation Act of 1974, February 20, 1974, pp. 2–3.
44. Memorandum from Hosmer to the members of the House Committee on Interior and Insular Affairs, February 25, 1974, on H.R. 11500 and H.R. 12898, pp. 3–4.
45. Memo from Morris Udall and Patsy Mink to the members of the House Committee on Interior and Insular Affairs, February 26, 1974, p. 1.
46. Ibid., p. 3.
47. Hosmer memo, p. 5.
48. Udall-Mink memo, p. 3.
49. "Congressional Report," Washington *Post*, February 22, 1974, p. A15.
50. "House Interior Unit Delays Action on Strip-Mine Bill," *New York Times*, February 22, 1974, p. 4.
51. Ibid.
52. George C. Wilson, "House Unit Set to Vote on Strip Mining Bill," *Washington Post*, February 27, 1974, p. A17.
53. Ibid.
54. Udall-Mink memo, p. 2–3.
55. Letter from John C. Whitaker, Undersecretary of the Interior, to Chairman Haley, February 6, 1974, p. 1.
56. Ibid., p. 4.
57. Ibid., p. 3.
58. Ben A. Franklin, "House Unit Backs Strip-Mine Curbs," *New York Times*, February 28, 1974, p. 23.
59. Telegram from Walter N. Heine to Representative Morris Udall, February 26; 1974.
60. George C. Wilson, "Substitute Strip Mine Bill Loses," *Washington Post*, February 28, 1974, p. 2.

CHAPTER 4.   THIS LAND WAS THEIR LAND: LITTLE WHITE LIES, GREAT WHITE FATHER

1. "Indian Treaties A Hundred Years Later," *Race Relations Reporter*, March 1974, vol. 5, no. 5, p. 32.

2. Sven Holmes and Charles J. Brown, Congress Project Profile on James A. Haley, *Citizens Look at Congress* (Washington: Grossman Publishers, 1972), p. 6.

3. Ralph Nader, "Lo, the Poor Indian," *New Republic*, March 30, 1968, p. 15.

4. Vine Deloria, Jr., *Custer Died for Your Sins* (New York: Avon Books, 1969), p. 78.

5. Ibid., p. 79.

6. Ibid.

7. S.J. Res. 133, 93rd Cong., 1st sess., p. 4.

8. Abourezk's press release, "Abourezk Says Justice Department Investigation Needed to Avert Violence in Yellow Thunder Case," March 10, 1971.

9. "Legend Lake Development Plan Ended," *Marinette* (Wisconsin) *Eagle-Star*, July 13, 1972, p. 6.

10. Ibid.

11. U.S., Congress, House, *House Concurrent Resolution 108*, 83rd Cong., 1st sess. (June 9, 1953), p. 1.

12. "Legend Lake Development Plan Ended."

13. "The Menominee Restoration Act: Legislation to Rectify the Effects of Termination upon the Menominee Indian Tribe of Wisconsin," mimeograph issued by the Menominee Determination Committee, Washington, p. 1.

14. Kirke Kickingbird and Karen Ducheneaux, *One Hundred Million Acres* (New York: Macmillan, 1973), p. 146.

15. Deborah Shames, ed., *Freedom with Reservation* (Madison, Wisc.: National Committee to Save the Menominee People and Forests, 1972), p. 7.

16. Shames, *Freedom with Reservation*, p. 8.

17. *Congressional Record*, June 18, 1954, p. H.8538.

18. Eisenhower's statement when signing the Menominee Termination Bill (H.R. 2828), June 17, 1954.

19. Shames, *Freedom with Reservation*, p. 13.

20. Kickingbird and Ducheneaux, *One Hundred Million Acres*, p. 152.

21. Ibid., p. 155.

22. "Recommendations for Indian Policy," message from the President of the United States, July 8, 1970, 91st Cong., 2nd sess., pp. 1–2.

23. *Congressional Record*, July 24, 1972, p. S.11577.

24. "Indians, Alaska Natives and Hawaiians," plank of the 1972 Republican Party platform, August 22, 1972, distributed by the Republican Party, p. 1.

25. *Congressional Record*, May 2, 1973, pp. H.3274–3275.

26. Ibid., p. S8161.

27. Jay Billington, "In the Wake of Wounded Knee," *Washington Evening Star*, June 5, 1973, p. 2.

28. "Jackson Backs Menominee Bid," *Milwaukee Journal*, June 26, 1973, p. 18.

29. "Secretary Morton urges support of Menominee Restoration Act," Department of the Interior news release, June 28, 1973, p. 1.

30. Weinberger's letter to House Interior Committee Chairman James Haley, July 11, 1973.

31. Laird's statement on Restoration of Reservation Status for the Menominee Indian Tribe of Wisconsin, August 31, 1973, pp. 1–2.

32. William Areider, "New Spirit in Congress Brightens Outlook for Indian Legislation," *Washington Post*, July 8, 1973, p. G1.

33. *Congressional Record*, October 16, 1973, p. H.9007.

34. Ibid., p. H.9098.

35. Ibid., p. H.9104.

36. Ibid., p. H.9098.

37. Ibid., p. H.9104.

38. Richard Bradee, "House Passes Menominee Bill," *Milwaukee Sentinel*, October 17, 1973 (in the files of the National Committee to Save the Menominee People and Forests, Inc., Washington.)

39. Statement by the President, December 22, 1973, upon signing the Menominee De-Termination Act.

40. Edward H. Blackwell, "New Life for Menominees," *Milwaukee Journal*, December 28, 1973, p. 1.

41. "Imposing Alien Values," reprinted from the *Wall Street Journal* in *Green Bay* (Wisc.) *Press Gazette*, January 12, 1974 (in the files of the National Committee to Save the Menominee People and Forests, Inc., Washington.)

CHAPTER 5.   BLUEPRINT FOR A NEW LANDSCAPE: ARE THE TIMES A-CHANGIN'?

1. *Committee Reform Amendments of 1974*, Report of the Select Committee on Committees, U.S. House of Representatives (Washington: Government Printing Office, 1974), p. 64.

Part II. The House Agriculture Committee and the Senate Agriculture and Forestry Committee

CHAPTER 6.   THE AGRICULTURE COMMITTEES OF CONGRESS

1. U.S., Congress, House, Committee on Agriculture, *Committee on Agriculture—150th Anniversary*, Committee Print, 91st Cong., 2nd sess. (May 3, 1970), p. 1.

2. Ibid.
3. Louis Hartz, *The Liberal Tradition in America* (New York: Harcourt, Brace, 1955).
4. Nick Kotz, *Let Them Eat Promises* (Englewood Cliffs, N.J.: Prentice-Hall, 1969).
5. Based on voting record analyses by the Americans for Constitutional Action (conservative) and the Americans for Democratic Action (liberal); compiled by Congress Project staff.
6. *Committee on Agriculture—150th Anniversary*, pp. 2–3.
7. Samuel Lubell, *The Future of American Politics* (New York: Harper's, 1952).
8. Congress Project Profile, *Citizens Look at Congress*, Ralph Nader Congress Project (Washington: Grossman Publishers, 1972).
9. Based on voting record analyses by the Americans for Democratic Action; compiled by Congress Project staff.
10. Congress Project Profiles, *Citizens Look at Congress*.
11. Richard Fenno, *Congressmen in Committees* (Boston: Little, Brown, 1973); U.S., Congress, House of Representatives, Agriculture Committee Print 62-453, 92nd Cong., 1st sess. (July 1, 1971), p. 117.
12. U.S., Congress, House, Judiciary Committee, Antitrust Subcommittee, *Continuation of the Family Farm and to Prevent Monopoly: Hearings*, 92nd Cong., 2nd sess. (March, 1972).
13. Ibid.
14. J. Phil Campbell, Undersecretary of Agriculture, Agriculture Department press release, 1973.
15. *1969 Congressional Staff Directory*, Charles B. Brownson, Washington, D.C.
16. *1973 Congressional Staff Directory*, Charles B. Brownson, Washington, D.C.
17. Congress Project Profile on Herman E. Talmadge, *Citizens Look at Congress*, p. 10.
18. Anne L. Millet, Congress Project Profile on W. R. Poage, *Citizens Look at Congress*.
19. Confidential interview with member of the House Agriculture Committee, July 18, 1973.
20. Ibid.
21. Ibid.
22. Confidential interview with former House Agriculture Committee member, August 20, 1973.
23. Ibid.
24. U.S., Congress, House, Agriculture Committee Print 62-453, 92nd Cong., 1st sess. (July 1, 1971), p. 117.
25. Peter H. Schuck, director, *The Judiciary Committees: A Study of the House and Senate Judiciary Committees* (New York: Grossman Publishers, 1975).
26. Confidential interview with Agriculture Committee staff member.
27. Richard Fenno, *The Power of the Purse* (Boston: Little, Brown, 1966).

28. Anne L. Millet, Congress Project Profile on W. R. Poage, *Citizens Look at Congress*, p. 17.
29. U.S., Congress, House, Government Operations Committee, *Deficiencies in Administration of Federal Insecticide, Fungicide, and Rodenticide Act: Hearings*, 91st Cong., 1st sess. (May 7, June 24, 1969).
30. U.S., Congress, House, Interstate and Foreign Commerce Committee, *Hearings on hormones in poultry*, 92nd Cong., 1st sess. (1971).
31. Confidential interview with Agriculture Committee staff member, August 1973.
32. Interview with Hyde Murray, associate counsel, House Agriculture Committee, June 1973.
33. Interview with James Thornton, staff, Senate Agriculture Committee, 1973.
34. Confidential interview with personal staff of Senate Agriculture Committee member, 1973.
35. Hearings include *School Lunch Programs*, 1971, full committee; *Financial Needs of Rural Electric Cooperatives*, 1971, Subcommittee on Agriculture Credit and Rural Electrification; *Implementation of the Rural Development Act*, 1973, Subcommittee on Rural Development; *Impact of Fuel Shortage on Agriculture*, 1973, Subcommittee on Agricultural Research and General Legislation; *Forest Service Reorganization and Forestry Programs*, 1973, Subcommittee on Environment, Soil Conservation and Forestry. See *CIS/Annuals* for 1971, 1972, 1973; Congressional Information Service, Washington.
36. *Congressional Quarterly Weekly Report*, August 18, 1973, pp. 2252–2265.
37. Confidential interview with House Agriculture Committee member.
38. Ibid.
39. H. Wellford, *Sowing the Wind: Food Safety and the Chemical Harvest* (New York: Grossman Publishers, 1972), pp. 256–259.
40. *Congressional Quarterly Almanac, 1971*, pp. 484–485.
41. Ross B. Talbot and Don Hadwiger, *The Policy Process of American Agriculture* (San Francisco: Chandler Publishing Company, 1968), Chapter 5.
42. *Congressional Quarterly Almanac, 1971*, pp. 484–485.
43. Interview with Julius L. Katz.
44. *Congressional Quarterly Weekly Report*, February 16, 1974, p. 366.
45. Ibid., March 9, 1974, p. 629.
46. Ibid., June 1, 1974, p. 1436.
47. Ibid., June 8, 1974, p. 1529.
48. "Milk Group Gave $462,000 Just Before The Election," *Congressional Quarterly Weekly Report*, March 17, 1973, p. 568.
49. Frank Wright, "The Dairy Lobby Buys the Cream of the Congress," *Washington Monthly*, May 1971, p. 17.
50. Ibid.
51. Ibid., pp. 18–19.
52. "Milk Group Gave $462,000 Just Before Election," pp. 571–573.

53. Interview with A. L. McWilliams.
54. Harold S. Nelson, "General Manager's Report," *Dairymen's Digest,* May 1971.
55. *Dairymen's Digest,* October 1971, pp. 4–9.

CHAPTER 7. BENEFITS FOR FARMERS: A REVIEW OF COMMITTEE PRIORITIES

1. The Agriculture Department was criticized severely for its apparent inefficiency in controlling the fertilizer, grain storage, and cotton allotment schemes of Billie Sol Estes, a Texas businessman. Estes was arrested in 1962 on charges of fraud in the sale of mortgages on nonexistent fertilizer tanks to finance companies. Estes used the cash to build and purchase grain storage facilities which he then leased to the Commodity Credit Corporation.

Estes was also exposed in a plan to circumvent the Department's prohibition of the sale of cotton allotments. Estes sold land in Pecos and Reeves County, Texas, to farmers who had allotments eligible for transfer to new land (because they had lost their land by eminent domain condemnation). The installment contract on the land sales specified that default on the first payment would return the land to Estes. Estes leased the land back from the farmers, made a payment on the lease, and then arranged with the farmer for his voluntary default on the first sales installment payment. The land—with the allotment—then went to Estes, who in effect had obtained the allotment for the price of the lease payment. By this device Estes increased his cotton allotment from 2,000 to 5,000 acres.

Senate and House Republicans criticized the Department for failing to rescind Estes' allotments, and for failing to check Estes' financial worth before accepting his bonds for grain storage. Charges of favoritism and small bribes led to the resignation of an Assistant Secretary of Labor and a deputy administrator of the Agriculture Soil Conservation Service, and several personnel transfers. See *Congressional Quarterly Almanac,* 1962, pp. 988–1002.
2. Varden Fuller, "Political Pressures and Income Distribution in Agriculture," *Journal of Farm Economics,* 47:5, 1965, p. 1246. Despite his rhetorical flourish, Fuller is correct in noting that "the victory of the nonrecourse loan system over the compensatory-payment system is one of the major triumphs of American farm politics."
3. Quoted ibid.
4. Ibid., p. 1248.
5. James T. Bonnen, "The Absence of Knowledge of Distributional Impacts: An Obstacle to Effective Public Program Analysis and De-

cisions" in U.S., Congress, Joint Economic Committee, *The Analysis and Evaluation of Public Expenditures: The PPB System*, Joint Economic Committee Print (Washington: Government Printing Office, 1969), I, pp. 419–450. See also note 12.

6. Ibid., p. 439.

7. K. L. Robinson, "An Examination of Past Farm Programs from the Standpoint of Equity," draft of remarks presented to the North Central Regional Farm Policy Research Committee, NCR-50 (Chicago: Farm Foundation, March 11, 1969), p. 16.

8. Bonnen, "The Absence of Knowledge of Distributional Impacts," p. 440.

9. Ibid., p. 439.

10. Don Paarlberg, *American Farm Policy* (New York: John Wiley and Sons, 1964), pp. 42, 130.

11. Glen T. Barton, "Impact of Farm Programs on Incomes of Low-Income Farmers," unpublished memorandum to Walter W. Wilcox, director, Agricultural Economics, Agriculture Department, August 11, 1968.

12. Marion Clawson, "A New Policy Direction for American Agriculture," *Journal of Soil and Water Conservation* 25:1, 1970.

13. W. L. Gibson, "Tobacco Allotments and the Price of Farm Land," in *The Tobacco Industry in Perspective* (Raleigh, N.C.: Agricultural Policy Institute, North Carolina State University, May 1964), p. 135.

14. Milton Shuggett and Josiah Hoskins, "Capitalization of Burley Tobacco Allotment Rights into Farmland Values," *American Journal of Agricultural Economics* 59:2, 1969, pp. 471–474.

15. U.S., Congress, Senate, Committee on Appropriations, Subcommittee on Agricultural Appropriations, *Proposed Limitation on Payments to Producers for Fiscal 1970: Hearings on H.R. 11612*, 91st Cong., 1st sess. (1969), pp. 32–33. The double-dip provision instituted in the 1965 Food and Agriculture Act was omitted from the 1970 farm bill. Under the 1965 cotton program a regular farmer received commodity loans on the output from his entire allotment and an additional direct payment on the "domestic portion" (65 percent) of his allotment. He was free to divert voluntarily up to 35 percent (the nondomestic portion) of his allotment in exchange for cash diversion payments (25 percent of the parity price). A small farmer, however, who produced on an allotment of ten acres or less or made under 3,600 pounds of cotton was eligible to receive diversion payments on 35 percent of his allotment *without* actually diverting the acreage from production. If he did divert, he received two diversion payments, a "double dip."

16. Interview with Horace D. Godfrey, former administrator, ASCS, Washington, July 30, 1969.

17. Ibid.

18. Ibid.

19. Ibid.

20. *Code of Federal Regulations* 701.29.

21. *Code of Federal Regulations* 701.28. If the government share of the

cost of the conservation project would be less than $200 when calculated on a 50 percent share, the government pays somewhat more than 50 percent on a graduated scale.

22. Raphael Fitzgerald, letter to Mrs. Marion P. Yankauer on nonwhite participation in the Agricultural Conservation Program, June 9, 1968.

23. John Schnittker, *1972 Budget Issues: Agriculture and Food*, unpublished study prepared for the Brookings Institution, 1971, pp. 14–15. See also Charles L. Schultze, et al, *Setting National Priorities—The 1972 Budget* (Washington: Brookings Institution, 1971), pp. 303–304.

24. See Table 1, rows 2 and 9.

25. Interview with William Shofner, former deputy director of the Program and Policy Division, ASCS, Washington, August 15, 1969.

26. Robinson, "An Examination of Past Farm Programs from the Standpoint of Equity," pp. 1–2.

27. Paarlberg, *American Farm Policy*, p. 42.

28. Distribution of Farms by Sales Class

Gross Sales	*Number of Farms (thousands)*		
(in 1954 prices)	*1939*	*1950*	*1959*
Under $2,500	4185	3295	1638
$2,500–$4,999	1015	882	618
$5,000–$9,999	585	721	654
$10,000 and over	312	484	794
Total	6097	5382	3704

SOURCE: Committee for Economic Development, *An Adaptive Program for Agriculture* (New York: Committee for Economic Development, 1962), p. 61.

29. U.S., Congress, Senate, *Parity Returns Positions of Farmers*, Senate Document 44, 90th Cong., 1st sess. (1967).

30. Ibid., p. 14. This is *not* the usual use of the term "parity" in farm policy debate. "Parity" generally refers to a "standard to measure the degree to which farm prices, or purchasing power, are in line with what the Congress has defined as a fair goal or objective." Specifically, the parity price of a commodity is the current dollar price that gives the same purchasing power, in terms of goods and services bought by farmers, that the commodity had in a 1900–1914 base period. See ASCS, *Farm Commodity and Related Programs: Agriculture Handbook No. 345* (Washington: Government Printing Office, undated), p. 8.

31. Ibid., p. 25.

32. Statement of W. R. Poage, "The Case Against Limiting Farm Program Payments," *Congressional Record*, July 31, 1968, p. 7914.

CHAPTER 8. THE POLITICS OF SUBSIDY LIMITATION

1. Charles L. Schultze, *Distribution of Farm Subsidies* (Washington: Brookings Institution, 1971), p. 1.
2. Ibid.
3. Ibid., p. 25, 30.
4. Ibid., p. 30.
5. *Congressional Record*, September 15, 1970, p. S.31780.
6. *Congressional Record*, March 24, 1970, p. S.8843.
7. Ibid.
8. U.S. Department of Agriculture, Agriculture Stabilization and Conservation Service, *Frequency Distribution of all ASCS Producer Payments Excluding Price Support Loans for Calendar Year 1970*, p. 1.
9. Schultze, *The Distribution of Farm Subsidies*, pp. 31–40.
10. *Congressional Quarterly Almanac, 1969*, p. 332.
11. Ibid. See also *Congressional Quarterly Almanac, 1971*, p. 215. of 1970, H. Rept. 91-1329, 91st Cong., 2nd sess. (1970), p. 15.
12. *Congressional Quarterly Almanac, 1968*, p. 459.
13. *Congressional Quarterly Almanac, 1969*, p. 327.
14. U.S., Congress, House, Committee on Agriculture, *Agriculture Act of 1970*, H. Rept. 91-1329, 91st Cong., 2nd sess. (1970), p. 15.
15. Ibid., pp. 14–15.
16. Ibid., p. 16.
17. Doane Agricultural Service, Inc., "Agricultural Opinion Survey," *Doane's Agricultural Report* 31:30, pp. 9–10, October 16, 1968.
18. Charles L. Schultze, *Setting National Priorities—The 1971 Budget* (Washington: Brookings Institution, 1970), pp. 144–146. This estimate of potential savings from a payment limitation of $20,000 assumes that total farm payments would otherwise be equal to the level of 1969–1970.
19. Ibid.
20. Clifford M. Hardin, "Position of the Department of Agriculture on Payment Limitations as Proposed in the Findley Amendment to the Agriculture Appropriations Bill," Department of Agriculture press release, May 26, 1969.
21. Ibid.
22. Ibid.
23. Clifford M. Hardin, letter to Representative Silvio O. Conte on proposed $110,000 payment limit, March 6, 1970.
24. Clifford M. Hardin, "Statement Supporting the $55,000 Limit," Department of Agriculture press release, July 10, 1970.
25. Burt Schoor, "Nixon Stand May Produce $20,000 Ceiling on Farm Payments, Despite Pleas by Hardin," *Wall Street Journal*, August 3, 1970.
26. President Richard M. Nixon, letter to Representative Page Belcher supporting the $55,000 payment limit, August 4, 1970.

27. It may be argued that the Nixon administration genuinely preferred a lower payment limit but could not approve it because of supply control problems. This was Nixon's claim in his August 4 letter to Page Belcher (see note 26). It is true that when payments are limited, larger growers have diminished incentive to participate in voluntary adjustment programs unless compensatory provision is made. Both the Goodell $10,000 limit and the Conte $5,000 limit allowed overplanting (outside allotments) as compensation to sustain larger growers' participation.

   Such provisions were not included in the Conte-Findley limit of $30,000 per farm, and some of the projected savings from a limit would have been lost in paying smaller feed-grain and wheat farmers to increase their acreage diversion. If the compensatory allowance had been granted, a smaller portion of the savings would have gone to maintain supply control. Even so, Undersecretary Schnittker concluded that wheat and cotton payments could be reduced by one third with little effect on acreage and production. Most of the savings, Brookings economist Charles Schultze concludes, could have been preserved "given appropriate statutory language and administrative regulation to control evasion." (Schultze, *Setting National Priorities—The 1971 Budget*, p. 145.) Secretary Hardin's own testimony before the House Agriculture Committee in 1969 implied that a large portion of the payments made under the cotton and wheat programs were *not* needed for supply control. (Statement before the Senate Subcommittee on Agriculture Appropriations in U.S. Congress, Senate, Committee on Appropriations, *Proposed Limitation on Payments to Producers for Fiscal 1970*, p. 8; Table 2, p. 32.) For all programs, Hardin noted, only 65 percent of total payments were needed for resource adjustment. Though that figure assumes the ability to target payments with discrimination, it implies the possibility of savings far greater than the 2 percent reduction of the Nixon-Hardin proposal.

   It may be contended that Nixon was instead worried by the so-called "snap-back provision" of the 1965 Act (Section 402(12), P.L. 89-321), which required that if payment limitations were authorized, an older and more expensive system of cotton price supports would go into effect. These supports would have been at high price levels, requiring the CCC to buy most cotton and sell it back at world prices. This provision could have been repealed, however, on a simple floor vote, before or after passage of the $20,000 limit.

28. U.S., Congress, House, Committee on Agriculture, *Agriculture Act of 1970*, H. Rept. 91-1329, 91st Cong., 2nd sess. (1970), p. 16.

29. Ibid.

30. Ibid., p. 18.

31. Ibid., p. 17.

32. *Agriculture Adjustment Act of 1938*, U.S. Code, Ch. 30, 52, Stat. 31, sec. 344(b), 1938.

33. Ibid., sec. 344(b)(v).

34. Ibid., sec. 344(b)(vii).

35. Ibid., sec. 344(b)(iv).
36. Ibid., sec. 344(b)(ii).
37. USDA, "Regulations on Payment Limitation," Part 795, in *Federal Register* 35:247, pp. 19339–19341, December 22, 1970.
38. Ibid., 795.6.
39. Ibid., 795.7.
40. Ibid., 795.12.
41. *Congressional Record*, August 4, 1970, p. H.7687.
42. Ibid., p. H.7688.
43. *Congressional Record*, August 5, 1970, p. H.7761.
44. Ibid., p. H.7759–7777.
45. *Congressional Record*, July 8, 1970, p. H.23266.
46. *Congressional Record*, August 5, 1970, p. H.7777.
47. Ibid., p. 27471.
48. U.S., Congress, Senate, Committee on Agriculture and Forestry, *Agriculture Act of 1970*, 91-1154, 91st Cong., 2nd sess. (1970), p. 7.
49. Department of Agriculture, *Farm Payment Limitations* (Washington: Government Printing Office, 1972), p. 6.
50. Confidential interview.
51. *Congressional Record*, September 15, 1970, p. S.15517.
52. Ibid., p. S.31815.
53. *Congressional Record*, July 15, 1971, p. S.11197.
54. Ibid., p. S11228.
55. Department of Agriculture, *Farm Payment Limitations*, p. 2.
56. U.S., General Accounting Office, *Payment Limitation Under 1971 Cotton, Wheat, and Feed Grain Programs Had Limited Effect on Reducing Expenditures*, B-142011.
57. Ibid.
58. Ibid.
59. Ibid., p. 2.
60. *Congressional Record*, June 29, 1972, p. H.6295.
61. Interview with Hyde H. Murray, associate counsel, House Agriculture Committee.
62. *Congressional Record*, March 9, 1972, p. H.2219.
63. Ibid.
64. *Congressional Quarterly Almanac, 1972*, p. 346.
65. *Congressional Quarterly Almanac, 1973*, p. 131–132.
66. Ibid., pp. 300–301.

CHAPTER 9.   COMMODITY POLITICS: THE PASSAGE OF THE FARM BILL, 1970–73

1. Charles M. Hardin, *Food and Fiber in the Nation's Politics* (Washington: Government Printing Office, 1967), p. 119.

2. U.S., General Accounting Office, *Report to the Congress B-14201* (Washington: Government Printing Office, April 12, 1972), p. 11.
3. Department of Agriculture, Agriculture Stabilization and Conservation Service, *Frequency Distribution of All ASCS Producer Payments Excluding Price Support Loans for Calendar Year 1970*, p. 2.
4. Ibid.
5. Glenn L. Johnson and Leroy Quance, editors, *The Overproduction Trap in U.S. Agriculture* (Washington: Resources for the Future, Johns Hopkins University Press, 1972), p. 3.
6. Department of Agriculture, *Agriculture Statistics, 1969*, p. 458.
7. U.S. Department of Agriculture, Economic Research Service, *U.S. Demand for Cotton: Trends and Prospects*, November 1971, pp. 13–14.
8. Ibid., p. 13.
9. Ibid., p. 15.
10. *Congressional Quarterly Weekly Report*, May 12, 1973, p. 1154.
11. Rodney Whitaker, "The Cotton Surplus Problem 1930–1966," in *Cotton and Other Fiber Problems and Policies in the United States* (Washington: Government Printing Office, July 1967), pp. 126–142.
12. Ibid., p. 126.
13. Ibid., pp. 126–27.
14. Ibid., p. 126.
15. Ibid., p. 127.
16. David Eugene Conrad, *The Forgotten Farmer* (Urbana, Ill.: University of Illinois Press, 1965), Chapter 3.
17. Soil Conservation and Domestic Allotment Act, Public Law 46, 74th Cong., 49 Stat. 1148, approved Feb. 29, 1936.
18. Charles L. Schultze, *The Distribution of Farm Subsidies* (Washington: Brookings Institution, 1971), p. 11.
19. Agriculture Adjustment Act of 1965, Public Law 89-321, 79 Stat. 1187, approved November 3, 1965.
20. Agriculture Adjustment Act of 1970, Public Law 91-524, approved November 30, 1970.
21. Of 4,049 pages of hearings involving the 1973 Agriculture Appropriations bill before the House Appropriations Subcommittee on Agriculture, only 77 pages, less than 2 percent, concern the farm subsidy programs. These hearings mainly involve the administration of the program rather than the provisions. U.S., Congress, House, Committee on Appropriations, *Agriculture—Environmental and Consumer Protection Appropriations for 1973: Hearings Before a Subcommittee of the Committee on Appropriations*, 92nd Cong., 2nd sess. (1972).
22. U.S., Congress, House, Committee on Agriculture, *Agriculture Act of 1970*, H. Rept. 91-1329, 91st Cong., 2nd sess. (1970), pp. 9, 15.
23. *Congressional Record*, October 13, 1970, p. H.10062.
24. Confidential interview.
25. Interview with Hyde Murray.
26. Ibid.
27. Confidential interview, 1972.

28. Confidential interview.

29. U.S., Congress, House, Committee on Agriculture, *Agriculture Act of 1970*, H. Rept. 91-1329, 91st Cong., 2nd sess. (1970), p. 4.

30. Ibid., p. 3.

31. U.S., Congress, Senate, Committee on Agriculture and Forestry, *Agriculture Act of 1970*, S. Rept. 91-1154, 91st Cong., 2nd sess. (1970), p. 11.

32. Ibid., p. 13.

33. Ibid., pp. 7–10. According to administration estimates, the Senate bill would increase costs for wheat by $634 million, for feed grains by $1,097 million, and for cotton by $150 million.

34. Ibid.

35. *Congressional Record*, September 15, 1970, p. S.11519.

36. U.S., Congress, House, Committee on Agriculture, *Agriculture Act of 1970*, H. Rept. 91-1594, 91st Cong., 2nd sess. (1970), p. 27.

37. U.S., Congress, Senate, Senator Ellender speaking against the conference report for the Agriculture Act of 1970, 91st Cong., 2nd sess. (November 19, 1970); *Congressional Record*, p. S.18525.

38. Ibid., p. S18524.

39. Confidential interview.

40. Representatives attending the 1970 Agriculture Act conference served on an average of 1.6 committees; participating senators served on an average of 3.3.

41. Interview with Hyde Murray.

42. U.S., Congress, House, Representative Poage (October 13, 1970), *Congressional Record*, p. H.10057.

43. Ibid., Representative Belcher, p. H.10057.

44. Confidential interview.

45. *Congressional Record*, November 19, 1970, p. S.18531.

46. Ibid., p. S.18523.

47. Confidential interview.

48. *Congressional Record*, November 19, 1970, p. S.18531.

49. Ibid., p. S.18533.

50. Ibid.

51. According to Department of Agriculture figures, costs of the acreage diversion and price support programs and the wheat program in 1970 were feed grains $1,268 million, wheat $449 million, and cotton $820 million. Estimated payments for 1972 were feed grains $1,000 million, wheat $397 million, and cotton $843 million. U.S., Congress, House, Committee on Agriculture, *Food Costs—Farm Prices*, Committee Print, 92nd Cong., 1st sess. (1971), p. 24.

CHAPTER 10. THE FORGOTTEN CONSTITUENCY: THE AGRICULTURE COMMITTEES AND THE POOR

This chapter is based primarily on the following sources:

Harrison Wellford, "Food for Peace," unpublished paper prepared for Harvard University, 1969.

Hearings on P. L. 480 before the House Committee on Agriculture and the Senate Committee on Agriculture and Forestry, 1968–72.

Hunger USA: A Report by the Citizens' Board of Inquiry into Hunger and Malnutrition in the United States, 1968.

Hunger USA Revisited, 1972.

Nick Kotz, *Let Them Eat Promises* (Englewood Cliffs, N.J.: Prentice-Hall, 1969).

Reports by and hearings before the Senate Select Committee on Nutrition and Human Needs, 1969–73.

Randall B. Ripley, "Legislative Bargaining and the Food Stamp Act of 1964," in F. N. Cleaveland, *Congress and Urban Problems* (Washington: Brookings Institution, 1969).

Interviews with congressmen, administrators, and lobbyists involved in the food stamp, school lunch, and Food for Peace programs.

Part III. The House Science and Astronautics Committee and the Senate Aeronautical and Space Sciences Committee

---

CHAPTER 12. SCIENCE AND SPACE

---

1. Trevor Gardner, "How We Fell Behind in Guided Missiles," *Air Power Historian*, January 1958, p. 10.

2. James Killian, in *Science*, January 6, 1961, pp. 24–25; from a speech delivered at the Massachusetts Institute of Technology Club of New York, Dec. 13, 1960.

3. The National Advisory Committee on Aeronautics was established in 1915.

4. Thomas Jahnigne, "Congress and Space" (Ph.D. dissertation, Claremont Graduate School, 1965), p. 33.

5. Ibid., p. 36. Jahnigne cites U.S., Congress, Senate Special Committee on Space and Astronautics, *Final Report* (Senate Report No. 100), 86th Cong., 1st sess. (1958).

6. Ibid., p. 38.

7. Vernon Van Dyke, *Pride and Power* (Urbana, Ill.: University of Illinois Press, 1964), p. 20.

8. Jahnige, "Congress and Space," p. 54. The description of this maneuver is based on rumor, but a widely reported rumor. See Neil MacNeil, *The Forge of Democracy* (New York: Van Rees Press, 1963), p. 159; and Allison Griffith, *The National Aeronautics and Space Act* (Washington: Public Affairs Press, 1962), p. 68.

9. Hugo Young, Bryan Silcock, and Peter Dunn, *Journey to Tranquility* (New York: Doubleday, 1970), p. 34.

10. Hugo Young, Bryan Silcock, and Peter Dunn, "Why We Went to the Moon," *Washington Monthly*, April 1970, p. 34.

11. Young, Silcock, and Dunn, *Journey to Tranquility*, p. 166.

12. U.S., Congress, House, Committee on Science and Astronautics, *Missile Development and Space Sciences*, 86th Cong., 1st sess. (1959), p. 20.

13. Young, Silcock, and Dunn, "Why We Went to the Moon," p. 43.

14. "Technology Incentives: NSF Gropes for Relevance," *Science*, March 16, 1973, p. 1106.

15. Young, Silcock, and Dunn, *Journey to Tranquility*, p. 133.

16. Ibid., p. 135.

17. Ibid., p. 163.

18. Ibid., p. 165.

19. Ibid., p. 166.

CHAPTER 13.   THE SPACE COMMITTEES IN ORBIT

1. House committee rules adopted in 1971 are listed in Appendix 1, p. 345. For a complete listing see U.S., Congress, House, Committee on Science and Astronautics, *Legislative Calendar*, 92nd Cong., 2nd sess. (March 31, 1972); and U.S., Congress, Senate, Committee on Aeronautical and Space Sciences, *Legislative Calendar*, 92nd Cong., 1st sess. (Dec. 31, 1971).

2. Robert Buchanan, "Looking Down Is Up," *Washington Star & Daily News*, March 4, 1973, p. E-5.

3. U.S., Congress, House, Committee on Science and Astronautics, Technology: *Annotated Bibliography and Inventory of Congressional Organization for Science and Technology*, 91st Cong., 2nd sess. (July 15, 1970).

4. *Aviation Week*, February 8, 1971.

5. U.S., Congress, Senate, Committee on Rules and Administration, *Senate Inquiries and Investigations*, a staff study (Washington: Government Printing Office, 1973), pp. 2–10.

6. See *Citizens Look at Congress*, Ralph Nader Congress Project (Washington: Grossman, 1972) for paperbound profiles of individual committee members.

7. Buchanan, "Looking Down Is Up."
8. Claude A. Barfield, "Space Report: NASA Gambles Its Funds, Future, in Reusable Shuttle Program," *National Journal*, March 13, 1971, p. 539.
9. Ibid.
10. Letter of Representative Ken Hechler to Representative Frank Thompson, February 7, 1972.
11. *Congressional Record*, March 12, 1973, p. S.4371.
12. *Congressional Record*, statement by Representative H. R. Gross, February 8, 1972, p. H.877.
13. Hugh Folk, "The Role of Technology Assessment," a paper presented at the 1969 meeting of the American Association for the Advancement of Science.
14. *Aviation Week*, February 8, 1971.

CHAPTER 14. THE STAR ISSUE

1. Claude Barfield, "Space Shuttle Go-Ahead Marked by Heated Battles," *National Journal*, August 12, 1972, p. 1290.
2. *Congressional Quarterly*, Feb. 26, 1972, p. 435.
3. John M. Logsdon, "Shall We Build the Space Shuttle?" *Technology Review*, October-November 1971, p. 51.
4. "Space Shuttle: Billions Were Up for Grabs," *New York Times*, July 30, 1972.
5. Logsdon, "Shall We Build the Space Shuttle?," p. 52.
6. *Economic Analysis of New Space Transportation Systems*, prepared for NASA under Contract NASW-2081 (Princeton, N.J.: Mathematica, Inc., May 31, 1971), vol. 1, p. 9.
7. Everly Driscoll, "The Story of an Evolving Shuttle," *Science News*, April 1, 1972, p. 220.
8. Klaus P. Heiss and Oskar Morgenstern, *Economic Analysis of the Space Shuttle System*, prepared for NASA under Contract NASW-2081 (Princeton, N.J.: Mathematica, Inc., Jan. 31, 1972), p. 1.
9. *National Journal*, August 12, 1972, p. 1296.
10. "Should Congress Approve the Space Shuttle?," *The Advocates* (Public Broadcasting System: WETA-TV, Washington, April 11, 1972).
11. "Space Shuttle: Why? An Exclusive Interview with NASA Administrator, Dr. James C. Fletcher," *Skyline*, (California: North American Rockwell), vol. 30, no. 2 (1972), p. 9.
12. Thomas Paine, "What Lies Ahead in Space," speech presented at the Economic Club of Detroit, September 14, 1970.
13. *Congressional Record*, June 28, 1971, p. S.10085.

14. U.S., Congress, Senate, Committee on Aeronautical and Space Sciences, *1973 NASA Authorization: Hearings on S.3094*, 92nd Cong., 2nd sess. (1972), p. 218.

15. U.S., Congress, House, Committee on Science and Astronautics, *1973 NASA Authorization: Hearings on H.R. 12824* (superseded by 14070), 92nd Cong., 2nd sess. (1972), part 2, p. 707.

16. *Congressional Record*, December 7, 1970, p. S.40069.

17. *Congressional Record*, May 4, 1972, p. S.7293.

18. U.S., Congress, Senate, *1973 NASA Authorization: Hearings*, p. 1039.

19. *Congressional Record*, May 4, 1972, p. S.57296.

20. "Space Shuttle: Why?" *Skyline*, p. 9.

21. U.S., Congress, Senate, *1973 NASA Authorization: Hearings*, p. 1114.

22. U.S., Congress, Senate, *1973 NASA Authorization: Hearings*, p. 1110.

23. Heiss and Morgenstern, *Economic Analysis*, vol. 11, pp. 4–280.

24. U.S., Congress, House, *1973 NASA Authorization: Hearings*, p. 1065.

25. U.S., Congress, Senate, *1973 NASA Authorization: Hearings*, p. 1065.

26. Logsdon, "Shall We Build the Space Shuttle?," p. 51.

27. "Should Congress Approve the Space Shuttle?," *The Advocates*.

28. Robert S. Benson and Harold Wolman, eds., *Counterbudget: A Blueprint for Changing National Priorities* (New York: Praeger, 1969), p. 210.

29. U.S., Congress, Senate, Committee on Rules and Administration, *Senate Inquiries and Investigations*, a staff study (Washington: Government Printing Office, 1973), p. 692.

30. "Should Congress Approve the Space Shuttle?," *The Advocates*.

31. U.S., Congress, Senate, *1973 NASA Authorization: Hearings*, p. 1026.

32. U.S., Congress, Senate, Committee on Rules and Administration, *Senate Inquiries and Investigations*, a staff study (Washington: Government Printing Office, 1973), pp. 2–10.

33. U.S., Congress, House, *1973 NASA Authorization: Hearings*, Part 2, p. 702.

34. U.S., Congress, Senate, *1973 NASA Authorization: Hearings*, pp. 1071–1072.

35. "New Means of Energy Conversion," an address by Representative Mike McCormack, *Congressional Record*, Sept. 28, 1972.

36. *Washington Post*, Aug. 6, 1973.

37. *National Journal,* Aug. 12, 1972, p. 1294.

CHAPTER 15.   SCIENCE, THE NEW BATTLEGROUND

1. U.S., Congress, House, Committee on Committees, *Hearings*, 93rd Cong., 1st sess. (May 1973), mimeo, statement of Representative Charles Mosher of Ohio.

2. The National Academy of Sciences *Annual Report, 1968–69* includes

a prefatory note from President Phillip Handler dated February 1972. (Nonprofit organizations are usually required to furnish annual reports each year.)

3. U.S., Congress, House, Committee on Science and Astronautics, Subcommittee on Science Research and Development, *The National Science Foundation: Its Present and Future*, 89th Cong., 2nd sess., doc. 318 (1966); *The National Science Foundation Act of 1950 to Make Improvements in the Organization and Operation of the Foundation*, 89th Cong., 2nd sess., H. Rept. No. 1650 (1966).

4. *New York Times*, Jan. 1, 1966, p. 38.

5. U.S., Congress, House, Committee on Committees, *Hearings*, 93rd Cong., 1st sess. (May 1973), mimeo. statement of Representative John Davis.

6. "National Science Foundation—Authorization," *National Journal*, May 8, 1971, p. 1018.

7. "National Science Foundation—Notes—Budget Request," *National Journal*, Feb. 6, 1971, p. 311.

8. U.S., Congress, House, Committee on Science and Astronautics, *1973 National Science Foundation Authorization: Hearings on H.R. 12753* (superseded by H.R. 14108), 92nd Cong., 2nd sess. (1972), p. 44.

9. *Science*, March 2, 1973, p. 879.

10. Claude E. Barfield, "Science Report/Presidential revamping of science tasks upgrades National Science Foundation role," *National Journal*, March 31, 1973, p. 461.

11. Ibid., p. 460.

12. Ibid., p. 461.

13. Ibid.; quoted from *Science*, March 16, 1973.

14. *Science*, August 3, 1973, p. 423.

15. *National Science Foundation Authorization: Hearings*, p. 184.

CHAPTER 16. CONCLUSIONS

1. *Congressional Quarterly Almanac, 1967*, p. 427.

2. U.S., Congress, Senate, Committee on Aeronautical and Space Sciences, *Apollo 204 Accident Report* (Senate Report No. 956), January 30, 1968.

3. Hugo Young, Bryan Silcock, and Peter Dunn, *Journey to Tranquility* (New York: Doubleday, 1970).

4. *New York Times*, March 9, 1972, p. 18.

5. Claude E. Barfield, "Science Report/Presidential revamping of science tasks upgrades National Science Foundation role," *National Journal*, March 31, 1973, p. 463.

Index